A TEXT BOOK OF

PRINCIPLES OF CONCURRENT AND DISTRIBUTED PROGRAMMING

FOR SEMESTER – II

THIRD YEAR DEGREE COURSE IN COMPUTER ENGINEERING
According to New Revised Syllabus of
Savitribai Phule, Pune University
[2012 Pattern]

N. N. SAKHARE
M.E. (C N)
Assistant Professor,
Deptt. of Computer Engg.
Vishwakarma Institute of Information Technology
Kondhwa, Pune.

S. B. GUJA
M.E. (C E)
Assistant Professor,
Deptt. of Computer Engg.
NBN Sinhgad School of Engineering,
Ambegoan (BK), Pune

V. V. MESHRAM
M.E. (C E)
Assistant Professor,
Deptt. of Computer Engg.
Vishwakarma Institute of Information Technology
Kondhwa, Pune

S. A. CHIWHANE
M.Tech. (C S & E)
Assistant Professor,
Deptt. of Computer Engg.
NBN Sinhgad School of Engineering,
Ambegoan (BK), Pune

N 3316

PRINCIPLES OF CONCURRENT & DISTRIBUTED PROGRAMMING
(TE COMPUTER SEM. II - PU)

ISBN : 978-93-5164-366-1

First Edition : January 2015

© : **Authors**

The text of this publication, or any part thereof, should not be reproduced or transmitted in any form or stored in any computer storage system or device for distribution including photocopy, recording, taping or information retrieval system or reproduced on any disc, tape, perforated media or other information storage device etc., without the written permission of Authors with whom the rights are reserved. Breach of this condition is liable for legal action. Every effort has been made to avoid errors or omissions in this publication. In spite of this, errors may have crept in. Any mistake, error or discrepancy so noted and shall be brought to our notice shall be taken care of in the next edition. It is notified that neither the publisher nor the authors or seller shall be responsible for any damage or loss of action to any one, of any kind, in any manner, therefrom.

Published By :
NIRALI PRAKASHAN
Abhyudaya Pragati, 1312, Shivaji Nagar,
Off J.M. Road, PUNE – 411005
Tel – (020) 25512336/37/39, Fax – (020) 25511379
Email : niralipune@pragationline.com

Printed By :
REPRO INDIA LTD.
50/2 T.T.C. MIDC,
Industrial Area, Mahape, Navi Mumbai
Tel – (022) 2778 2011

DISTRIBUTION CENTRES

PUNE

Nirali Prakashan
119, Budhwar Peth, Jogeshwari Mandir Lane
Pune 411002, Maharashtra
Tel : (020) 2445 2044, 66022708, Fax : (020) 2445 1538
Email : bookorder@pragationline.com

Nirali Prakashan
S. No. 28/25, Dhyari,
Near Pari Company, Pune 411041
Tel : (020) 24690204 Fax : (020) 24690316
Email : dhyari@pragationline.com
bookorder@pragationline.com

MUMBAI

Nirali Prakashan
385, S.V.P. Road, Rasdhara Co-op. Hsg. Society Ltd.,
Girgaum, Mumbai 400004, Maharashtra
Tel : (022) 2385 6339 / 2386 9976, Fax : (022) 2386 9976
Email : niralimumbai@pragationline.com

DISTRIBUTION BRANCHES

NAGPUR
Pratibha Book Distributors
Above Maratha Mandir, Shop No. 3, First Floor,
Rani Jhanshi Square, Sitabuldi, Nagpur 440012,
Maharashtra, Tel : (0712) 254 7129

BENGALURU
Pragati Book House
House No. 1, Sanjeevappa Lane, Avenue Road Cross,
Opp. Rice Church, Bengaluru – 560002.
Tel : (080) 64513344, 64513355,
Mob : 9880582331, 9845021552
Email:bharatsavla@yahoo.com

JALGAON
Nirali Prakashan
34, V. V. Golani Market, Navi Peth, Jalgaon 425001,
Maharashtra, Tel : (0257) 222 0395
Mob : 94234 91860

KOLHAPUR
Nirali Prakashan
New Mahadvar Road,
Kedar Plaza, 1st Floor Opp. IDBI Bank
Kolhapur 416 012, Maharashtra. Mob : 9855046155

CHENNAI
Pragati Books
9/1, Montieth Road, Behind Taas Mahal, Egmore,
Chennai 600008 Tamil Nadu, Tel : (044) 6518 3535,
Mob : 94440 01782 / 98450 21552 / 98805 82331, Email : bharatsavla@yahoo.com

RETAIL OUTLETS

PUNE

Pragati Book Centre
157, Budhwar Peth, Opp. Ratan Talkies,
Pune 411002, Maharashtra
Tel : (020) 2445 8887 / 6602 2707, Fax : (020) 2445 8887

Pragati Book Centre
Amber Chamber, 28/A, Budhwar Peth,
Appa Balwant Chowk, Pune : 411002, Maharashtra,
Tel : (020) 20240335 / 66281669
Email : pbcpune@pragationline.com

Pragati Book Centre
676/B, Budhwar Peth, Opp. Jogeshwari Mandir,
Pune 411002, Maharashtra
Tel : (020) 6601 7784 / 6602 0855

PBC Book Sellers & Stationers
152, Budhwar Peth, Pune 411002, Maharashtra
Tel : (020) 2445 2254 / 6609 2463

MUMBAI
Pragati Book Corner
Indira Niwas, 111 – A, Bhavani Shankar Road, Dadar (W), Mumbai 400028, Maharashtra
Tel : (022) 2422 3526 / 6662 5254, Email : pbcmumbai@pragationline.com

www.pragationline.com

info@pragationline.com

PREFACE

It gives us immense pleasure to present this book **"Principles of Concurrent And Distributed Programming"** to the Students of Third Year (TE) Degree Course in Computer Engineering of Savitribai Phule Pune University.

The book is written strictly as per New Revised Syllabus (2012 Pattern) which has been implemented from Academic Year (2014-2015).

As per New Revised Examination Scheme which has been implemented from this academic year, **In-semester Examination carries 30 Marks**, over First Three units and **End Semester Examination carries 70 Marks** over entire syllabus of which First Three Units will carry 20 Marks and Units 4, 5, 6 will carry 50 Marks.

The objectives of this text are :

- **Unit I** : It covers basic concepts of Different Computation Models and the concept of different programming environmental tools.
- **Unit II** : It covers Concurrent Programming Techniques.
- **Unit III** : It covers concept of Parallel Computing and the CUDA programming techniques.
- **Unit IV** : It covers the concept of Distributed Computing System.
- **Unit V** : It covers the concept of Virtualization and the Xen-Overview of Virtualization.
- **Unit VI** : It covers the concept of clounad and Mobile Computing. It also covers the Multi-GPU concepts.

We have included Two In-Semester Model Question Papers (30 Marks) for University Examination.

We would like to extend our sincere thanks to Management of VIIT (BRACT), Dr. Mrs. B. S. Karkare (Principal VIIT), Dr. Mr. S. D. Markande (Principal NBNSSOE), Dr. Mr. S. R. Sakhare (Head, Comp. Dept., VIIT) and Dr. Mr. R. S. Prasad (Head, Comp. Dept., NBNSSOE) for their untiring support in our work.

We take this opportunity to express thanks to all members of Nirali Prakashan for their excellent co-operation. A special thanks to Publisher Mr. Dineshbhai Furia, Mr. Jignesh Furia and Mr. M. P. Munde and team namely Mrs. Deepali Lachake (Co-ordinator), Mrs. Neeta Kulkarni, Mrs. Shilpa Kale, Mrs. Pratibha Bele, Mrs. Roshan Khan for showing full faith in us to write this book.

Suggestions and comments are always welcome for the improvement of this book.

January 2015

Pune   **Authors**

SYLLABUS

Unit I (6 Hours)
Concepts, Overview, Programming Environments: Computation Models, Distributed programming languages LISP, YACC, Programming environmental tools, Open GL, MPI Java.

Unit II (8 Hours)
Concurrent grammar, communication and synchronization of concurrent tasks process/Thread System process migration, shared memory, Concurrent LISP, Concurrent YACC, Concurrent java.

Unit III (8 Hours)
The death of single core solution, NVIDA and CUDA, GPU hardware, alternatives to CUDA, Understanding parallelism with GPUs, CUDA hardware overview, Parallel architectures and Programming principles-Parallel computing, Parallel architecture, Architectural classification scheme, Parallel programming models, Parallel algorithms, Performance analysis of parallel algorithms.

Unit IV (6 Hours)
Distributed Computing Systems, models, Issues in designing distributed operating systems, DCE.

Unit V (6 Hours)
Virtualization and programming for XEN-Overview of virtualization, resource virtualization, need and advantages of Virtualization, XEN-overview and X86 virtualization, XEN and virtualization resources, installation and Configuration, Virtual Machine booting and Configuration.

Unit VI (6 Hours)
Cloud and Mobile Computing Principles, CUDA Blocks and Treads, Memory handling with CUDA, Multi-CPU and Multi-GPU solution.

CONTENTS

Unit 1 : Concepts, Overview and Programming Environments   1.1-1.66
1.1 Computation Models   1.1
     1.1.1 Declarative Programming Techniques   1.1
     1.1.2 Declarative Concurrency   1.4
     1.1.3 Object Oriented Programming   1.13
     1.1.4 Relational Programming   1.16
     1.1.5 Message Passing Concurrency   1.17
     1.1.6 Shared State Concurrency Programming   1.19
     1.1.7 Graphical User Interface Programming   1.21
     1.1.8 Distributed Programming   1.22
1.2 Lisp   1.24
     1.2.1 Syntax and Semantics   1.25
     1.2.2 Advantages of Lisp   1.26
     1.2.3 Lisp Applications   1.27
     1.2.4 Distributed Programming Language : Lisp   1.27
1.3 Lex and Yacc   1.32
     1.3.1 Lex   1.33
     1.3.2 Yacc : Yet Another Compiler   1.35
1.4 Open CL   1.57
     1.4.1 OpenCL Development Framework   1.58
     1.4.2 OpenCL Platform Model   1.58
     1.4.3 OpenCL Execution Model   1.59
     1.4.4 OpenCL Memory Model   1.62
     1.4.5 OpenCL Framework   1.63
     1.4.6 Steps for Program   1.63
     1.4.7 Restrictions of OpenCl C Language   1.65
- Questions   1.65

Unit 2 : Concurrent Programming   2.1-2.24
2.1 Communication and Synchronization of Concurrent Tasks   2.1
     2.1.1 Communication and Synchronization   2.1
     2.1.2 Synchronizing Concurrency   2.15
- Questions   2.24

Unit 3 : Parallel Architectures and Programming Principles   3.1-3.64
3.1 Introduction   3.1
3.2 Introduction to Graphics Processing Units (GPUs)   3.2
     3.2.1 The Death of The Single-Corer Solution   3.2
3.3 NVIDIA and CUDA   3.3
     3.3.1 GPU Hardware   3.5

3.4 Alternatives to CUDA	3.6
3.4.1 OpenCL	3.6
3.4.2 Direct Compute	3.7
3.5 CPU Alternatives	3.7
3.5.1 Message Passing Interface	3.7
3.5.2 Open Multi-Processing (OpenMP)	3.8
3.5.3 Pthreads	3.8
3.5.4 ZeroMQ	3.8
3.5.5 Hadoop	3.8
3.5.6 Directives and Libraries	3.8
3.6 Understanding Parallelism with GPUs	3.9
3.6.1 Conventional Serial Programming	3.9
3.6.2 Problems with Serial and Parallel Computing	3.11
3.6.3 Parallelism with GPUs	3.11
3.7 CUDA Hardware Overview	3.12
3.7.1 CUDA Physical Architecture	3.13
3.8 Parallel Computing	3.14
3.8.1 Serial Computing	3.14
3.8.2 Parallel Computing	3.15
3.8.3 Parallel Computers	3.16
3.8.4 Need of Parallel Computing	3.17
3.8.5 Uses of Parallel Computing	3.18
3.9 Parallel Architecture and Classification	3.18
3.9.1 Pipelined Architectures	3.20
3.9.2 Synchronous Multiprocessors/Array Processor	3.21
3.9.3 Shared Memory Multiprocessor Architecture	3.22
3.9.4 Conventional Multiprocessors	3.23
3.9.5 Data Flow Computers	3.25
3.9.6 Systolic Architectures	3.27
3.9.7 Neural Network	3.27
3.10 Classifications	3.29
3.10.1 Classification of Parallel Architectures by Flynn	3.30
3.10.2 Classification of Parallel Architectures Based on Memory Arrangement and Communication Among Processing Elements	3.35
3.10.3 Classification of Parallel Architectures Based on Interconnections Between Processing elements and Memory Modules	3.37
3.10.4 Classification of Parallel Architectures Based on Characteristic Nature of Processing Elements	3.45
3.10.5 Specific Types of Parallel Architectures	3.47
3.10.6 Shore's Classification	3.47
3.10.7 Feng's Classification	3.49
3.10.8 Handler's Classification	3.50
3.11 Parallel Programming Models	3.53

3.12 Parallel Algorithms	3.58
3.13 Performance Analysis of Parallel Algorithms	3.62
3.13.1 Performance Metrics	3.62
• Questions	3.64
Unit 4 : Distributed Computing Systems	**4.1-4.24**
4.1 Introduction	4.1
4.2 Distributed Computing Systems	4.2
4.3 Architecture	4.3
4.4 Guidelines for Organising the Distributed Computing System	4.6
4.5 Distributed Computing System Models	4.6
4.5.1 Minicomputer Model	4.6
4.5.2 Workstation Model	4.7
4.5.3 Workstation-server model	4.9
4.5.4 Processor Pool Model	4.10
4.5.5 Hybrid Model	4.11
4.6 Distributed Operating System	4.11
4.7 Issues in Designing A Distributed Operating System	4.13
4.7.1 Transparency	4.14
4.7.2 Performance Transparency	4.15
4.7.3 Scaling Transparency	4.15
4.7.4 Reliability	4.15
4.7.5 Fault Handling Mechanisms	4.16
4.7.6 Flexibility	4.18
4.7.7 Performance	4.20
4.7.8 Scalability	4.20
4.7.9 Heterogeneity	4.21
4.7.10 Security	4.21
4.8 Distributed Computing Environment	4.22
• Questions	4.24
Unit 5 : Virtualization and Programming for XEN	**5.1-5.52**
5.1 Introduction	5.1
5.2 Overview of Virtualization	5.1
5.3 The Virtual Server	5.3
5.4 Types of virtualization	5.8
5.4.1 Emulation	5.8
5.4.2 Full virtualization	5.9
5.4.3 Para virtualization	5.10
5.4.4 Operating System level virtualization	5.11
5.4.5 Application level virtualization	5.12
5.5 Need and Advantages of Virtualization	5.13
5.5.1 Need of virtualization	5.13
5.5.2 Advantages of virtualization	5.14
5.5.3 Limitations of virtualization	5.14

5.6 Xen Overview 5.15
    5.6.1 Introduction to XEN 5.15
    5.6.2 Basic Components of XEN Environment 5.15
    5.6.3 Xen Operation 5.20
    5.6.4 Understanding Virtualization Modes 5.21
    5.6.5 The Virtual Machine Interface 5.21
    5.6.6 Xen architecture 5.25
5.7 x86 Virtualization 5.27
    5.7.1 Introduction to x86 virtualization 5.27
    5.7.2 x86 Architecture- History 5.28
    5.7.3 VMware ESX 5.28
    5.7.4 Virtualizing 32- and 64-bit CPUs 5.29
    5.7.5 Execution Modes 5.29
5.8 Installation and Configuration 5.37
    5.8.1 Installation 5.37
    5.8.2 Installing from Binary Tarball 5.38
    5.8.3 Installing from RPMs 5.38
    5.8.4 Installing from Source 5.38
    5.8.5 Configuration 5.40
    5.8.6 Booting Xen 5.42
    5.8.7 Booting Guest Domains 5.43
    5.8.8 Domain management tools 5.44
5.9 Virtual Machine Booting and Configuration 5.49
    5.9.1 Creating Up Hardware Profiles in Virtual Machines 5.51
- Questions 5.52

Unit 6 : Cloud, Mobile Computing and CUDA Principles   6.1-6.70

6.1 Introduction to Cloud Computing 6.1
    6.1.1 Services provided by Cloud Computing 6.2
    6.1.2 Characteristics of the Cloud Computing 6.4
    6.1.3 Understanding Public and Private Clouds 6.5
    6.1.4 Cloud Computing Benefits 6.6
    6.1.5 Cloud Computing Challenges 6.8
6.2 Introduction to Mobile Computing 6.9
    6.2.1 Basic components of Mobile Computing System 6.10
    6.2.2 Mobile Computing Current Trends 6.11
    6.2.3 Mobile Computing Classification 6.12
    6.2.4 Mobile Computing Major Advantages 6.13
    6.2.5 Mobile Computing Security Issues 6.14
    6.2.6 Mobile Computing Future Trends 6.15
    6.2.7 Limitations of Mobile Computing 6.16

6.2	CUDA Blocks and Threads	6.17
	6.3.1 Introduction to CUDA	6.17
	6.3.2 CUDA physical Architecture	6.18
	6.3.3 CPUs vs. GPUs	6.20
	6.3.4 CUDA Logical Architecture and GPU Programming	6.22
6.4	Memory Handling with DUDA	6.38
6.5	Multi-CPU and Multi-GPU Solution	6.56
	6.5.1 Introduction	6.56
	6.5.2 Locality	6.56
	6.5.3 Multi-CPU Systems	6.57
	6.5.4 Multi-GPU Systems	6.58
	6.5.5 Algorithms on Multiple GPUs	6.58
	6.5.6 Choice of GPU	6.59
	6.5.7 Single-Node Systems	6.60
	6.5.8 Streams	6.61
	6.5.9 Multiple-Node Systems	6.65
•	Questions	6.70

•	**Model Question Papers For In-Semester University Exam. (30 Marks)**	**MQP-1**

UNIT - I
CONCEPTS, OVERVIEW AND PROGRAMMING ENVIRONMENTS

1.1 COMPUTATION MODELS

Programming consists of three things :
- A computation model is a formal system which defines a language and how that language is executed by an abstract machine line by line. e.g., expressions and statements.
- A programming model is always built on top of a computation model. A a set of programming techniques and design principles used to write programs in the language of the computation model.
- Programming language describe the degree of success with which a programming language meets its goals both in its faithfulness to the underlying model of computation and in its utility for human programmers.
- Computation models are divided into two parts. General Computation Model and Special Computation Models.
- Section 1.1.1 to 1.1.6 include general computation model and section 1.1.7 to 1.1.9 include special computation model.

GENERAL COMPUTATION MODELS

1.1.1 Declarative Programming Techniques

Declarative programming is a programming paradigm, a style of building the structure and elements of computer programs, that expresses the logic of a computation without describing its control flow. Many languages applying this style attempt to minimize or eliminate side effects by describing *what* the program should accomplish in terms of the problem domain, rather than describing how to go about accomplishing it as a sequence of the programming language primitives.

Declarative programming often considers programs as theories of a formal logic, and computations as deductions in that logic space. Declarative programming may greatly simplify writing parallel programs.

1.1.1.1 Declarative Operations
- An operation is declarative if whenever it is called with the same arguments, it returns the same results independent of any other computation state.
- A declarative operation is :
  - Independent (depends only on its arguments, nothing else)

- Stateless (no internal state is remembered between calls)
- Deterministic (call with same operations always give same results)
- Declarative operations can be composed together to yield other declarative components.
  - All basic operations of the declarative model are declarative and combining them always gives declarative components.

Declarative programming contrasts with imperative programming and procedural programming. Declarative programming is a non-imperative style of programming in which programs describe their desired results without explicitly listing commands or steps that must be performed. Functional and logical programming languages are characterized by a declarative programming style. In logical programming languages, programs consist of logical statements, and the program executes by searching for proofs of the statements.

1.1.1.2 Sub Programming Techniques
- Constraint programming
- Domain-specific languages
- Functional programming
- Hybrid languages
- Logic programming
- Modeling

(a) Constraint Programming

Constraint programming is a technology for declarative description and solving of hard combinatorial problems. The user just states the constraints over the problem variables and the system finds a valuation of the variables satisfying the constraints.

Constraint Satisfaction Problems (CSP)

Fundamental concept in Constraint Programming
- CSP is defined by a set of variables Each variable X_i has a non-empty domain D_i of possible values.

Constraint Satisfaction Problem consists of :
- Finite set of variables $x_1, x_2, ..., x_n$.
- For each variable x_1, a finite set D_i of possible values (its domain).
- Set of constraints restricting the values that the variables can take.

Once CSP is represented, solving process include :
- Determining whether the CSP has a solution (check for consistency).
- Finding a solution – A solution to a CSP is a complete consistent assignment of variables.
- Finding all solutions.
- Finding an optimal solution.
- Finding all optimal solutions.
- Finding a good solution.

Classify CSPs on the basis of :
- Domain over which the CSP is defined.
- Syntax of the used constraint.

Constraint Satisfaction Problems can be classified into four categories depending on the types of domains over which the variables range :

1. CSP on integers   –   Variables range over integer domains
2. CSP on reals   –   Variables range over real domains
3. Boolean CSP   –   Variables range over the binary domain [0..1]
4. Symbolic CSP   –   Variables range over non-numeric domains

Example :

The n Queens Problem

Given any integer N, the problem is to place N queens on squares in an N*N chessboard.

Constraint

No queens threaten each other (no two queens on the same row, column or diagonal).

N >= 3

Model :

1. Assume each queen is in a different column.
2. Assign a variable R_i (with domain 1...N) to the queen in the i-th column indicating the position of the queen in the row.

(b) Functional Programming

It is a programming paradigm, a style of building the structure and elements of computer programs, that treats computation as the evaluation of mathematical functions and avoids changing-state and mutable data. It is a declarative programming paradigm, which means programming is done with expressions. Functional programming is so called because its fundamental operation is the application of functions to arguments. A main program itself is written as a function that receives the program's input as its argument and delivers the program's output as its result. Functional programming good illustration of the declarative style of programming. A program is viewed as a function from input to output.

Example :

Facorial Program

```
int factorial(int n);
int main()
{
    int n;
    printf("Enter an positive integer: ");
```

```
   scanf("%d",&n);
   printf("Factorial of %d = %ld", n, factorial(n));
   return 0;
}
int factorial(int n)
{
   if(n!=1)
     return n*factorial(n-1);
}
```

1.1.2 Declarative Concurrency

Declarative Concurrency is a deterministic model of concurrency, compatible with Declarative Programming. A program is said to be declaratively concurrent if for all inputs, the program does the following. All the executions either

(1) fail to terminate.

(2) terminate and are logically equivalent.

1.1.2.1 Partial Termination

fun {Double L} case L of nil then nil else H|T then 2*H | {Double T} end end Y = {Double X}. If X keeps growing, then so does Y. But if X does not change, then Y stops growing and the program remains unchanged.

If the inputs do not change, the program stops executing any further. This is called partial termination.

1.1.2.2 Logical Equivalence

A set of store bindings: constraint.

For each variable x and constraint c, values (x,c) is the set of all possible values x can have, given that c holds.

Two constraints c1 and c2 are logically equivalent if (1) They contain the same variables and (2) For each variable x, values(x, c1) = values(x,c2)

For example,

x = rec(a b) and a = d is

equivalent to

x = rec(d b) and a = d

1.1.2.3 Failure and Confinement

If a declarative concurrent program results in a failure for a given set of inputs, then all possible executions with that set will fail.

For example, the bindings in :

```
thread X=1 end
thread Y=X+1 end
thread X=Y end
```

will eventually conflict. The program terminates.

One way to handle this is using exceptions. But, with these, the executions are no longer declarative, since the store after different execution sequences could be different. For example, Y might be bound to 1 or to 2 before the execution fails in the example above.

Hiding the nondeterminism in case of failure: This is up to the programmer.

```
declare X Y
local XTrial YTrial StatusX StatusY StatusV in
  thread
    try
      XTrial = 1
      StatusX = success
    catch _ then StatusX=error end
  end
  thread
    try
      YTrial = XTrial+1
      StatusX = success
    catch _ then StatusX=error end
  end
  thread
    try
      XTrial = YTrial
      StatusX = success
    catch _ then StatusV=error end
  end
  if StatusX==error orelse
     StatusY==error orelse
     StatusV==error then
    X=1
    Y=1
```

```
else
   X=XTrial
   Y=YTrial
  end
end
% Rest of the code using X and Y
```

Programming with threads

```
proc {ForAll Xs P}
   case Xs of nil then skip
   [] X|Xr then {P X} {ForAll Xr P} end
end
declare L in
thread {ForAll L Browse} end
end
Now, bind L
declare L1 L2 in
thread L = 1|L1 end
thread L1 = 2|L2 end
thread L2 = 3|nil end
```

The effect is the same as sequential execution, but the results can be computed incrementally.

1.1.2.4 Time Slices

Allowing each process to run for one step can increase the overload on the scheduler, or in other cases, hog the processor for too long executing an intensive step. The Mozart scheduler uses a preemptive scheduling based on timers. Allowing one whole computation step leads to a deterministic scheduler. Running the threads multiple times preempts the threads exactly at the same steps. The timer based-approach is hardware-implemented, hence more efficient. This is however, nondeterministic, and depends on external events in the system as well. Either the thread itself, or the scheduler can keep track of the time a thread has run. The second is easier to implement. A short time slice :

- responsive system.
- large overhead for thread switches.

Large number of threads with long timeslices (~10 ms)? == if the threads are interdependent, then long timeslices are ok. == if the threads are independent, long timeslices are not ok. You need a hard-real-time OS.

1.1.2.5 Priority Levels

Provides more control over how processor time is shared between threads. Three priority levels in Mozart: high, medium, low. Each has a guaranteed lower bound on processor time share. 100:10:1. When a thread creates a child thread, then child thread inherits the parent's priority. This is important for threading high-priority applications.

1.1.2.6 Cooperative vs. Competitive Concurrency

Threads are cooperative in completing a global task. On the other hand, you can have a competitive model where entities compete to complete a task. Usually those are OS processes. Competitive Concurrency in Mozart - distributed computation model and Remote module. The distributed model is network-transparent.

1.1.2.7 Streams

A potentially unbounded list of messages. Its **tail** is an unbound dataflow variable (not a general partial value). Sending a message: Send one element to the stream. Bind the tail to a list pair consisting of the element, and a new unbound tail. Receiving a message: read one stream element.

A thread communicating through streams : Stream Object.

No locking or mutual exclusion is necessary since each variable is bound by only one thread.

Stream-based programming : e.g. Unix Pipes.

Summary--what's most important.

To put my strongest concerns into a nutshell :

1. We should have some ways of coupling programs like garden hose--screw in another segment when it becomes when it becomes necessary to massage data in another way. This is the way of IO also.
2. Our loader should be able to do link-loading and controlled establishment.
3. Our library filing scheme should allow for rather general indexing, responsibility, generations, data path switching.
4. It should be possible to get private system components (all routines are system components) for buggering around with.

(a) Basic Producer/Consumer

The function which produced the stream of random bits is like a producer, and the function which computed running averages is like the consumer. This shows how to form a basic producer/consumer style program in the declarative model with threads.

You can also have multiple consumers without affecting the execution in any way.

```
local Xs S1 S2 in
   thread Xs={GenerateRandom} end
```

```
   thread S1={Average Count1} end
   thread S2={Average Count2} end
end
```

(b) Transducers

We can put many other stream objects between a producer and a consumer. These are called Transducers. A sequence of stream objects each of which feeds the next is called a pipeline. The simplest stream is a filter.

Sum of odd numbers in a stream

```
%-----------
% Producer
%-----------
fun {Generate N Limit}
   if N<Limit
   then N|{Generate N+1 Limit}
   end
end
%-----------
% Consumer
%-----------
fun {Sum Xs Accumulator}
   case Xs
   of X|Xr then {Sum Xr X+Accumulator}
   [] nil then Accumulator
   end
end
%-----------
% A filter in between producer and consumer
%-----------
local Xs Ys S in
   thread Xs={Generate 0 1000000} end
   thread Ys={Filter Xs
              fun {$ X} X mod 2\=0 end} end % Take odd numbers
   thread S={Sum Ys 0} end
end
```

This can be represented graphically using the following diagram (sometimes called a Henderson Diagram.) The dashed arrows represent stream inputs, and the dotted arrow represents non-stream inputs.

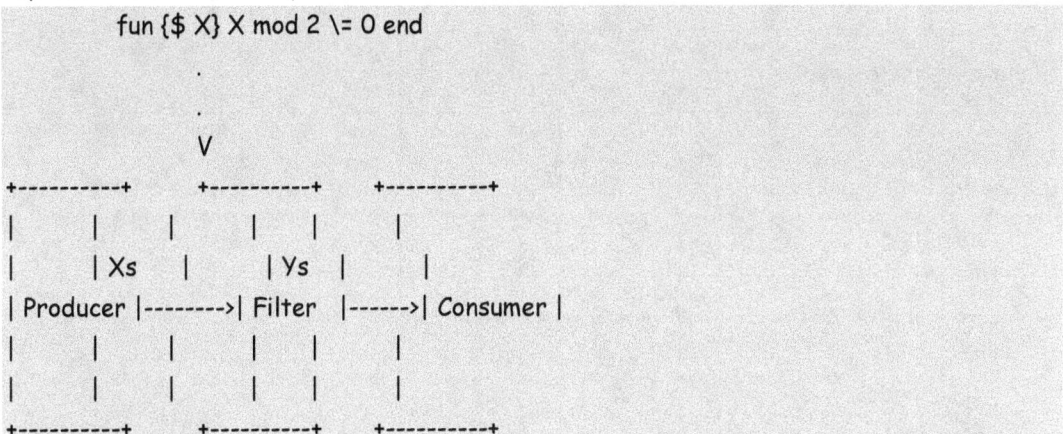

Eratosthenes Sieve

We implement the Eratosthenes' Sieve as a stream-based program. The Sieve generates prime numbers, starting from 2. The algorithm works as follows. First, we consider all consecutive numbers from 2, and remove multiples of 2 from this. At any stage, we pick the first number say n from the list whose multiples have not yet been removed, and remove all its multiples from the list, except for n itself. This process is iterated. The ultimate stream will consist of prime numbers only.

We can program this in the stream model as follows.

```
%---------------
% Returns an infinite stream of integers starting from N
%---------------
fun {IntsFrom N}
   N|{IntsFrom N+1}
end
%-------------------
% Returns a function which checks whether its argument is a multiple
% of N
%-------------------
fun {NonMultiple N}
   fun {$ M}
```

```
      M mod N \= 0
   end
end
%--------------------
% Sieve of Eratosthenes
%--------------------
fun {Sieve Xs}
   case Xs
   of X|Xr then
      thread
         Ys = {Filter Xr {NonMultiple X}} % Remove multiples of X
      end
      X|{Sieve Ys}
   [] nil then nil
   end
end
%--------------------
% Example Execution
%--------------------
local Xs Ys in
   thread Xs={IntsFrom 2} end
   thread Ys={Sieve Xs} end
   {Browse Ys}
end

% Think about why the usage code was not simply
% local Ys in
%    Ys = {Sieve {IntsFrom 2}} % Eager version
% end
```

(c) Stream Objects

As an abstraction, we can introduce a new concept called a **Stream Object**. A stream object is a recursive procedure, which executes in its own thread, communicates with other stream objects via input and output streams, and finally, maintains a state.

```
proc {StreamObject InStream CurrentState ?OutStream}
  case InStream
  of InMsg|InStreamTail then
     NextState OutMsg OutStreamTail
  in
     % NexStateProcedure is the transition procedure
     {NextStateProcedure InMsg CurrentState OutMsg NextState}
     OutStream = OutMsg|OutStreamTail % Why is this done before recursing?
     {StreamObject InStreamTail NextState OutStreamTail}
  end
end
```

1.1.2.8 Using the declarative Concurrent model directly

We can use the declarative concurrent model directly without relying on to Streams or Stream Objects. The ingredients are partial values, and threads. We consider a few examples.

(a) Concurrent Composition

We can create new threads using a thread statement. In a system with threading, the two important operations that are usually supported are thread creation, and thread join. Joining is the process whereby the creator of the new thread waits until the newly created thread is destroyed, before it continues.

The basic idea is for the creator thread to Wait for the binding of an unbound variable, which is bound by the newly created thread just before it terminates. The procedure {Wait X} blocks until X is bound, and gets unblocked when X is bound.

```
local X in
  thread {P1} X=unit end
  {Wait X} % Creator thread blocks until X is bound
end
```

This is easily extended to multiple processes.

```
local X1 X2 X3 in
  thread {P1} X1=unit end
  thread {P2} X2=X1  end
  thread {P3} X3=X2  end
  {Wait X3} % blocks until X3 is bound,
        % which happens only when all three new threads terminate.
end
```

We can abstract this into a procedure {Barrier Procs}, which takes in a list Procs of procedures. This executes each procedure in the list in its own thread, and blocks until all the threads have terminated.

The procedure merely generalizes the methodology described above.

```
proc {Barrier Procs}
   %------------------------
   % Takes a finite list of procedures, and a variable L used for
   % synchronizing.
   %
   % Runs each process in its own thread,
   % creates a new variable M, binds it to L, and passes M recursively
   % to run other procedures.
   %
   % Return value is L if there is no procedure to execute,
   % and the result of the recursive call otherwise.
   %------------------------
   fun {BarrierLoop Procs L}
      case Procs
      of Proc|Procr then
         M
      in
         thread {Proc} M=L end
         {BarrierLoop Procr M}
      [] nil then L
      end

   S = {BarrierLoop Procs unit}
in
   {Wait S}
end

%------------- Example Usage-------------------
{Barrier [ proc {$} X = 1 end
          proc {$} {Browse X} end]}
```

1.1.3 Object Oriented Programming

The use of Object Oriented (OO) design and Object Oriented Programming (OOP) are becoming increasingly popular. Thus, it is useful to have an introductory understanding of OOP and some of the programming features of OO languages. You can develop OO software in any high level language, like C or Pascal. However, newer languages such as Ada, C++, and F90 have enhanced features that make OOP much more natural, practical, and maintainable.

Modern OO languages provide the programmer with three capabilities that improve and simplify the design of such programs: encapsulation, inheritance, and polymorphism. Objects, classes, and data hiding are other important concepts in Object Oriented Programming.

1.1.3.1 Object

An object is an encapsulation of data. The concept of object relates to both data abstraction and to procedural abstraction. An object is a data abstraction in that it contains data elements that retain their values or state between references to the object. An object is a procedural abstraction, in that the principal means of getting information from it, or of changing its state, is through the invocation of procedures.

1.1.3.2 Class

A class is a collection of objects (or values) and a corresponding set of methods. A class encapsulates the data representation and makes data access possible at a higher level of abstraction. Class is composed of three things: a name, attributes, and operations.

The following Bicycle class is one possible implementation of a bicycle :

```
class Bicycle {

  int cadence = 0;
  int speed = 0;
  int gear = 1;

  void changeCadence(int newValue) {
     cadence = newValue;
  }

  void changeGear(int newValue) {
     gear = newValue;
  }

  void speedUp(int increment) {
```

```
    speed = speed + increment;
}

void applyBrakes(int decrement) {
    speed = speed - decrement;
}

void printStates() {
    System.out.println("cadence:" +
        cadence + " speed:" +
        speed + " gear:" + gear);
    }
}
```

1.1.3.3 Encapsulation and Data Hiding

Encapsulation are supported using classes in most object-oriented programming languages. Encapsulation can be used to hide data member and member function. Under this definition, encapsulation means that the internal representation of an object is generally hidden from view outside of the object's definition. Typically, only the object's own methods can directly inspect or manipulate its fields. Some languages like Smalltalk and Ruby only allow access via object methods, but most others (e.g. C++, C# or Java) offer the programmer a degree of control over what is hidden, typically via keyword like private. Data hiding allows one the means to protect information in one part of a program from access, and especially from being changed in other parts of the program.

Below is an example in Java:

```
public class Employee {
    private BigDecimal salary = new BigDecimal(50000.00);

    public BigDecimal getSalary() {
        return salary;
    }
    public static void main() {
        Employee e = new Employee();
        BigDecimal sal = e.getSalary();
    }
}
```

1.1.3.4 Inheritance

When a class acquire the property of another class is known as inheritance. Inheritance is process of object reusability.

C++ Program :

```
public class ParentClass
{
public ParentClass()
{
Console.WriteLine("Parent Constructor.");
}
public void print()
{
Console.WriteLine("I'm a Parent Class.");
}
}
public class ChildClass : ParentClass
{
public ChildClass()
{
Console.WriteLine("Child Constructor.");
}
public static void Main()
{
ChildClass child = new ChildClass();
child.print();
}
}
```

Output :
Parent Constructor.
Child Constructor.
I'm a Parent Class.

1.1.3.5 Polymorphism

Polymorphism means one name many forms. One function behaves different forms. In other words, "Many forms of a single object is called Polymorphism."

(a) Function Onerloading

It is a type of polymorphism to refer to polymorphic functions which can be applied to arguments of different types, but which behave differently depending on the type of the argument to which they are applied (also known as function overloading or operator overloading).

e.g. int area(int a);
       int area (int a,int b);

(b) Parametric Polymorphism

Parametric polymorphism allows a function or a data type to be written generically, so that it can handle values *identically* without depending on their type Parametric polymorphism is a way to make a language more expressive, while still maintaining full static type-safety.

1.1.4 Relational Programming

Relational programming is based on the mathematical relation. A relation is a table of which has a column, or columns for inputs and a column for outputs. A function is a type of relation. Relational programming is an approach to programming where procedures are thought of as relations between values, and where no clear distinction between input and output is made. We have used functions to compute and return values, and procedures to perform side effects. In a declarative model, a function always returns the same output given the same input. In a non-declarative model, a function may return different values on different calls with the same input, but the function still works one way. In relational programming, procedures are used to assert or query relations between arguments.

Example   (Function Prepend)
code/prepend-fun.oz
fun {Prepend Head Tail}
 Head|Tail end
 {Browse {Prepend 1 [2 3]}}
 % prints [1 2 3]
 The function Prepend :

- takes two arguments—a value and a list
- returns a result—a list with the value in front of the input list.

In most programming languages this would define a one-way procedure: take input, then return output.

1.1.4.1 Logic and Logic Programming

Logic programming is a programming paradigm based on form a logic. A program written in a logic programming language is a set of sentences in logical form, expressing facts and rules about some problem domain. Major logic programming language families include Prolog, Answer set programming (ASP) and Datalog.

A logic program is a statement of logic that is given an operational semantics, i.e., it can be executed on a computer. If the operational semantics is well-designed, then the execution has two properties: it is correct, i.e.it respects the logical semantics and it is efficient, i.e.it allows to write programs that execute with the expected time and space complexity. There are many different logics. E.g. there is propositional logic. Propositional formulas consist of expressions combining symbols such as p, q, r and so forth together with the connectors ∧ ("and"), ∨ ("or"), ↔ ("if and only if"), → ("implies"), and ¬ ("not"). The symbols p, q, r and so forth are called atoms in logic. An atom in logic is the smallest indivisible part of a logical formula. This should not be confused with an atom in a programming language, which is a constant uniquely determined by its print representation. e.g. Let a and b are the atoms in logic. Following table shows the result of operations.

a	b	a ∧ b	a ∨ b	a ↔ b	a → b	¬ a
False	False	False	False	True	True	True
False	True	False	True	False	True	True
True	False	False	True	False	False	False
True	True	True	True	True	True	False

1.1.4.2 Prolog in Logic Programming

The relational computation model provides a form of nondeterministic logic pro- gramming that is very close to what Prolog provides.

Rules are written in the form of clauses :

H : B_1, ..., B_n.

Rules are read declaratively as logical implications :

H if B_1 and ... and B_n.

H is called the *head* of the rule and B_1, ..., B_n is called the *body*. Facts are rules that have no body, and are written in the simplified form :

H.

In the simplest case in which H, B_1, ..., B_n are all atomic formulae, these clauses are called definite clauses or <u>Horn clauses</u>. However, there exist many extensions of this simple case, the most important one being the case in which conditions in the body of a clause can also be negations of atomic formulae. Logic programming languages that include this extension

1.1.5 Message Passing Concurrency

In Message passing programming technique, a program consists of several processors, each with own memory that interact by sending each other messages asynchronously, i.e., without waiting for a reply. It has no concept of a shared memory space or of processors accessing each other's memory directly. Any processor can send messages to the channel at any time and the receiving processor can read all the messages from the channel. Simple kind of channel called port has an associated port. After sending a message to the port, message appear on the port's stream. Associate a port with a stream object. We call the resulting entity a port object. A port object reads all its messages from the port's stream, and sends messages to other port objects through their ports.

(1) Ports

A port is an ADT with two operations, creating a channel and sending message to it. {NewPort S P}: create a new port with entry point P and stream S. {Send P X}: append X to the stream corresponding to the entry point P. A port is an asynchronous FIFO (first-in, first-out) communication channel. Successive sends from the same thread appear on the stream in the same order in which they were executed.

e.g. declare S P in
{NewPort S P}
{Browse S}
{Send P a}
{Send P b}

(2) Port objects

A port object is a combination of one or more ports and a stream object.
This extends stream objects in two ways.

(a) Many-to-one communication :

Many threads can reference a given port object and send to it independently. This is not possible with a stream object because it has to know where its next message will come from.

(b) Port objects can be embedded inside data structures (including messages).This is not possible with a stream object because it is referenced by astream that can be extended by just one thread. In the message-passing model, a program consists of a set of port objects for sending and receiving messages. Port objects can create new port objects. Port objects can send messages containing references to other port objects. This means that the set of port objects forms a graph that can evolve during execution.

A port object has the following structure :
declare P1 P2 ... Pn in
local S1 S2 ... Sn in
{NewPort S1 P1}
{NewPort S2 P2}
...
{NewPort Sn Pn}
thread {RP S1 S2 ... Sn} end
end

(c) Message Passing Protocols

Port objects work together by exchanging messages. Different message passing protocols such as the Internet protocols (TCP/IP, HTTP, FTP, etc.) or LAN (local area network) protocols such as Ethernet, DHCP (Dynamic Host Connection Protocol) are used in message passing model.

Message passing system provides following information to specify the message transfer :
– Which processor is sending the message
– Where is the data on the sending processor
– What kind of data is being sent
– How much data is there
– Which processor(s) are receiving the message
– Where should the data be left on the receiving processor
– How much data is receiving processor prepared to accept

1.1.6 Shared State Concurrency Programming

The shared-state concurrent model

The shared-state concurrent model is an extension to declarative concurrent model which adds explicit state in the form of cells, which are a kind of mutable variable .

1.1.6.1 Shared-state concurrency

Shared state is another basic programming style in the stateful concurrent model. A set of shared passive objects are accessed by a set of threads. The threads coordinate among each other while accessing the shared objects. They do this by means of coarse-grained atomic actions, e.g., locks, monitors, or transactions.

(1) Programming with atomic actions
(a) Locks
(b) Monitors
(c) Transactions

(a) Locks

Any resource can only be used by one thread at a time. Many times number of threads wants to access a shared resource .Therefore, a language concept called lock is introduced, to control access to the resource. A lock dynamically controls access to part of the program through critical region. The basic operation of the lock is to ensure mutual exclusive access to the critical region, i.e., that only one thread at a time can be executing inside it.

The shared resource can be either inside the program (e.g. an object) or outside it (e.g. an operating system resource). Locks can help in both cases. For the resource is inside the program, then the programmer can guarantee that it cannot be referenced outside the critical region, using lexical scoping. This kind of guarantee can in general not be given for

resources outside of the program. For those resources, locks are an aid to the programmer, but he must follow the discipline of only referencing the resource inside the critical region. Different kinds of locks are provided for different kinds of access control. Most of them can be implemented in Oz using language entities (i.e., cells, threads, and dataflow variables). But one useful kind of lock, the thread-reentrant lock, is directly supported by the language. Following operations are the provided lock operation :
- {NewLock L} : It returns a new lock.
- {IsLock X} : It returns true if and only if X references a lock.
- lock X then <S> end guards <S> with lock X. If no thread is currently executing any statement guarded by lock X, then any thread can enter. If a thread is currently executing a guarded statement, then the same thread can enter again, if it encounters the same lock in a nested execution. A thread suspends if it attempts to enter a guarded statement while there is another thread in a statement guarded by the same lock.

(b) Monitors

A monitor is a lock extension. It provides program control over how waiting threads enter and exit the lock. This control makes it possible to use the monitor as a resource that is shared among concurrent activities. Typically, a monitor has either one set of waiting threads or several queues of waiting threads. Following operations are the provided lock operation :
- The wait operation does the following :
– The current thread is suspended.
– The thread is placed in the object's internal wait set.
– The lock for the object is released.
- The notify operation does the following :
– If one exists, an arbitrary thread T is removed from the object's internal wait set.
– T proceeds to get the lock, just as any other thread. This means that T will always suspend for a short time, until the notifying thread releases the lock.
– T resumes execution at the point it was suspended.
- The notifyAll operation is similar to notify except that it does the all steps of notify operation for all threads in the internal wait set.

e.g. M={NewMonitor} creates a monitor with operations {M.'lock'}.
  {M.'lock'}   monitor lock procedure
  {M.wait}   wait operation
  {M.notify}   notify operation
  {M.notifyAll} notifyAll operation

(c) Transactions

Transactions were introduced as a basic concept for the management of large shared databases. Databases must provide a high rate of concurrent up-dates while keeping the data coherent and surviving system crashes through ACID property.

ACID is an acronym :

Atomic : Any transaction involves several low level operations but this property states that a transaction must be treated as an atomic unit, that is, either all of its operations are executed or none. There must be no state in database where the transaction is left partially completed. States should be defined either before the execution of the transaction or after the execution/abortion/failure of the transaction..

Consistent : This property states that after the transaction is finished, its database must remain in a consistent state. There must not be any possibility that some data is incorrectly affected by the execution of transaction. If the database was in a consistent state before the execution of the transaction, it must remain in consistent state after the execution of the transaction.

Isolation : In a database system where more than one transaction are being executed simultaneously and in parallel, the property of isolation states that all the transactions will be carried out and executed as if it is the only transaction in the system. No transaction will affect the existence of any other transaction.

Durability : This property states that in any case all updates made on the database will persist even if the system fails and restarts. If a transaction writes or updates some data in database and commits that data will always be there in the database. If the transaction commits but data is not written on the disk and the system fails, that data will be updated once the system comes up.

SPECIAL COMPUTATION MODELS

1.1.7 Graphical User Interface Programming

Computer users today expect to interact with their computers using a graphical user interface (GUI). Java can be used to write GUI programs ranging from simple applets which run on a Web page to sophisticated stand-alone applications.

GUI programs differ from traditional "straight-through" programs .One big difference is that GUI programs are event-driven. That is, user actions such as clicking on a button or pressing a key on the keyboard generate events, and the program must respond to these events as they occur.

(a) Basic concepts
- **The declarative approach** defines a set of possibilities for different attributes. The developer chooses among this set and defines a data structure that describes the interface. A purely declarative approach makes it easy to manipulate the user interface definitions, e.g., to translate raw data into a user interface or to change representations.
- **The procedural approach** gives a set of primitive operations and the ability to write programs with that operations. These programs construct the interface.

In GUI Programming, Procedures are executed when external events happen. These procedures are called actions. Events are external activities that are detected by the window. Objects that can be called to change the interface in various ways. These objects are called handlers.

The GUI model of this chapter has five basic elements:
- **Windows :** A window is a rectangular area of the screen that contains a set of widgets arranged hierarchically according to a particular layout.
- **Widgets :** A widget is a GUI primitive that is represented visually on the screen and that contains an interaction protocol, which defines its interactions with a human user. A widget is specified by a record, which gives its type, initial state, a reference to its handler, and some of the actions it can invoke.
- **Events :** An event is an interaction by the external world on the user interface. An event is defined by its type, the time at which it occurs, and possibly some additional information (such as the mouse coordinates).
- **Actions :** An action is a procedure that is invoked when a particular event occurs. Event invokes an action.
- **Handlers :** A handler is an object with which the program can control a widget. Each widget can have a corresponding handler.

In case of creating GUI for the class, we need to write a source code performing the following steps :
- Create an empty form;
- Add a layout manager;
- For each needed attribute add a widget which will show its content and will allow edition;
- For each widget add a describing label;
- For each widget add a code which will read the value of a particular attribute and will put it into the widget;

1.1.8 Distributed Programming

Distributed system is the system in which hardware and software components located at networked computers communicate and coordinate their actions only by message passing.

(1) Taxonomy of distributed systems

Figure 1.7 shows four types of distributed system. For each type, there is a simple diagram to illustrate it. In these diagrams, circles are processors or computers, the rectangle is memory, and connecting lines are communication links (a network).

Shared-memory multiprocessor, which is a computer that consists of several processors attached to a memory that is shared between all the processors. Communication between processors is extremely fast, one processor writes to a memory cell and another to read it from the cell. Coordinating the processors, so that, e.g., they all agree to do the same operation at the same time, is efficient.

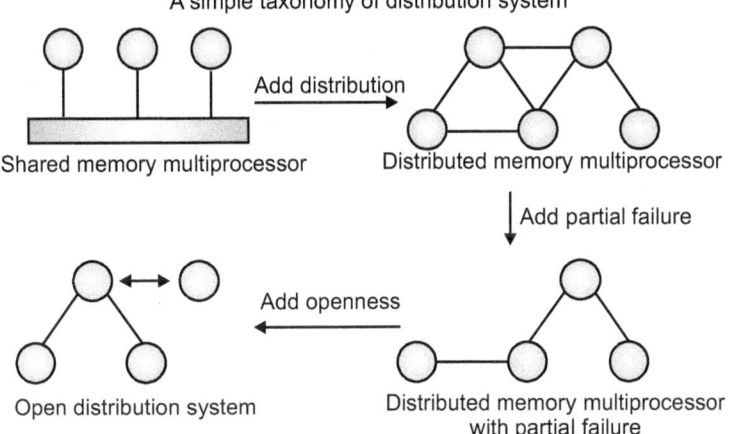

Fig. 1.1 : Simple Taxonomy of Distributed System

A more popular solution is to connect a set of independent computers through their I/O channels. Another popular solution is to connect off-the-shelf computers with a high-speed network. The network can be implemented as a shared bus (similar to Ethernet) or be point-to-point (separately connecting pairs of processors). It can be custom or use standard LAN (local-area network) technology. All such machines are usually called clusters or distributed-memory multiprocessors. They usually can have partial failure, i.e., where one processor fails while the others continue. In the figure, a failed computer is a circle crossed with a large X. With appropriate hardware and software the cluster can keep running, albeit with degraded performance, even if some processors are failed. That is, the probability that the cluster continues to provide its service is close to one even if part of the cluster is failed. This property is called high availability. A cluster with the proper hardware and software combines high performance with high availability.

In the last step, the computers are connected through a wide-area network (WAN) such as the Internet. This adds openness, in which independent computations or computers can find each other, connect, and collaborate meaningfully.

(2) Distribution of Declarative Data
(a) Open Distribution and Global Naming

A distributed computation is open if a process can connect independently with other processes running a distributed computation at run time. A distributed computation is closed if it is arranged in such a way that a single process starts and then spawns other processes on various computers. An important issue in open distributed computing is naming. While communicating with each other independent computations should avoid confusion. They do so by using globally-unique names for things. For example, instead of using print representations (character strings) to name procedures, ports, or objects, we use globally-unique names instead. The uniqueness should be guaranteed by the system.

Global naming is provided with the following name entities :

References : A reference is used to access any language entity. In programs, a reference is transparent, i.e., it is dereferenced when needed to access the entity. References can be local, to an entity on the current process, or remote, to an entity on a remote process. For example, a thread can reference an entity that is localized on another process. The language does not distinguish local from remote references.

Names : A name is a constant that is used to implement abstract data types. Names can be used for different kinds of identity and authentication abilities. All language entities with token equality, e.g., objects, classes, procedures, functions, etc., implement their identity by means of a name embedded inside them .

Tickets : A ticket, is a global means to access any language entity. A ticket is similar to a reference, except that it is valid anywhere including outside a Mozart process. It is represented by an ASCII string, it is explicitly created and de-referenced, and it is forgeable. A computation can get a reference to an independent computation by getting a ticket from that computation. The ticket is communicated using any communication protocol between the processes (e.g., TCP, IP, SMTP, etc.) or between the users of these processes (e.g,telephone, PostIt notes, etc.).

URLs (Uniform Resource Locators) : A URL is a global reference to a file. The file must be accessible by a World-Wide Web server. A URL encodes the hostname of a machine that has aWeb server and a file name on that machine. URLs are used to exchange persistent information between processes. A common technique is to store a ticket in a file addressed by URL.

1.2 LISP

Lisp is the second-oldest high-level programming language in widespread use today. The name *LISP* derives from "LISt Processing". Linked lists are one of Lisp language's major data structures, and Lisp source code is itself made up of lists.

As a result, Lisp programs can manipulate source code as a data structure, giving rise to the macro systems that allow programmers to create new syntax or new domain-specific languages embedded in Lisp.

Lisp is a pioneer of many ideas in computer science, including tree data structures, automatic storage management, dynamic typing, conditionals, higher-order functions, recursion, and the self-hosting compiler etc.

1.2.1 Syntax and Semantics

1.2.1.1 Symbolic expressions (S-expressions)

Lisp is an expression-oriented language. There is no any distinction between "expressions" and "statements", all code and data are written as expressions. When an expression is *evaluated*, it produces a value (in Common Lisp, possibly multiple values), which then can be embedded into other expressions. Each value can be of any data type.

1.2.1.2 Lists

A Lisp list is written with its elements separated by whitespace, and surrounded by parentheses. For example, (1 2 mul) is a list whose elements are three *atoms*: the values 1, 2, and mul. These values are implicitly typed: they are respectively two integers and a Lisp-specific data type called a "symbolic atom". The empty list () is also represented as the special atom nil. This is the only entity in Lisp which is both an atom and a list.

Expressions are written as lists, using prefix notation. The first element in the list is the name of a form, i.e., a function, operator, macro, or "special operator". The remainder of the list are the arguments.

For example, the function list returns its arguments as a list, so the expression :

(list 'X 'Y 'Z)= (X Y Z)

(list (+ 2 3)(* 2 3))= (5 6)

A Lisp list is a singly linked list. Each cell of this list is called a cons, and is composed of two pointers, called the car and cdr.

These are respectively equivalent to the data and next fields in the linked list. Car returns first element of the list.cdr returns rest of the elements of the list except first element.

(car '(A B C)) = A
(car 'A) = Error: A is not a list
(cdr '(A B C)) = (B C)
(cdr (cdr '(A B C))) = C

1.2.1.3 Operators

Arithmetic operators are treated similarly. The expression

(+ 1 2 3 4)

evaluates to 10.

1.2.1.4 Atoms

In the original **LISP** there were two fundamental data types: atoms and lists. A list was a finite ordered sequence of elements, where each element is in itself either an atom or a list, and an atom was a number or a symbol. A symbol was essentially a unique named item used either as a variable name or as a data item in symbolic processing. For example, the list (FOO (BAR 1) 2) contains three elements: the symbol FOO, the list (BAR 1), and the number 2.

The main difference between atoms and lists was that atoms were immutable and unique.

1.2.1.5 List-processing procedures

Lisp provides many built-in procedures for accessing and controlling lists. Lists can be created directly with the list procedure, which takes any number of arguments, and returns the list of these arguments.

(list 1 2 'a 3)
Output: (1 2 a 3)

(list 1 '(2 3) 4)
Output: (1 (2 3) 4)

Because of the way that lists are constructed from cons pairs, the cons procedure can be used to add an element to the front of a list. Note that the cons procedure is asymmetric in how it handles list arguments, because of how lists are constructed.

(cons 1 '(2 3))
Output: (1 2 3)
(cons '(1 2) '(3 4))
Output: ((1 2) 3 4)

The append procedure appends two (or more) lists to one another. Because Lisp lists are linked lists, appending two lists has asymptotic time complexity.

(append '(1 2) '(3 4))
Output: (1 2 3 4)

(append '(1 2 3) '() '(a) '(5 6))
Output: (1 2 3 a 5 6)

1.2.2 Advantages of LISP

- Garbage Collection : Data storage is automatically recycled.
- Interaction : User can combine program writing ,compilation ,testing ,debugging, running in a single interactive session.
- Uniform Representation : Programs and Data look the same.
- Recursion : A program can call itself as a subroutine.

1.2.3 LISP Applications

- Artificial Intelligence.
- Automatic Programming.
- Robotics.
- Formal Logical Reasoning.
- Machine Translation.
- Perception(Vision, Speech Understanding).
- Symbolic Algebraic Manipulation.

1.2.4 Distributed Programming Language : LISP

1.2.4.1 Introduction

There is a great need for the development of distributed applications. These applications are found under different forms: email, web pages, newsgroups, chat rooms, games, telephony, file swapping, etc. All distributed applications share the property of being constituted from a set of processes executing concurrently on different computers and communicating in order to exchange data and coordinate their activities. The possibility of failure is always present in that setting, due to the unreliability of networks and computer hardware.

When building a distributed application, common practice is to use an ad-hoc approach for each particular problem. Much of the work has to be redone every time: how to serialize the application's data, how to synchronize the computation, how to deal with exceptional conditions like network failures, etc.

One of the main reasons for using Erlang instead of other functional languages is Erlang's ability to handle concurrency and distributed programming. Distributed programs written in Erlang typically combine techniques for symbolic functional programming with techniques for distributed programming.

1.2.4.2 Erlang with LISP List of Languages :

- ETOS, an Erlang to (Gambit) Scheme compiler, dating from 1997, was probably the first attempt to combine Erlang and Lisp.
- Erlisp was another attempt, this time in Common Lisp. It's a (partial) reimplementation of the Erlang concurrency model.
- CL-MUPROC is a Common Lisp library which strives to offer some of the multiprocessing abstractions found in Erlang, very much in the same way as Erlisp. It implements some of Erlang's fault-tolerance mechanisms, but not yet distributed operations.
- Distel, a distributed Emacs Lisp with Erlang-style processes and message passing, and the Erlang distribution protocol, originally developed by Luke Gorrie of LtU, SLIME, OLPC, and other fame.

- Termite, another Erlang-like distributed programming system, this time written in Gambit-C Scheme.
- Lisp Flavoured Erlang (LFE) is a Lisp syntax front-end to the Erlang compiler by Robert Virding (one of the inventors of Erlang). This is an interesting one, because it comes out of the Erlang community for a change, and instead of porting Erlang ideas to Lisp, it goes the other route: porting Lisp ideas to Erlang.
- Erlang-in-Lisp
- Erlang Server, Common Lisp Client by Berlin Brown appears to be the latest attempt of integrating Erlang and Lisp. They are connected via sockets and exchange messages in a custom protocol. This has the advantage that either side can easily be replaced by a different implementation.
- erlang-scheme is a port of Distel from ELisp to Scheme.
- Erlang-like Threads in Common Lisp

Here we are going to study some of the languages.

(1) Erlang in Lisp

Erlang-in-Lisp aims to copy the semantics of Erlang.

(a) Spawning a Process

To spawn a process, simply pass the spawn function a name for your new process, and it is to be executed inside this new process. For example, to create a simple hello world process:
(spawn 'hello-world #'(lambda () (format t "hello world~%")))
spawn returns a process identifier, or pid, that is used for sending messages to the process.

(b) Sending and Receiving Messages

Send

The send function is used to send a message to a process using its process id. With the pid you simple : (send pid 'this 'is 'my 'message) Anything following the pid is sent as the message.

Receive

Receiving messages from another process is simply a matter of calling the receive function with a block of code that contains the message patterns to match, and the code to execute when such a match is found. The receive pattern matching syntax follows that of fare-matcher. Receive is a blocking call, and will not continue until a match has been found. As an example, say we'd like to receive a message starting with the symbol hello followed by one variable(which we'll bind to a), and then print out that variable:

```
(receive
((list :hello a)
(format t "The value of a is: ~A~%" a)))
```

Receive-after

The receive-after function takes three parameters: a receive block, an integer timeout, and an after block. The recive block is the same as in the receive function, however, since receive-after is implemented with a destructuring bind, it is necessary to wrap the receive and after blocks in an extra set of parentheses. The receive-after function blocks for at least the number of seconds specified as the timeout. If a message is still not found, the code in the after block is executed. Now we extend our receive example above to print a timeout message after 10 seconds if a message has not been received:

```
(receive-after
(((list :hello a)
(format t "The value of a is: ~A~%" a)))
10
((format t "No message received.~%")))
```

Errors and Linking Processes

The Erlang-in-Lisp error system uses the condition system of Common Lisp directly. All errors that are not handled inside of a process are converted to messages and sent to linked processes. At the moment, this means that all processes behave like Erlang system processes. Below is the simple ping-pong example which implements the the ideas of Erlang. The ping function takes a pid and an integer, count as arguments. It then sends count messages to the pid, waiting after each message for a response.

The pong function simple accepts ping messages and responds to each with a pong until the receipt of a done message, at which point the process exits.

```
(defun ping (pong count)
(loop for iter from 1 to count
do (send pong :ping iter (self))
do (receive
((list :pong) (format t "PING -- Got pong.~%"))))
(send pong :done))
(defun pong ()
(receive
((list :ping iter ping)
(format t "PONG -- Got ping.~%")
(send ping :pong)
(format t "PONG -- Sent pong.~%")
(pong)) ;;check that this tail call can be eliminated.
((list :done)
(format t "PONG -- Got done."))))
(defun ping-pong (count)
```

```
(let* ((pong (spawn 'pong #'pong)))
(ping (spawn 'ping #'ping pong count))))
```

(1) Termite: a Lisp for Distributed Computing

Termite processes are lightweight. A Termite process is executed in the context of a node. Nodes are identified with a node identifier that contains information to locate a node physically and connect to it. Termite processes are identified with a process identifier or pid. Pids are universally unique.

(a) Sending and Receiving Messages

The message sending operation is asynchronous. When a process sends a message, this is done without the process blocking.

The message receiving operation is synchronous. A process attempting to retrieve a message from its mailbox will block if no acceptable message is available.

Here is an example showing the basic operators used in Termite. A process A spawns a new process B. The process B sends a message to A.

The process A waits until the message is received.

```
(let ((me (self))) (spawn (! me "Hello, world!")))
(?) ⇒ "Hello, world !"
```

The procedure self returns the pid of the current process. The procedure ! is the "send message" operation, while the procedure ? is the "retrieve the next message" operation.

(b) Making a "server" process

In the following code, we create a process called pong-server. This process will reply with the symbol pong to any message that is a list of the form (pid 'ping) where pid refers to the originating process :

```
(define pong-server
 (spawn
     (let loop ()
       (let ((msg (?)))
       (if (and (list? msg)
            (= (length msg) 2)
       (pid? (car msg))
             (eq? (cadr msg) 'ping))
             (let ((from (car msg)))
(! from 'pong)
 (loop))
(loop))))))
(! pong-server (list (self) 'ping))
(?)              ⇒ pong
```

(c) Selective message retrieval

While the ? operator retrieves the next available message in the process' mailbox, sometimes it can be useful to be able to choose the message to retrieve based on certain criteria. The selective message retrieval operator is ??. It takes a predicate for argument. The first message in the mailbox which satisfies that predicate will be retrieved.

Here's an example of the ?? procedure in use :

(! (self) 1)
(! (self) 2)
(! (self) 3)

(?)   ⇒ 1

(?? Odd?)   ⇒ 3

(?)   ⇒ 2

(d) Remote procedure call

Here is an example of an RPC server to which we make uniquely identified requests. In this case a synchronous call to the server is made :

```
(define rpc-server
    (spawn
      (let loop ()
        (recv
          ((from tag ('add a b))
            (! from (list tag (+ a b)))))
          (loop))))
      (let ((tag (make-tag)))
        (! rpc-server (list (self)
          tag
          (list 'add 21 21)))
        (recv
          ;; note the reference to tag in
          ;; the current lexical scope

          ((,tag reply reply))) ⇒ 42
```

The pattern of implementing a synchronous call by creating a tag and then waiting for the corresponding reply by testing for tag equality is frequent. This pattern is abstracted by the procedure !?. The following call is equivalent to the last let expression in the previous code:

(!? rpc-server (list 'add 21 21))

(e) Mutable Data Structure

Mutation isn't allowed in Termite in the same way that it is present in Scheme, but it is still possible to implement mu- table data structures using a suspended process to represent state. Here is an example of the implementation of a cell:

```
(define (make-cell content)
(spawn
   (let loop ((content content))
   (recv
       ((from tag 'ref)
           (! from (list tag content))
       (loop content))
       (('set! content)
(loop content))))))
(define (cell-ref cell)
(!? cell 'ref))
(define (cell-set! cell value)
(! cell (list 'set! value)))
```

Implementation :

A prototype Termite system has been implemented. It is built on top of Gambit-C . Two features of Gambit-C were very helpful when implementing the system: lightweight threads and object serialization. Gambit-C supports lightweight language-level threads as specified by SRFI-18 and SRFI-21 . It is possible to start millions of threads in a single program. This makes the Termite model applicable when used with Gambit. Serialization is also supported for an interesting subset of Gambit-C objects. In particular closure and continuation serialization is supported. This makes it possible to implement process migration in the language by using call/cc.

1.3 LEX AND YACC

Lex and yacc helps you to write programs which transforms structured input. This includes an enormous range of applications-anything from a simple text search program that looks for patterns in its input file to a C compiler that transforms a source program into optimized object code. Following Fig. shows the compilation sequence :

In programs with structured input, dividing the input into meaningful units, and then discovering the relationship among the units occurs. This division into units (which are usually called tokens) is known as lexical analysis. A set of descriptions of possible tokens are provided to the lex which produces a C routine, which we call a lexical analyzer, or a lexer, or a scanner, that can identify those tokens. The set of descriptions you give to lex is called a lex specifiication.

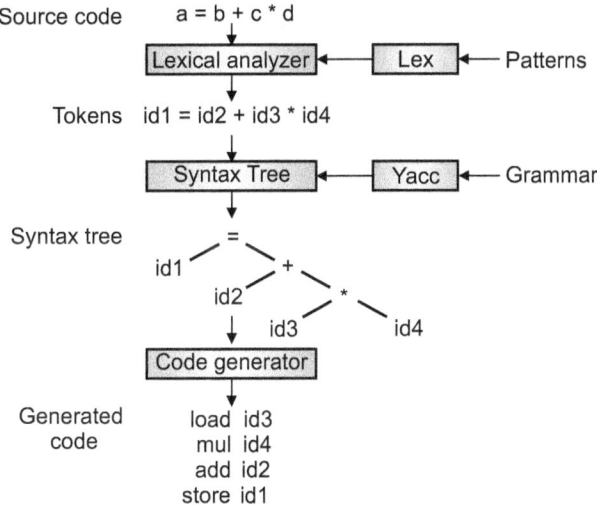

Fig. 1.2 : Compilation Sequence

The token descriptions that lex uses are known as regular expressions. Lex turns these regular expressions into a form that the lexer can use to scan the input text extremely fast, independent of the number of expressions that it is trying to match. A C compiler needs to find the expressions, statements, declarations, blocks, and procedures in the program. This task is known as parsing and the list of rules that define the relationships that the program understands is a grammar.

Description of a grammar is provided as a input to Yacc and produces a C routine that can parse that grammar, a parser. The Yacc parser automatically detects whenever a sequence of input tokens matches one of the rules in the grammar and also detects a syntax error whenever its input doesn't match any of the rules. The Depth First Search Technique is applied on Syntax tree which forms the generated code.

1.3.1 Lex

Lex is a program generator designed for lexical processing of character input streams. It accepts a high-level, problem oriented specification for character string matching, and produces a program in a general purpose language which recognizes regular expressions. The regular expressions are specified by the user in the source specifications given to Lex. The Lex written code recognizes these expressions in an input stream and partitions the input stream into strings matching the expressions. At the boundaries between strings program sections provided by the user are executed. The Lex source file associates the regular expressions and the program fragments. As each expression appears in the input to the program written by Lex, the corresponding fragment is executed.

The user supplies the additional code beyond expression matching needed to complete his tasks, possibly including code written by other generators. The program that recognizes the expressions is generated in the general purpose programming language employed for the user's program fragments.

Lex is not a complete language, but rather a generator representing a new language feature which can be added to different programming languages, called "host languages." Just as general purpose languages can produce code to run on different computer hardware, Lex can write code in different host languages.

The host language is used for the output code generated by Lex and also for the program fragments added by the user. Compatible run-time libraries for the different host languages are also provided.

This makes Lex adaptable to different environments and different users. Each application may be directed to the combination of hardware and host language appropriate to the task, the user's background, and the properties of local implementations. At present, the only supported host language is C.

1.3.1.1 Structure of a Lex File

Files are divided into three sections, separated by lines that contain only two percent signs, as follows :

```
Definition section
%%
Rules section
%%
C code section
```

- The definition section defines macros and imports header files written in C. It is also possible to write any C code here, which will be copied verbatim into the generated source file.
- The rules section associates regular expression patterns with C statements. When the lexer sees text in the input matching a given pattern, it will execute the associated C code.
- The C code section contains C statements and functions that are copied verbatim to the generated source file. These statements presumably contain code called by the rules in the rules section. In large programs it is more convenient to place this code in a separate file linked in at compile time.

1.3.1.2 Lexical Analyzer Source Code

Following are the contents of the calc.lex file. This file contains include statements for standard input and output, as well as for the y.tab.h file. The yacc program generates that file from the yacc grammar file information if you use the -d flag with the yacc command. The y.tab.h file contains definitions for the tokens that the parser program uses. In addition, calc.lex contains the rules to generate these tokens from the input stream.

```
%{
#include <stdio.h>
#include "y.tab.h"
int c;
extern int yylval;
%}
%%
" " ;
[a-z]   {
        c = yytext[0];
        yylval = c - 'a';
        return(LETTER);
        }
[0-9]   {
        c = yytext[0];
        yylval = c - '0';
        return(DIGIT);
        }
[^a-z0-9\b]  {
        c = yytext[0];
        return(c);
        }
```

1.3.2 YACC : Yet Another Compiler

Yacc provides a general tool for imposing structure on the input to a computer program. The Yacc user prepares a specification of the input process; this includes rules describing the input structure, code to be invoked when these rules are recognized, and a low-level routine to do the basic input. Yacc then generates a function to control the input process. This function, called a parser, calls the user-supplied low-level input routine (the lexical analyzer) to pick up the basic items (called tokens) from the input stream. These tokens are organized according to the input structure rules, called grammar rules; when one of these rules has been recognized, then user code supplied for this rule, an action, is invoked; actions have the ability to return values and make use of the values of other actions. Yacc is written in portable C. In addition to compilers for C, APL, Pascal, RATFOR, etc., Yacc has also been used for less conventional languages, including several desk calculator languages, a document retrieval system, and a Fortran debugging system.

Basic Specifications

Names in Yacc refer either tokens or nonterminal symbols. Yacc requires token names to be declared as such.It is often desirable to include the lexical analyzer as part of the specification file; it may be useful to include other programs as well. Thus, every specification file consists of three sections: the declarations, (grammar) rules, and programs. The sections are separated by double percent ``%%'' marks.

A full specification file looks like :

```
declarations
%%
rules
%%
Programs
```

The declaration part may be empty. If the programs section is omitted, the second %% mark may be omitted also;

Thus, the smallest legal Yacc specification is :

```
%%
Rules
```

The rules section is made up of one or more grammar rules. A grammar rule has the form:

```
    P : BODY ;
```

Here P represents a nonterminal name, and BODY represents a sequence of zero or more names and literals. The colon and the semicolon are Yacc punctuation.

Names are made up of characters along with letters, dot ``.'', underscore ``_'', and non-initial digits. Upper and lower case letters are distinct. The names used in the body of a grammar rule may represent tokens or nonterminal symbols.

A literal consists of a character enclosed in single quotes ``''''. As in C, the backslash ``\'' is an escape character within literals, and all the C escapes are recognized. Thus

```
    '\n'    newline
    '\t'    tab
```

```
'\r'    return
'\''    single quote `` ' ''
'\\'    backslash `` \ ''
'\f'    form feed
'\b'    backspace
'\xxx'  ``xxx'' in octal
```

If there are several grammar rules with the same left hand side, the vertical bar ``|'' can be used to avoid rewriting the left hand side. In addition, the semicolon at the end of a rule can be dropped before a vertical bar. Thus the grammar rules

```
P  :   Q R T ;
P  :   U V ;
P  :   W ;
```

can be given to Yacc as

```
P  :   Q R T
   |   U V
   |   W
   ;
```

Every name not defined in the declarations section is assumed to represent a nonterminal symbol. Every nonterminal symbol must appear on the left side of at least one rule. If a nonterminal symbol matches the empty string, this can be indicated in the obvious way:

```
empty : ;
```

Names representing tokens must be declared; this is most simply done by writing

```
%token  name1  name2 ...
```

in the declarations section. Every production rule is having a nonterminal symbol i.e. start symbol.. The parser is designed to recognize the start symbol; thus, this symbol represents the largest, most general structure described by the grammar rules. By default, the start symbol is taken to be the left hand side of the first grammar rule in the rules section. Declare the start symbol explicitly in the declarations section using the %start keyword:

```
%start  symbol
```

The end of the input to the parser is signaled by a special token, called the endmarker. If the tokens up to, but not including, the endmarker form a structure which matches the start symbol, the parser function returns to its caller after the endmarker is seen; it accepts the input. If the endmarker is seen in any other context, it is an error. It is the job of the user-supplied lexical analyzer to return the endmarker when appropriate. Usually the endmarker represents some reasonably obvious I/O status, such as ``end-of-file'' or ``end-of-record''.

Actions

With each grammar rule, the user may associate actions to be performed each time the rule is recognized in the input process. These actions may return values, and may obtain the values returned by previous actions. Moreover, the lexical analyzer can return values for tokens, if desired. An action is an arbitrary C statement, and as such can do input and output, call subprograms, and alter external vectors and variables. An action is specified by one or more statements, enclosed in curly braces ``{'' and ``}''. For example,

```
P    :    '(' Q ')'
          {   hello( 1, "abc" ); }
```

and

```
XXX  :    YYY ZZZ
          {   printf("a message\n");
              flag = 25; }
```

are grammar rules with actions.

To facilitate easy communication between the actions and the parser, the action statements are altered slightly. The symbol ``dollar sign'' ``$'' is used as a signal to Yacc in this context.

To return a value, the action normally sets the pseudovariable ``$$'' to some value. For example, an action that does nothing but return the value 1 is

```
{ $$ = 1; }
```

To obtain the values returned by previous actions and the lexical analyzer, the action may use the pseudo-variables $1, $2, . . ., which refer to the values returned by the components of the right side of a rule, reading from left to right. Thus, if the rule is

```
P    :    Q R T ;
```

for example, then $2 has the value returned by R, and $3 the value returned by T.

As a more concrete example, consider the rule

```
expr :    '(' expr ')' ;
```

The value returned by this rule is usually the value of the expr in parentheses. This can be indicated by

```
expr :    '(' expr ')'    { $$ = $2; }
```

By default, the value of a rule is the value of the first element in it ($1). Thus, grammar rules of the form

```
P    :    Q ;
```

frequently need not have an explicit action.

In the examples above, all the actions came at the end of their rules. Sometimes, it is desirable to get control before a rule is fully parsed. Yacc permits an action to be written in the middle of a rule as well as at the end. This rule is assumed to return a value, accessible through the usual mechanism by the actions to the right of it. In turn, it may access the values returned by the symbols to its left. Thus, in the rule

```
P    :    Q
              { $$ = 1; }
          R
              { x = $2; y = $3; }
     ;
```

the effect is to set x to 1, and y to the value returned by R. Actions that do not terminate a rule are actually handled by Yacc by manufacturing a new nonterminal symbol name, and a new rule matching this name to the empty string. The interior action is the action triggered off by recognizing this added rule. Yacc actually treats the above example as if it had been written :

```
$ACT  :    /* empty */
              { $$ = 1; }
      ;

P     :    Q $ACT R
              { x = $2; y = $3; }
      ;
```

In many applications, output is not done directly by the actions; rather, a data structure, such as a parse tree, is constructed in memory, and transformations are applied to it before output is generated. Parse trees are particularly easy to construct, given routines to build and maintain the tree structure desired. For example, suppose there is a C function node, written so that the call

```
node( L, n1, n2 )
```

creates a node with label L, and descendants n1 and n2, and returns the index of the newly created node. Then parse tree can be built by supplying actions such as :

```
expr  :    expr '+' expr
              { $$ = node( '+', $1, $3 ); }
```

in the specification. The user may define other variables to be used by the actions. Declarations and definitions can appear in the declarations section, enclosed in the marks ``%{'' and ``%}''. These declarations and definitions have global scope, so they are known to the action statements and the lexical analyzer. For example,

```
%{ int variable = 0; %}
```

could be placed in the declarations section, making variable accessible to all of the actions. The Yacc parser uses only names beginning in ``yy''; the user should avoid such names.

Lexical Analysis

The user must supply a lexical analyzer to read the input stream and communicate tokens (with values, if desired) to the parser. The lexical analyzer is an integer-valued function called yylex. The function returns an integer, the token number, representing the kind of token read. If there is a value associated with that token, it should be assigned to the external variable yylval.

The parser and the lexical analyzer must agree on these token numbers in order for communication between them to take place. The numbers may be chosen by Yacc, or chosen by the user. In either case, the ``# define'' mechanism of C is used to allow the lexical analyzer to return these numbers symbolically. For example, suppose that the token name DIGIT has been defined in the declarations section of the Yacc specification file. The relevant portion of the lexical analyzer might look like:

```
yylex(){
    extern int yylval;
    int c;
    ...
    c = getchar();
    ...
    switch( c ) {
        ...
        case '0':
        case '1':
        ...
        case '9':
            yylval = c-'0';
            return( DIGIT );
        ...
    }
    ...
```

Return a token number of DIGIT, and a value equal to the numerical value of the digit. Provided that the lexical analyzer code is placed in the programs section of the specification file, the identifier DIGIT will be defined as the token number associated with the token DIGIT. This mechanism leads to clear, easily modified lexical analyzers. Avoid using any token names in the grammar that are reserved or significant in C or the parser; for example, the use of token names if or while will almost certainly cause severe difficulties when the lexical analyzer is compiled. The token name error is reserved for error handling.

The token numbers may be chosen by Yacc or by the user. In the default situation, the numbers are chosen by Yacc. The default token number for a literal character is the numerical value of the character in the local character set. Other names are assigned token numbers starting at 257.

To assign a token number to a token (including literals), the first appearance of the token name or literal in the declarations section can be immediately followed by a nonnegative integer. This integer is taken to be the token number of the name or literal. Names and literals not defined by this mechanism retain their default definition. It is important that all token numbers be distinct.

A very useful tool for constructing lexical analyzers is the Lex program developed by Mike Lesk. These lexical analyzers are designed to work in close harmony with Yacc parsers. The specifications for these lexical analyzers use regular expressions instead of grammar rules. Lex can be easily used to produce quite complicated lexical analyzers, but there remain some languages (such as FORTRAN) which do not fit any theoretical framework, and whose lexical analyzers must be crafted by hand.

How the Parser Works

Yacc turns the specification file into a C program, which parses the input according to the specification given. The algorithm used to go from the specification to the parser is complex. The parser itself, however, is relatively simple, and understanding how it works, while not strictly necessary, will nevertheless make treatment of error recovery and ambiguities much more comprehensible.

The parser produced by Yacc consists of a finite state machine with a stack. The parser is also capable of reading and remembering the next input token i.e. lookahead token. The current state is always the one on the top of the stack. The states of the finite state machine are given small integer labels; initially, the machine is in state 0, the stack contains only state 0, and no lookahead token has been read.

The machine has only four actions available to it, called shift, reduce, accept, and error. A move of the parser is done as follows :

1. Based on its current state, the parser decides whether it needs a lookahead token to decide what action should be done; if it needs one, and does not have one, it calls yylex to obtain the next token.

2. Using the current state, and the lookahead token if needed, the parser decides on its next action, and carries it out. This may result in states being pushed onto the stack, or popped off of the stack, and in the lookahead token being processed or left alone.

The shift action is the most common action the parser takes. Whenever a shift action is taken, there is always a lookahead token. For example, in state 56 there may be an action:

    IF   shift 34

which says, in state 56, if the lookahead token is IF, the current state (56) is pushed down on the stack, and state 34 becomes the current state (on the top of the stack). The lookahead token is cleared.

The reduce action keeps the stack from growing without bounds. Reduce actions are appropriate when the parser has seen the right hand side of a grammar rule, and is prepared to announce that it has seen an instance of the rule, replacing the right hand side by the left hand side. It may be necessary to consult the lookahead token to decide whether to reduce, but usually it is not; in fact, the default action (represented by a ``.'') is often a reduce action.

Reduce actions are associated with individual grammar rules. Grammar rules are also given small integer numbers, leading to some confusion. The action

    .   reduce 18

refers to grammar rule 18, while the action

    IF   shift 34

refers to state 34.

Suppose the rule being reduced is P : x y z ;

The reduce action depends on the left hand symbol (P in this case), and the number of symbols on the right hand side (three in this case). To reduce, first pop off the top three states from the stack (In general, the number of states popped equals the number of symbols on the right side of the rule). In effect, these states were the ones put on the stack while recognizing x, y, and z, and no longer serve any useful purpose. After popping these states, a state is uncovered which was the state the parser was in before beginning to process the rule. Using this uncovered state, and the symbol on the left side of the rule, perform what is in effect a shift of P. P new state is obtained, pushed onto the stack, and parsing continues. There are significant differences between the processing of the left hand symbol and an ordinary shift of a token, however, so this action is called a goto action. In particular, the lookahead token is cleared by a shift, and is not affected by a goto. In any case, the uncovered state contains an entry such as:

    P   goto 20

causing state 20 to be pushed onto the stack, and become the current state.

In effect, the reduce action ``turns back the clock'' in the parse, popping the states off the stack to go back to the state where the right hand side of the rule was first seen. The parser then behaves as if it had seen the left side at that time. If the right hand side of the rule is empty, no states are popped off of the stack: the uncovered state is in fact the current state.

The reduce action is also important in the treatment of user-supplied actions and values. When a rule is reduced, the code supplied with the rule is executed before the stack is adjusted. In addition to the stack holding the states, another stack, running in parallel with it, holds the values returned from the lexical analyzer and the actions. When a shift takes place, the external variable yylval is copied onto the value stack. After the return from the user code, the reduction is carried out. When the goto action is done, the external variable yyval is copied onto the value stack. The pseudo-variables $1, $2, etc., refer to the value stack.

The other two parser actions are conceptually much simpler. The accept action indicates that the entire input has been seen and that it matches the specification. This action appears only when the lookahead token is the endmarker, and indicates that the parser has successfully done its job. The error action, on the other hand, represents a place where the parser can no longer continue parsing according to the specification. The inputtokens it has seen, together with the lookahead token, cannot be followed by anything that would result in a legal input. The parser reports an error, and attempts to recover the situation and resume parsing.

Consider the specification

```
%token DING DONG DELL
%%
rhyme   :   sound place
        ;
sound   :   DING DONG
        ;
place   :   DELL
        ;
```

When Yacc is invoked with the -v option, a file called y.output is produced, with a human-readable description of the parser. The y.output file corresponding to the above grammar (with some statistics stripped off the end) is:

```
state 0
    $accept : _rhyme $end

    DING shift 3
    . error

    rhyme goto 1
    sound goto 2
```

```
state 1
    $accept : rhyme_$end

    $end  accept
    .  error

state 2
    rhyme :  sound_place

    DELL  shift 5
    .  error

    place  goto 4

state 3
    sound :  DING_DONG

    DONG  shift 6
    .  error

state 4
    rhyme :  sound place_   (1)

    .  reduce 1

state 5
    place :  DELL_   (3)

    .  reduce 3

state 6
    sound :  DING DONG_   (2)
    .  reduce 2
```

In addition to the actions for each state, there is a description of the parsing rules being processed in each state. The _ character is used to indicate what has been seen, and what is yet to come, in each rule. Suppose the input is

DING DONG DELL

It is instructive to follow the steps of the parser while processing this input.

Initially, the current state is state 0. The parser needs to refer to the input in order to decide between the actions available in state 0, so the first token, DING, is read, becoming the lookahead token. The action in state 0 on DING is is ``shift 3'', so state 3 is pushed onto the stack, and the lookahead token is cleared. State 3 becomes the current state. The next token, DONG, is read, becoming the lookahead token. The action in state 3 on the token DONG is ``shift 6'', so state 6 is pushed onto the stack, and the lookahead is cleared. The stack now contains 0, 3, and 6. In state 6, without even consulting the lookahead, the parser reduces by rule 2.

sound : DING DONG

This rule has two symbols on the right hand side, so two states, 6 and 3, are popped off of the stack, uncovering state 0. Consulting the description of state 0, looking for a goto on sound,

sound goto 2

is obtained; thus state 2 is pushed onto the stack, becoming the current state.

In state 2, the next token, DELL, must be read. The action is ``shift 5'', so state 5 is pushed onto the stack, which now has 0, 2, and 5 on it, and the lookahead token is cleared. In state 5, the only action is to reduce by rule 3. This has one symbol on the right hand side, so one state, 5, is popped off, and state 2 is uncovered. The goto in state 2 on place, the left side of rule 3, is state 4. Now, the stack contains 0, 2, and 4. In state 4, the only action is to reduce by rule 1. There are two symbols on the right, so the top two states are popped off, uncovering state 0 again. In state 0, there is a goto on rhyme causing the parser to enter state 1. In state 1, the input is read; the endmarker is obtained, indicated by ``$end'' in the y.output file. The action in state 1 when the endmarker is seen is to accept, successfully ending the parse.

The reader is urged to consider how the parser works when confronted with such incorrect strings as DING DONG DONG, DING DONG, DING DONG DELL DELL, etc. A few minutes spend with this and other simple examples will probably be repaid when problems arise in more complicated contexts.

Ambiguity and Conflicts

A set of grammar rules is ambiguous if there is some input string that can be structured in two or more different ways. For example, the grammar rule

expr : expr '-' expr

is a natural way of expressing the fact that one way of forming an arithmetic expression is to put two other expressions together with a minus sign between them. Unfortunately, this grammar rule does not completely specify the way that all complex inputs should be structured. For example, if the input is

```
expr - expr - expr
```

the rule allows this input to be structured as either

```
( expr - expr ) - expr
```

or as

```
expr - ( expr - expr )
```

Yacc detects such ambiguities when it is attempting to build the parser. It is instructive to consider the problem that confronts the parser when it is given an input such as

```
expr - expr - expr
```

When the parser has read the second expr, the input that it has

seen:

```
expr - expr
```

matches the right side of the grammar rule above. The parser could reduce the input by applying this rule; after applying the rule; the input is reduced to expr(the left side of the rule).

The parser would then read the final part of the input:

```
- expr
```

and again reduce. The effect of this is to take the left associative interpretation.

Alternatively, when the parser has seen

```
expr - expr
```

it could defer the immediate application of the rule, and continue reading the input until it had seen

```
expr - expr - expr
```

It could then apply the rule to the rightmost three symbols, reducing them to expr and leaving

```
expr - expr
```

Now the rule can be reduced once more; the effect is to take the right associative interpretation. Thus, having read

```
expr - expr
```

the parser can do two legal things, a shift or a reduction, and has no way of deciding between them. This is called a shift / reduce conflict. It may also happen that the parser has a choice of two legal reductions; this is called a reduce / reduce conflict. Note that there are never any ``Shift/shift'' conflicts. When there are shift/reduce or reduce/reduce conflicts, Yacc still produces a parser. It does this by selecting one of the valid steps wherever it has a choice. A rule describing which choice to make in a given situation is called a disambiguating rule.

Yacc invokes two disambiguating rules by default:
1. In a shift/reduce conflict, the default is to do the shift.
2. In a reduce/reduce conflict, the default is to reduce by the earlier grammar rule (in the input sequence).

Rule 1 implies that reductions are deferred whenever there is a choice, in favor of shifts. Rule 2 gives the user control over the behavior of the parser in this situation, but reduce/reduce conflicts should be avoided whenever possible. Conflicts may arise because of mistakes in input or logic, or because the grammar rules, while consistent, require a more complex parser than Yacc can construct. The use of actions within rules can also cause conflicts, if the action must be done before the parser can be sure which rule is being recognized. In these cases, the application of disambiguating rules is inappropriate, and leads to an incorrect parser. For this reason, Yacc always reports the number of shift/reduce and reduce/reduce conflicts resolved by Rule 1 and Rule 2.

In general, whenever it is possible to apply disambiguating rules to produce a correct parser, it is also possible to rewrite the grammar rules so that the same inputs are read but there are no conflicts. For this reason, most previous parser generators have considered conflicts to be fatal errors. Our experience has suggested that this rewriting is somewhat unnatural, and produces slower parsers; thus, Yacc will produce parsers even in the presence of conflicts.

As an example of the power of disambiguating rules, consider a fragment from a programming language involving an ``if-then-else'' construction:

```
stat  :   IF '(' cond ')' stat
      |   IF '(' cond ')' stat ELSE stat
      ;
```

In these rules, IF and ELSE are tokens, cond is a nonterminal symbol describing conditional (logical) expressions, and stat is a nonterminal symbol describing statements. The first rule will be called the simple-if rule, and the second the if-else rule.

These two rules form an ambiguous construction, since input of the form

```
    IF ( C1 ) IF ( C2 ) S1 ELSE S2
```

can be structured according to these rules in two ways:

```
    IF ( C1 ) {
        IF ( C2 ) S1
    }
```

```
    ELSE S2
```
or
```
    IF ( C1 ) {
        IF ( C2 ) S1
        ELSE S2
    }
```

The second interpretation is the one given in most programming languages having this construct. Each ELSE is associated with the last preceding "un-ELSE'd" IF. In this example, consider the situation where the parser has seen

```
    IF ( C1 ) IF ( C2 ) S1
```

and is looking at the ELSE. It can immediately reduce by the simple-if rule to get

```
    IF ( C1 ) stat
```

and then read the remaining input,

```
    ELSE S2
```

and reduce

```
    IF ( C1 ) stat ELSE S2
```

by the if-else rule. This leads to the first of the above groupings of the input.

On the other hand, the ELSE may be shifted, S2 read, and then the right hand portion of

```
    IF ( C1 ) IF ( C2 ) S1 ELSE S2
```

can be reduced by the if-else rule to get

```
    IF ( C1 ) stat
```

which can be reduced by the simple-if rule. This leads to the second of the above groupings of the input, which is usually desired.

Once again the parser can do two valid things - there is a shift/reduce conflict. The application of disambiguating rule 1 tells the parser to shift in this case, which leads to the desired grouping. This shift/reduce conflict arises only when there is a particular current input symbol, ELSE, and particular inputs already seen, such as

```
    IF ( C1 ) IF ( C2 ) S1
```

In general, there may be many conflicts, and each one will be associated with an input symbol and a set of previously read inputs. The previously read inputs are characterized by the state of the parser.

The conflict messages of Yacc are best understood by examining the verbose (-v) option output file.

For example, the output corresponding to the above conflict state might be :

23: shift/reduce conflict (shift 45, reduce 18) on ELSE
state 23
stat : IF (cond) stat_ (18) stat : IF (cond) stat_ELSE stat
ELSE shift 45 . reduce 18

The first line describes the conflict, giving the state and the input symbol. The ordinary state description follows, giving the grammar rules active in the state, and the parser actions. Recall that the underline marks the portion of the grammar rules which has been seen. Thus in the example, in state 23 the parser has seen input corresponding to

    IF (cond) stat

and the two grammar rules shown are active at this time. The parser can do two possible things. If the input symbol is ELSE, it is possible to shift into state 45. State 45 will have, as part of its description, the line

    stat : IF (cond) stat ELSE_stat

since the ELSE will have been shifted in this state. Back in state 23, the alternative action, described by ``.'', is to be done if the input symbol is not mentioned explicitly in the above actions; thus, in this case, if the input symbol is not ELSE, the parser reduces by grammar rule 18 :

    stat : IF '(' cond ')' stat

Once again, notice that the numbers following ``shift'' commands refer to other states, while the numbers following ``reduce'' commands refer to grammar rule numbers. In the y.output file, the rule numbers are printed after those rules which can be reduced. In most one states, there will be at most reduce action possible in the state, and this will be the default command. The user who encounters unexpected shift/reduce conflicts will probably want to look at the verbose output to decide whether the default actions are appropriate..

Precedence

There is one common situation where the rules given above for resolving conflicts are not sufficient; this is in the parsing of arithmetic expressions. Most of the commonly used constructions for arithmetic expressions can be naturally described by the notion of precedence levels for operators, together with information about left or right associativity. It turns out that ambiguous grammars with appropriate disambiguating rules can be used to create parsers that are faster and easier to write than parsers constructed from unambiguous grammars. The basic notion is to write grammar rules of the form

    expr : expr OP expr

and

    expr : UNARY expr

for all binary and unary operators desired. This creates a very ambiguous grammar, with many parsing conflicts. As disambiguating rules, the user specifies the precedence, or binding strength, of all the operators, and the associativity of the binary operators. This information is sufficient to allow Yacc to resolve the parsing conflicts in accordance with these rules, and construct a parser that realizes the desired precedences and associativities.

The precedences and associativities are attached to tokens in the declarations section. This is done by a series of lines beginning with a Yacc keyword: %left, %right, or %nonassoc, followed by a list of tokens. All of the tokens on the same line are assumed to have the same precedence level and associativity; the lines are listed in order of increasing precedence or binding strength. Thus,

```
%left '+' '-'
%left '*' '/'
```

describes the precedence and associativity of the four arithmetic operators. Plus and minus are left associative, and have lower precedence than star and slash, which are also left associative. The keyword %right is used to describe right associative operators, and the keyword %nonassoc is used to describe operators, like the operator .LT. in Fortran, that may not associate with themselves; thus,

```
A .LT. B .LT. C
```

is illegal in Fortran, and such an operator would be described with the keyword %nonassoc in Yacc. As an example of the behavior of these declarations, the description

```
%right '='
%left '+' '-'
%left '*' '/'

%%

expr :    expr '=' expr
     |    expr '+' expr
     |    expr '-' expr
     |    expr '*' expr
     |    expr '/' expr
     |    NAME
     ;
```

might be used to structure the input

```
a = b = c*d - e - f*g
```

as follows :

a = (b = (((c*d)-e) - (f*g)))

When this mechanism is used, unary operators must, in general, be given a precedence. Sometimes a unary operator and a binary operator have the same symbolic representation, but different precedences. An example is unary and binary '-'; unary minus may be given the same strength as multiplication, or even higher, while binary minus has a lower strength than multiplication. The keyword, %prec, changes the precedence level associated with a particular grammar rule. %prec appears immediately after the body of the grammar rule, before the action or closing semicolon, and is followed by a token name or literal. It causes the precedence of the grammar rule to become that of the following token name or literal. For example, to make unary minus have the same precedence as multiplication the rules might resemble :

```
%left  '+'  '-'
%left  '*'  '/'

%%

expr  :     expr '+' expr
      |     expr '-' expr
      |     expr '*' expr
      |     expr '/' expr
      |     '-' expr   %prec '*'
      |     NAME
      ;
```

A token declared by %left, %right, and %nonassoc need not be, but may be, declared by %token as well. The precedences and associativities are used by Yacc to resolve parsing conflicts; they give rise to disambiguating rules. Formally, the rules work as follows:

1. The precedences and associativities are recorded for those tokens and literals that have them.
2. A precedence and associativity is associated with each grammar rule; it is the precedence and associativity of the last token or literal in the body of the rule. If the %prec construction is used, it overrides this default. Some grammar rules may have no precedence and associativity associated with them.
3. When there is a reduce/reduce conflict, or there is a shift/reduce conflict and either the input symbol or the grammar rule has no precedence and associativity, then the two

disambiguating rules given at the beginning of the section are used, and the conflicts are reported.

4. If there is a shift/reduce conflict, and both the grammar rule and the input character have precedence and associativity associated with them, then the conflict is resolved in favor of the action (shift or reduce) associated with the higher precedence. If the precedences are the same, then the associativity is used; left associative implies reduce, right associative implies shift, and nonassociating implies error.

Conflicts resolved by precedence are not counted in the number of shift/reduce and reduce/reduce conflicts reported by Yacc. The y.output file is very useful in deciding whether the parser is actually doing what was intended.

Error Handling

When an error is found, for example, it may be necessary to reclaim parse tree storage, delete or alter symbol table entries, and, typically, set switches to avoid generating any further output. Its better to stop all processing when an error is found; it is more useful to continue scanning the input to find further syntax errors. This leads to the problem of getting the parser ``restarted'' after an error. A general class of algorithms to do this involves discarding a number of tokens from the input string, and attempting to adjust the parser so that input can continue.

To allow the user some control over this process, Yacc provides a simple, but reasonably general, feature. The token name ``error'' is reserved for error handling. This name can be used in grammar rules; in effect, it suggests places where errors are expected, and recovery might take place. The parser pops its stack until it enters a state where the token ``error'' is legal. It then behaves as if the token ``error'' were the current lookahead token, and performs the action encountered.

The lookahead token is then reset to the token that caused the error. If no special error rules have been specified, the processing halts when an error is detected.

In order to prevent a cascade of error messages, the parser, after detecting an error, remains in error state until three tokens have been successfully read and shifted. If an error is detected when the parser is already in error state, no message is given, and the input token is quietly deleted.

As an example, a rule of the form

    stat :   error

would, in effect, mean that on a syntax error the parser would attempt to skip over the statement in which the error was seen. More precisely, the parser will scan ahead, looking for three tokens that might legally follow a statement, and start processing at the first of these; if the beginnings of statements are not sufficiently distinctive, it may make a false start in the middle of a statement, and end up reporting a second error where there is in fact no error.

Actions may be used with these special error rules. These actions might attempt to reinitialize tables, reclaim symbol table space, etc.

Error rules such as the above are very general, but difficult to control. Somewhat easier are rules such as

    stat :   error ';'

Here, when there is an error, the parser attempts to skip over the statement, but will do so by skipping to the next ';'. All tokens after the error and before the next ';' cannot be shifted, and are discarded. When the ';' is seen, this rule will be reduced, and any ``cleanup'' action associated with it performed.

Another form of error rule arises in interactive applications, where it may be desirable to permit a line to be reentered after an error. A possible error rule might be

    input :   error '\n' { printf("Reenter last line: "); } input
                { $$ = $4; }

There is one potential difficulty with this approach; the parser must correctly process three input tokens before it admits that it has correctly resynchronized after the error. If the reentered line contains an error in the first two tokens, the parser deletes the offending tokens, and gives no message; this is clearly unacceptable. For this reason, there is a mechanism that can be used to force the parser to believe that an error has been fully recovered from. The statement

    yyerrok ;

in an action resets the parser to its normal mode. The last example is better written

    input :   error '\n'
              {   yyerrok;
                printf("Reenter last line: "); }
        input
            { $$ = $4; }
    ;

As mentioned above, the token seen immediately after the ``error'' symbol is the input token at which the error was discovered. Sometimes, this is inappropriate; for example, an error recovery action might take upon itself the job of finding the correct place to resume input. In this case, the previous lookahead token must be cleared. The statement

    yyclearin ;

in an action will have this effect. For example, suppose the action after error were to call some sophisticated resynchronization routine, supplied by the user, that attempted to advance the input to the beginning of the next valid statement. After this routine was called, the next token returned by yylex would presumably be the first token in a legal statement; the old, illegal token must be discarded, and the error state reset. This could be done by a rule like

```
stat  :  error
         {   resynch();
             yyerrok ;
             yyclearin ;  }
      ;
```

These mechanisms are admittedly crude, but do allow for a simple, fairly effective recovery of the parser from many errors; moreover, the user can get control to deal with the error actions required by other portions of the program.

The Yacc Environment

When the user inputs a specification to Yacc, the output is a file of C programs, called y.tab.c on most systems. The function produced by Yacc is called yyparse; it is an integer valued function. When it is called, it in turn repeatedly calls yylex, the lexical analyzer supplied by the user to obtain input tokens. Eventually, either an error is detected, in which case yyparse returns the value 1, or the lexical analyzer returns the endmarker token and the parser accepts. In this case, yyparse returns the value 0.

The user must provide a certain amount of environment for this parser in order to obtain a working program. For example, as with every C program, a program called main must be defined, that eventually calls yyparse. In addition, a routine called yyerror prints a message when a syntax error is detected.

These two routines must be supplied in one form or another by the user. To ease the initial effort of using Yacc, a library has been provided with default versions of main and yyerror. The name of this library is system dependent; on many systems the library is accessed by a -ly argument to the loader. To show the triviality of these default programs, the source is given below :

```
main(){
    return( yyparse() );
}
```

and

```
# include <stdio.h>

yyerror(s) char *s; {
    fprintf( stderr, "%s\n", s );
}
```

The argument to yyerror is a string containing an error message, usually the string ``syntax error''. The average application will want to do better than this. Ordinarily, the program should keep track of the input line number, and print it along with the message when a syntax error is detected. The external integer variable yychar contains the lookahead token number at the time the error was detected; this may be of some interest in giving better diagnostics. Since the main program is probably supplied by the user (to read arguments, etc.) the Yacc library is useful only in small projects, or in the earliest stages of larger ones.

The external integer variable yydebug is normally set to 0. If it is set to a nonzero value, the parser will output a verbose description of its actions, including a discussion of which input symbols have been read, and what the parser actions are. Depending on the operating environment, it may be possible to set this variable by using a debugging system.

Advanced Features of Yacc

Simulating Error and Accept in Actions

The parsing actions of error and accept can be simulated in an action by use of macros YYACCEPT and YYERROR. YYACCEPT causes yyparse to return the value 0; YYERROR causes the parser to behave as if the current input symbol had been a syntax error; yyerror is called, and error recovery takes place. These mechanisms can be used to simulate parsers with multiple endmarkers or context-sensitive syntax checking.

Support for Arbitrary Value Types

By default, the values returned by actions and the lexical analyzer are integers. Yacc can also support values of other types, including structures. In addition, Yacc keeps track of the types, and inserts appropriate union member names so that the resulting parser will be strictly type checked. The Yacc value stack is declared to be a union of the various types of values desired. The user declares the union, and associates union member names to each token and nonterminal symbol having a value. When the value is referenced through a $$ or $n construction, Yacc will automatically insert the appropriate union name, so that no unwanted conversions will take place. In addition, type checking commands such as Lint will be far more silent. There are three mechanisms used to provide for this typing. First, there is a way of defining the union; this must be done by the user since other programs, notably the lexical analyzer, must know about the union member names. Second, there is a way of associating a union member name with tokens and nonterminals. Finally, there is a mechanism for describing the type of those few values where Yacc can not easily determine the type.

To declare the union, the user includes in the declaration section :

```
%union {
    body of union ...
}
```

This declares the Yacc value stack, and the external variables yylval and yyval, to have type equal to this union. If Yacc was invoked with the -d option, the union declaration is copied onto the y.tab.h file. Alternatively, the union may be declared in a header file, and a typedef used to define the variable YYSTYPE to represent this union. Thus, the header file might also have said :

```
typedef union {
    body of union ...
} YYSTYPE;
```

The header file must be included in the declarations section, by use of %{ and %}. Once YYSTYPE is defined, the union member names must be associated with the various terminal and nonterminal names. The construction

```
< name >
```

is used to indicate a union member name. If this follows one of the keywords %token, %left, %right, and %nonassoc, the union

member name is associated with the tokens listed. Thus, saying

```
%left <optype> '+' '-'
```

will cause any reference to values returned by these two tokens to be tagged with the union member name optype. Another keyword, %type, is used similarly to associate union member names with nonterminals. Thus, one might say

```
%type <nodetype> expr stat
```

There remain a couple of cases where these mechanisms are insufficient. If there is an action within a rule, the value returned by this action has no a priori type. Similarly, reference to left context values (such as $0 - see the previous subsection) leaves Yacc with no easy way of knowing the type. In this case, a type can be imposed on the reference by inserting a union member name, between < and >, immediately after the first $. An example of this usage is

```
rule :   aaa { $<intval>$ = 3; } bbb
         {   fun( $<intval>2, $<other>0 ); }
         ;
```

The facilities in this subsection are not triggered until they are used: in particular, the use of %type will turn on these mechanisms. When they are used, there is a fairly strict level of checking.

For example, use of $n or $$ to refer to something with no defined type is diagnosed. If these facilities are not triggered, the Yacc value stack is used to hold int's, as was true his.

1.4 OPEN CL

Introduction :
- Graphics Processing Unit (GPU) is normally used for graphics rendering operations.
- GPUs are high performance multicore processors that can be used to accelerate the execution performance of wide variety of applications using parallel computing.
- GPUs are basically high speed co-processors.
- Few years ago computer applications were able to scale up with advances in CPU technologies. But most of the modern applications such as 3D animations, machine designs, HD videos, and games are not compatible with advances in CPU technologies.
- To achieve the greater performance system often needs computational units other than traditional CPU.
- This creates the need for heterogeneous computing.
- Heterogeneous computing involves the use of various types of computational units such as general purpose processing units – CPU, Graphics Processing Units, Special purpose processing units such as digital signal processors (DSP).
- Heterogeneous computing allows application developer to select most suitable computational unit to achieve the better results. Heterogeneous computing gives the freedom to developer to utilize most beneficial computing unit based on his requirement.
- Open Computing Language (OpenCL) is a framework for writing programs that execute across heterogeneous platforms consisting of central processing units (CPUs), graphics processing units (GPUs), digital signal processors (DSPs), field-programmable gate arrays (FPGAs) and other processors.
- OpenCL is basically a open source parallel computing API designed to enable GPUs and other co-processors to work in association with CPU.
- This mechanism provides the additional computing power which results in acceleration of performance by parallel processing.
- OpenCL enables all computational resources such as multicore CPUs and GPUs as peer computational units.
- OpenCL also provides cross vendor software portability. All the hardware implementation details such as drivers and runtimes are invisible to software programmers which allows them to take the advantage of best underlying hardware.
- OpenCL includes a language for programming these devices, and application programming interfaces (APIs) to control the platform and execute programs on the compute devices. OpenCL provides parallel computing using task-based and data-based parallelism.

1.4.1 OpenCL Development Framework

- OpenCL development framework has following three important components.
  1. Language Specification.
  2. Platform API.
  3. Runtime API.
- Language specification describes the syntax and programming interfaces for writing the kernel functions.
- Kernel functions are like normal C language functions which are to be run on supporting acceleration devices such as GPU, multi core CPU or any special purpose processor.
- C language is base for OpenCL. This OpenCL programming environment is based on OpenCL C programming language.
- Platform API gives the developer access to software applications that can query the system for the existence of OpenCL supported devices.
- Platform API can also be used for initializing OpenCL devices, submitting the workload to these OpenCL supported devices and enabling the data transfer to and from the devices.
- Runtime API can be used for managing one or more OpenCL devices. This API also manages memory objects, kernel objects. Runtime API is responsible executing the kernel functions on or more OpenCL supporting devices.

1.4.2 OpenCL Platform Model

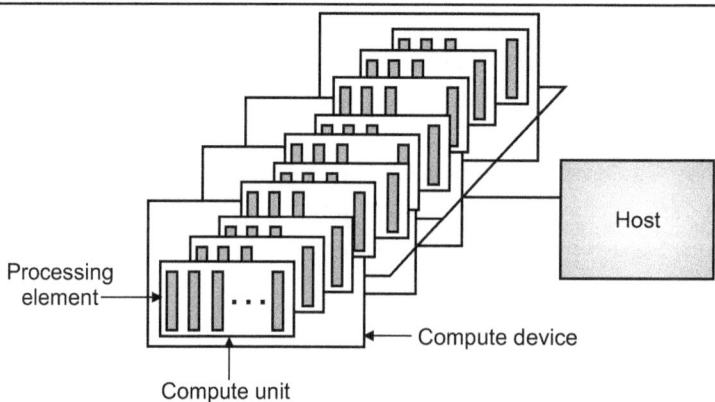

Fig. 1.3 : OpenCL Platform Model

- In platform model a host is connected to one or more OpenCL devices.
- A host is any computer with a CPU running standard operating system
- OpenCL compute devices are GPU, multi core CPU, DSP, etc.
- Each OpenCL compute device consists of a collection of one or more computing units called as cores.

- These computing units consist of one or more processing elements.
- These processing elements execute the instructions in SIMD or SPMD manner.
- SPMD instructions are typically executed on CPU and SIMD instructions are executed on GPUs.
- Serial code is always executed on CPU and parallel code is always executed on GPU.

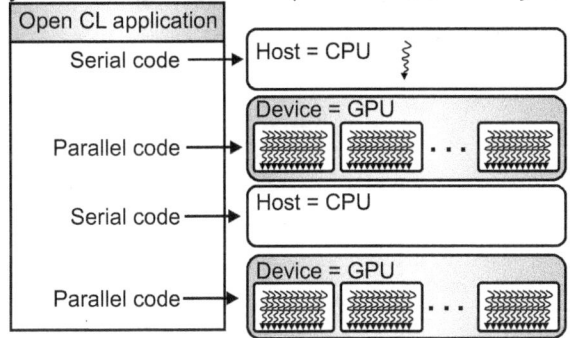

Fig. 1.4 : Execution of Serial and Parallel Code

1.4.2.1 Specifications of ATI Radeon HD 5870 in Terms of Processing Units

- GPU available on ATI Radeon HD 5870 is made up of 20 SIMD units. These 20 SIMD units corresponds to 20 compute units in terms of OpenCL
- Each SIMD unit contains 16 stream cores and each core has 5 processing elements
- This each computing unit in this graphics card has 16*5 = 80 processing elements.

1.4.3 OpenCL Execution Model

- OpenCL execution model consists of 2 components: kernels and host programs.
- Kernels are the basic unit of executable code that runs on one or more OpenCL devices.
- These kernels are similar to C functions.
- Host programs get execute on host system and they decide which kernel to be executed on which OpenCL device.
- If multiple kernels are available then these kernels are queued in order.
- But while execution they can be executed in order or out of order.

1.4.3.1 Kernels

- OpenCL exhibits parallel computation on compute devices by defining the problem into n dimensional space.
- When a kernel is queued for execution by the host program, an index space is defined
- Each independent element of execution in this index space is called a work item.
- Each work item executes the same kernel but on different data.

Index space must be defined to let the device keep track of the total number of work items that require execution.
- Value for N in N dimensional workspace
  N = 1 for processing a linear array of data
  N = 2 for processing 2 dimensional array of data. Say image
  N = 3 for processing 3 D objects.
- Consider processing of 1024*1024 image.

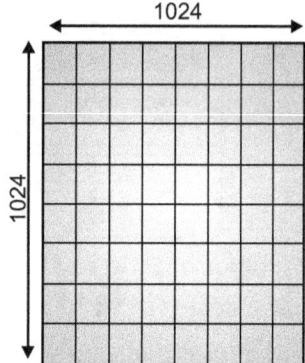

Fig. 1.5 : 2 Dimensional Workspace of Size 1024*1024

- Index space is 2 dimensional space of 1024*1024 with 1 kernel execution per pixel.
- Within this index space each work item is assigned a unique global ID.
- Within its local workgroup each work item is known by a local ID.
- OpenCL allows grouping of work items together in work group
- All work items in the same workgroup are executed together on the same device.
- The reason for such execution is to allow work items from same workgroup to share local memory and synchronization.
- Global work items are independent and cannot be synchronized.
- Consider 2 D image with global size 1024 (9 * 9).
- Index space is divided into 9 groups. Thus each workgroup will be of size 9 (3*3).
- Each group has its ID and local size.
- Each work item is addressed with its local ID and global ID
- Global ID is calculated at the workspace level whereas local ID is calculated at the workgroup level.
- OpenCL execution model supports two types of kernels

1. **OpenCL kernels**
- OpenCL kernels are written in OpenCL C language and compiled with OpenCL compiler
- Devices that support OpenCL can execute OpenCL kernels.

2. Native kernels
- These are usually special functions exported from library designed for particular application.
- OpenCL provides functionality to determine which native kernels are supported.

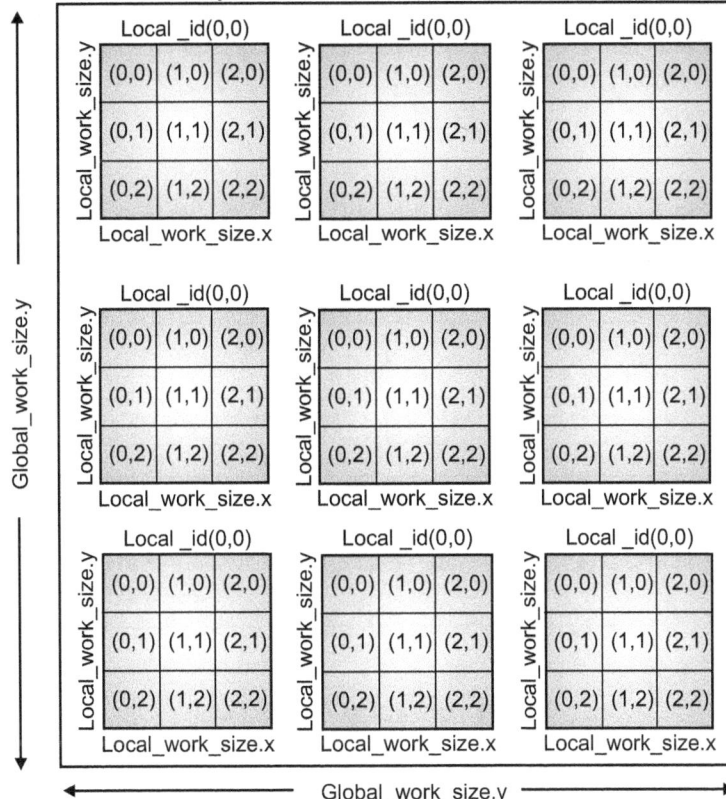

Fig. 1.6 : Dividing Single 9*9 Workspace into nine 3*3 Workgroups

1.4.3.2 Host programs
- Host programs are the programs that run on host.
- These are responsible for managing the execution of kernels on OpenCL devices with the help of contexts.
- Using OpenCL API host can create the context with the help of following resources
    1. Devices – OpenCL supported devices that run kernels
    2. Program Objects – Objects that represent the kernel or collection of kernels
    3. Kernels – OpenCL functions that execute on the OpenCL devices
    4. Memory Objects – Objects that represent a set of memory buffers that is common to host and OpenCL devices

5. After the context is created queues are created to manage the execution of kernels on OpenCL devices

1.4.4 OpenCL Memory Model

- When common memory address space between host and OpenCL devices is not available, OpenCL memory model defines 4 regions of memory that is accessible to work items when executing a kernel
  1. Global memory
  2. Constant memory
  3. Local memory
  4. Private memory

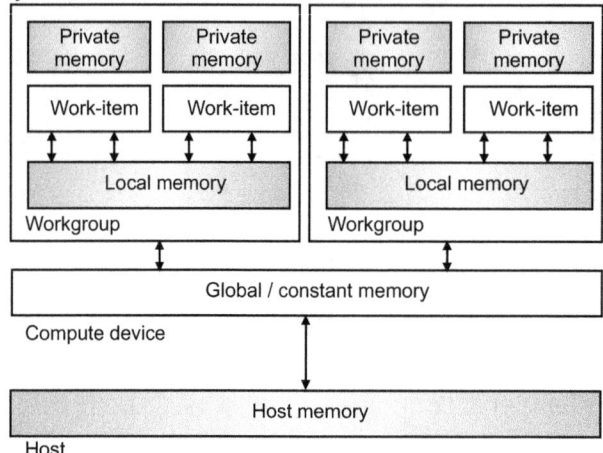

Fig. 1.7 : OpenCL Memory Model

- Global memory is a memory region in which all work items and work groups have read and write access.
- This memory region can be allocated by only host during run time.
- Constant memory is a region of global memory that is constant throughout the execution of kernel.
- Work items have read only access to this region
- Host can perform both read and write to this region
- Local memory is associated with workgroup
- Work items from the same work group have both read and write access in corresponding global memory.
- Private memory is associated with individual work item and work item can perform read and write in its private memory.

1.4.5 OpenCL Framework :

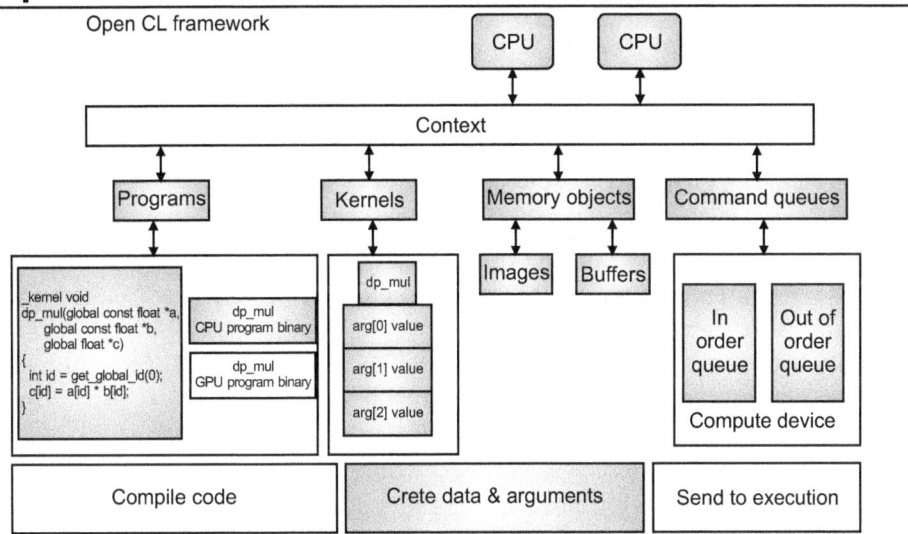

Fig. 1.8 : OpenCL Framework

1.4.6 Steps for Program

1. Obtain OpenCL platform
2. Obtain device id for at least one device (accelerator)
3. Create context for device
4. Create accelerator program from source code
5. Build the program
6. Create kernel(s) from program functions
7. Create command queue for target device
8. Allocate device memory / move input data to device memory
9. Associate arguments to kernel with kernel object
10. Deploy kernel for device execution
11. Move output data to host memory
12. Release context/program/kernels/memory.

Step 1 Obtain Platform :
- Platform id identifies vendor installation of OpenCL clGetPlatformIDs(1, &platform, NULL);
- Functions often used twice, first to get the number of platforms and then for allocation.

Step 2 Obtain Device Id for At Least One Device (Accelerator) :
- Use platform to get ID for device clGetDeviceIds(platform, CL_DEVICE_TYPE_GPU, 1, &device, NULL); device id is stored in "device" variable

- Functions often used twice, first to get the number of devices available and then for allocation.

Step 3 Create Context For Device - Context - Abstract Container Attached To Device :
- Contains program kernels, memory objects, etc .
- Holds command queue used for program execution.
  context = clCreateContext(NULL, 1, &device, NULL, NULL, &err);

Step 4 Create Accelerator Program from Source Code :
- Recommended to have a .cl file that contains kernels to run on accelerator .
- Read .cl file into a string on host ○ Create cl_program attached to context.
- program = clCreateProgramWithSource (context, 1, (const char**) &program_buffer, &program_size, &err);

Step 5 Build the Program - OpenCL Accelerator Code is Compiled at Run-time :
Host code will compile even if there are errors in accelerator code .
Need to check for errors during run-time compilation.
clBuildProgram(program, 0,..) .
Compilation error determined by error value returned from clBuildProgram
Calling clGetProgramBuildInfo() with the program object and the parameter CL_PROGRAM_BUILD_STATUS returns a string with the compiler output

Step 6 Create Cl_Kernel(S) From Program Functions :
- Use (now built) program as parameter to create kernel.
- kernel = clCreateKernel(program, "kernel_name", &err) .
- "kernel_name" is the name of the kernel function to be run in parallel.

Step 7 Create Command Queue for Kernel Dispatch
- Command queue is attached to specific device.
  Mechanism for request that action be performed by device.
  Requests include memory transfer, begin executing kernel, etc.
- Can support out-of-order execution and profiling ○ queue = clCreateCommandQueue(context, device, 0, &err).

Step 8 Allocate Device Memory / Move Input Data To Device
- memObject = clCreateBuffer (context, NULL, SIZE_N, NULL, &err) .
- clEnqueueWriteBuffer(command_queue, memObject, ..., TOTAL_SIZE, hostPointer, ...) .
- Memory objects can be buffers or images.

Check buffers and make sure that contiguous memory chunks on GPU (global memory) areRead/write capable.

Step 9 Associate Arguments To Kernel With Kernel Object
- cl_int clSetKernelArg (kernel, arg_index, arg_size, *arg_value) .
- arg_index is index of argument in function signature (0 if first argument into function, etc).

- Argument value is pointer to memory object if input parameter is array (buffer on GPU).
- Argument value is pointer to primitive if input parameter is primitive value (such as a char, int, float, etc).

Step 10 Deploy Kernel For Device Execution
- Using command_queue, kernel object, and global and local (workgroup) sizes.
  global_size = TOTAL_NUM_THREADS;
  local_size = WORKGROUP_SIZE;
- All threads in workgroup execute on same compute unit.
- Access to fast local memory (shared within workgroup) .
- Can synchronize between threads in workgroup.
  clEnqueueNDRangeKernel(command_queue, kernel, 1, NULL, &global_size, &local_size, 0, NULL, NULL);

Step 11 Write Output Device Data Back To Host
- clEnqueueReadBuffer(command_queue, memObject, blocking_read, offset, TOTAL_SIZE, hostPointer, 0, NULL, NULL) .

Notable parameters.
- command_queue
- memObject
- buffer size
- target pointer on host

Step 12 Release Context/Program/Kernels/Memory
- clReleaseMemObject(memObject) .
- clReleaseKernel(kernel).
- clReleaseProgram(program).
- clReleaseContext(context)

1.4.7 Restrictions of OpenCL C Language
- OpenCl C language does not support Recursion.
- It does not support Variable-length arrays and structures.
- It does not support Bit-fields.
- Pointers to pointers allowed within a kernel, but not as an argument
- 3D Image writes are not supported.

QUESTIONS	
1. What are the Different Computation Models? Explain in detail.	(12)
2. What is Iterative computation? How it works?	(6)
3. Explain classification of Declarative Programming.	(8)
4. Explain Declarative Concurrency.	(6)

5. Explain message passing concurrency. (8)
6. Explain Object Oriented Programming. (8)
7. Explain Shared-State Concurrency. (8)
8. Explain Programming with atomic actions in Shared-State Concurrency. (6)
9. Explain Relational Computational Model. (8)
10. Explain Graphical User Interface Programming. (8)
11. Explain Distribution of declarative data. (4)
12. Explain Constraint Programming. (8)
13. Explain Recursive Computation is Declarative Programming Technique. (8)
14. Explain distributed programming language Lisp. (8)
15. How processes spawn in Erlang Lisp? (6)
16. Explain Termite as a Lisp Programming language in Distributed Computing. (8)
17. How Remote Procedure Call works in Termite? (6)
18. Explain mutable data structure of termite. (4)
19. Explain Yacc actions. (4)
20. Explain Lexical Analysis. (6)
21. Explain How the parser works. (6)
22. Explain the ambiguities in grammar in yacc. How to remove these ambiguities? (8)
23. Explain the advance features of Yacc. (6)
24. Explain MPI java in detail. (6)
25. Explain data types of MPI in detail. (6)
26. How to send and receive messages in MPI? (6)
27. Write short notes on :
    (i) Collective Communications (ii) Groups (iii) Overlapping Communications (8)
28. What is OpenGL ? Explain its need. (4)
29. Explain OpenGL's Rendering Pipeline. (8)
30. Explain in detail Graphics Library of OpenGL. (8)
31. What are the different OpenGL drawing primitives ? (6)
32. What are the different features in OpenGL ? (6)

UNIT - II
CONCURRENT PROGRAMMING

2.1 COMMUNICATION AND SYNCHRONIZATION OF CONCURRENT TASKS

2.1.1 Communication and Synchronization

2.1.1.1 Dependency Relationships

Process or threads of a common process often require interaction and co-operation between each other so that they can achieve their common result. This interaction and cooperation is defined by dependency relationship. When we say process 2 depends on process1, it means process 2 requires some input from process1. Without the input from process1, process 2 cannot progress. When there are two process say process1 and process2 there could be any one of the four kinds of dependency relationship between them.

- Process1 -> Process 2: Process 1 depends on process 2 but process2 does not depend on process 1.
- Process 2-> Process1: Process 2 depends on process 1 but process1 does not depend on process 2.
- Process1<->Process2: Both processes depend on each other.
- There exists no dependency relationship between both processes.

Dependency relationship between two processes can be divided into two major parts :

- Communication Dependency: When process 1 requires data from process 2 we say there exists communication dependency between process1 and process2.

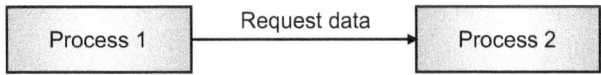

- Co-operation Dependency: When process1 requires any resource from process 2 we say there exists cooperation dependency between process1 and process2.

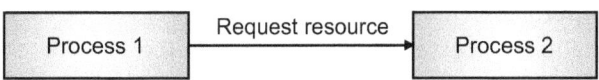

2.1.1.2 Interprocess Communication

In computer science, **inter-process communication** (**IPC**) is the activity of sharing data across multiple and commonly specialized processes using communication protocols. Typically, applications using IPC are categorized as clients and servers, where the client requests data and the server responds to client requests. Many applications are both clients and servers, as commonly seen in distributed computing. Methods for achieving IPC are divided into categories which vary based on software requirements, such as performance and modularity requirements, and system circumstances, such as network bandwidth and latency.

There are several reasons for implementing inter-process communication systems :

- Sharing information: for example, web servers use IPC to share web documents and media with users through a web browser.
- Distributing labor across systems :for example, Wikipedia uses multiple servers that communicate with one another using IPC to process user requests.[2]
- Privilege separation : for example, HMI software systems are separated into layers based on privileges to minimize the risk of attacks. These layers communicate with one another using encrypted IPC.

Following are the list of Types of IPC :

Method	Description
File	A record stored on disk, or a record synthesized on demand by a file server, which can be accessed by multiple processes.
Signal	A system message sent from one process to another, not usually used to transfer data but instead used to remotely command the partnered process.
Socket	A data stream sent over a network interface, either to a different process on the same computer or to another computer on the network.
Message queue	An anonymous data stream similar to a socket, usually implemented by the operating system, that allows multiple processes to read and write to the message queue without being directly connected to each other.
Pipe	A two way data stream between two processes interfaced through standard input and output and read in one character at a time.
Named Pipe	A pipe implemented through a file on the file system instead of standard input and output. Multiple processes can read and write to the file as a buffer for IPC data.
Semaphore	A simple structure that synchronizes multiple processes acting on shared resources.
Shared Memory	Multiple processes are given access to the same block of memory which creates a shared buffer for the processes to communicate with each other.
Message Passing	Allows multiple programs to communicate using channels, commonly used in concurrent models.
Memory Mapped File	A file mapped to RAM can be modified by changing memory addresses directly instead of outputting to a stream. This shares the same benefits as a standard file.

(a) Files

Files are used for the transfer and sharing of data between processes. Files can be used to transfer data between processes that are related or unrelated. They can allow processes that were not designed to work together to do so. When you use files to communicate between processes, you follow basic steps in the file - transferring process :

- Create a new file
- Change the access permissions and attributes of a file
- Open a file, which makes the file contents available to the program
- Read data from a file
- Write data to a file
- Close a file, terminating the association between it and the program

First, Create a file. The name of the file has to be communicated between the processes. Each file contained over a million strings. The posix_queue contained the names of the files. Filenames can also be passed to child processes by means of other IPC - like pipes.

When the process is accessing the file, if more than one process can also access the same file, you need provide synchronization. Leaving the file open can lead to data corruption and can prevent other processes from accessing the file. The processes that read or write to or from the file should know the file's file format in order to correctly process the file. The file's format refers to the file type and the file's organization. The file's type also implies the type of data in the file. The processes should also know the file layout or how the data is organized in the file.

(b) Pipes

A pipe is a communication device that permits unidirectional communication. Data written to the "write end" of the pipe is read back from the "read end." Pipes are serial devices; the data is always read from the pipe in the same order it was written. Typically, a pipe is used to communicate between two threads in a single process or between parent and child processes.

Fig. 2.1 : Pipe which Provides Inter-Process Communication Channel

There are two kinds of pipes :
(1) Un-named or Anonymous
(2) Named (also called FIFO)

(1) Un-named Pipes

Unnamed or anonymous pipes provide a means of one-to-one, one-way interprocess communication between different processes that are related by either a parent-child relationship, or by being children of a common parent that provides the pipe, such as a shell process. Because the processes are related, the association of file descriptors to the pipe can be implicit and does not require an object with a name that is external to the processes. An unnamed pipe exists only as long as the processes that use it maintain open file descriptors to the pipe. When the processes exit and the OS closes all of the file descriptors associated with the processes, the unnamed pipe is closed.

(2) Named Pipes

Named pipes are in fact FIFO's. These are persistent objects represented by nodes in the file system. A named pipe provides many-to-many, two-way communication between one or more processes that are not necessarily related and do not need to exist at the same time. The file name of the pipe serves as an address or contract between the processes for communication. If only one process writes to a named pipe and one other process reads from the named pipe, then the named pipe behaves in the same way as an unnamed pipe between the two related processes

Creating Pipes

To create a pipe, invoke the pipe command. Supply an integer array of size 2.The call to pipe stores the reading file descriptor in array position 0 and the writing file descriptor in position 1. For example, consider this code :

```
int pipefds[2];
int readfd;
int writefd;
pipe (pipefds);
readfd = pipefds[0];
writefd = pipefds[1];
```

Data written to the file descriptor readfd can be read back from writefd.

e.g. A pipe provides a one-way flow of data.

```
Int pipe (int * filedes); Int pipefd[2];
/* pipefd[0] is opened for reading;pipefd[1] is opened for writing */
```

Example to show how to create and use a pipe:

```
main()
{
int pipefd[2], n;
char buff[100];
if (pipe(pipefd) < 0 ) err_sys("pipe error");
printf("read fd = %d, write fd = %d\n", pipefd[0], pipefd[1]);
if (write(pipefd[1], "hello world\n", 12) != 12) err_sys("write error");
```

```
if ( (n=read(pipefd[0], buff, sizeof(buff))) <=0) err_sys("read error");
write(1, buff, n);
/*fd=1=stdout*/
}
result: hello world read fd=3, write df =4
```

FIFO Interface Class

A first-in, first-out (FIFO) file is a pipe that has a name in the filesystem. Any process can open or close the FIFO; the processes on either end of the pipe need not be related to each other. FIFOs are also called named pipes.

Here are the basic components of the FIFO model :

Input/output port.

Insertion and extraction operation.

Creation/initialization operation.

Buffer creation, insertion, extraction, destruction.

Creating a FIFO

Create a FIFO programmatically using the mkfifo function. The first argument is the path at which to create the FIFO; the second parameter specifies the pipe's owner, group, and world permissions, "Security," "File System Permissions." Because a pipe must have a reader and a writer, the permissions must include both read and write permissions. If the pipe cannot be created (for instance, if a file with that name already exists), mkfifo returns −1. Include <sys/types.h> and <sys/stat.h> if you call mkfifo.

Accessing a FIFO

Access a FIFO just like an ordinary file. To communicate through a FIFO, one program must open it for writing, and another program must open it for reading. Either low-level I/O functions (open, write, read, close, and so on, as listed in Appendix B, "Low-Level I/O") or C library I/O functions (fopen, fprintf, fscanf, fclose, and so on) may be used. For example, to write a buffer of data to a FIFO using low-level I/O routines, you could use this code :

```
int fd = open (fifo_path, O_WRONLY);
write (fd, data, data_length);
close (fd);
```

To read a string from the FIFO using C library I/O functions, you could use this code:

```
FILE* fifo = fopen (fifo_path, "r");
fscanf (fifo, "%s", buffer); fclose (fifo);
```

Message Queue

POSIX defines a set of nonblocking message-passing facilities known as *message queues*. Like pipes, message queues are named objects that operate with "readers" and "writers." As a priority queue of discrete messages, a message queue has more structure than a pipe and offers applications more control over communications. Message queues provide an asynchronous communications protocol, meaning that the sender and receiver of the message do not need to interact with the message queue at the same time. Messages placed onto the queue are stored until the recipient retrieves them. Message queues have implicit or explicit limits on the size of data that may be transmitted in a single message and the number of messages that may remain outstanding on the queue. Message Queues are Linked list of messages. When reading a message from the queue, the oldest message with the highest priority is returned. Each message in the queue has these attributes :

- A priority
- The length of the message
- The message or data

With a linked list the head of the list has the maximum number of messages allowed in the queue and the maximum size allowed for a message.

POSIX Message Queues

POSIX message queues provide a familiar interface for many realtime programmers. They are similar to the "mailboxes" found in many realtime executives. There's a fundamental difference between our messages and POSIX message queues. Our messages block — they copy their data directly between the address spaces of the processes sending the messages. POSIX messages queues, on the other hand, implement a store-and-forward design in which the sender need not block and may have many outstanding messages queued. POSIX message queues exist independently of the processes that use them. You would likely use message queues in a design where a number of named queues will be operated on by a variety of processes over time.

System calls to support messages queues :

(1) msgget : Create or open a message queue.

(2) msgsend : Send a message to a message queue.

(3) msgrcv : Receive a message from a message queue.

(4) msgctl : Control message queue information.

(1) msgget()

#include <sys/types.h>
#include <sys/msg.h>
#include <sys/ipc.h>
int msgget(key_t key, int flags);

key :

– An integer
– IPC_PRIVATE:

Create a new key and a new IPC

flags:
- IPC_CREAT: Create entry if key does not exist
- IPC_EXCL: Fail if key exists
- IPC_NOWAIT: Fail if request must wait

(2) msgctl()
```
#include <sys/types.h>
#include <sys/msg.h>
#include <sys/ipc.h>
int msgctl(int msgid, int cmd, struct msqid_ds *buffer);
```

(3) msgid
IPC ID

cmd:
- IPC_STAT:

Copy information from the kernel data structure associated with msqid into the msqid_ds structure pointed to by buffer.

- IPC_SET:

Write the values of some members of the msqid_ds structure pointed to by buffer to the kernel data structure associated with this message queue, updating also its msg_ctime member.

- IPC_RMID: Remove the message queue, awake all waiting reader and writer processes.

(3) msgsnd ()
```
#include <sys/types.h>
#include <sys/msg.h>
#include <sys/ipc.h>
int msgsnd(int msqid, void *msgp, size_t msgsz, int msgflg);
```

msqid : IPC ID

msgp : Pointer to the message data (can be anything): struct msgbuf { long mtype; /* message type, must be > 0 */ char *mtext; /* message data of size msgsz */ };

msgsz : Size of the message (bytes)

msgflg :
- IPC_NOWAIT: Immediate return if no message of the type is in queue
- MSG_EXCEPT: If (msgtyp > 0) read the first message in the queue.
- MSG_NOERROR: Truncate the message text if longer than msgsz bytes.

(a) msgrcv()

#include <sys/types.h>
#include <sys/msg.h>
#include <sys/ipc.h>
int msgrcv (int msqid, void *msgp, size_t msgsz, long msgtype, int msgflg);

msqid : IPC ID

msgp : Pointer to the message data (can be anything):

struct msgbuf { long mtype; /* message type, must be > 0 */ char *mtext; /* message data of size msgsz */ };

msgsz : Size of the message (bytes)

msgtype : Type of the message

msgflg :

- IPC_NOWAIT: Immediate return if no message of the type is in queue
- MSG_EXCEPT: If (msgtyp > 0) read the first message in the queue.
- MSG_NOERROR: Truncate the message text if longer than msgsz bytes.

Program :

```
struct mymsg
{
long mtype; char *mtext;
};
int main()
{
int msqid; struct mymsg msg;
char buffer[10] = "abcdefghi\0";
msg.mtype = 1;
msg.mtext = buffer;
/* Creation of the IPC */
if ((msqid = msgget(20, 0666 | IPC_CREAT)) == 1)
{
perror("mymsg");
exit(1);
}
/* Sending a message */
msgsnd(msqid, &msg, 3, 0); sleep(5);
```

```
/* Receiving a message */
msgrcv(msqid, &msg, 3, 1, 0);
printf("The message is: %s", msg.mtext); exit(0);
}
```

(a) Sockets

Sockets provide point-to-point, two-way communication between two processes. Sockets are very versatile and are a basic component of interprocess and intersystem communication. A socket is an endpoint of communication to which a name can be bound. It has a type and one or more associated processes.

Sockets exist in communication domains. A socket domain is an abstraction that provides an addressing structure and a set of protocols.

The UNIX domain provides a socket address space on a single system. UNIX domain sockets are named with UNIX paths. Sockets can also be used to communicate between processes on different systems.

Socket types define the communication properties visible to the application. Processes communicate only between sockets of the same type. There are different types of socket.

(1) A Stream Socket

Provides two-way, sequenced, reliable, and unduplicated flow of data with no record boundaries. A stream operates much like a telephone conversation. The socket type isSOCK_STREAM, which, in the Internet domain, uses Transmission Control Protocol (TCP).

(2) A Datagram Socket

Supports a two-way flow of messages. A on a datagram socket may receive messages in a different order from the sequence in which the messages were sent. Record boundaries in the data are preserved. Datagram sockets operate much like passing letters back and forth in the mail. The socket type is SOCK_DGRAM, which, in the Internet domain, uses User Datagram Protocol (UDP).

(3) A Sequential Packet Socket

Provides a two-way, sequenced, reliable, connection, for datagrams of a fixed maximum length. The socket type is SOCK_SEQPACKET.

(4) A Raw Socket

Provides access to the underlying communication protocols.

Socket Creation and Naming

Int socket(int domain, int type, int protocol) is called to create a socket in the specified domain and of the specified type. If a protocol is not specified, the system defaults to a protocol that supports the specified socket type. The socket handle (a descriptor) is returned. A remote process has no way to identify a socket until an address is bound to it.

Communicating processes connect through addresses. In the UNIX domain, a connection is usually composed of one or two path names. In the Internet domain, a connection is composed of local and remote addresses and local and remote ports. In most domains, connections must be unique.

int bind(int s, const struct sockaddr *name, int namelen) is called to bind a path or internet address to a socket. There are three different ways to call bind(), depending on the domain of the socket. For UNIX domain sockets with paths containing 14, or fewer characters, you can :

#include <sys/socket.h>

...

bind (sd, (struct sockaddr *) &addr, length);

If the path of a UNIX domain socket requires more characters, use:

#include <sys/un.h>

...

bind (sd, (struct sockaddr_un *) &addr, length);

For Internet domain sockets, use

#include <netinet/in.h>

...

bind (sd, (struct sockaddr_in *) &addr, length);

A socket communication is created by

#include <sys/socket.h>

#include <sys/types.h>

int socket(int domain, int type, int protocol);

The two most common domain (or address family) used are :

AF UNIX : The addresses are ordinary UNIX path name :

AF INET : The addresses are Internet addresses (four-byte numbers usually written as four decimal numbers separated by periods e.g. 192.9.200.10).

In addition to the machine address, there is also a port number which allows more than one AF INET socket on each machine.

There are two types of communication channels supported by sockets (selected with the argument type in socket function.

SOCK STREAM : It is a birectional continuous byte stream that guarantees the reliable delivery of data.

SOCK DGRAM : This type of connection is used to send distinct packets of information called datagrams.

The delivery of data is not guaranteed. protocol specifies a particular protocol to be used with the socket.

Steps in Server Process :
1. Call socket() with proper arguments to create the socket
2. Call bind() to bind the socket to an address (in our case it is just a pathname) in the Unix domain.
3. Call listen() to instruct the socket to listen for incoming connections from client programs.
4. Call accept(): to accept a connection from a client.
5. Handle the connection and loop back to accept().
6. Close the connection.

Steps in Client Process
1. Call socket() to get a Unix domain socket to communicate through.
2. Set up a struct sockaddr un with the remote address (where the server is listening) and call connect() with that as an argument.
3. Assuming no errors, you're connected to the remote side! Use send() and recv() to communicate.

Program :
Server code Echo back the message sent by the client

```
#include <stdio.h>
#include <stdlib.h>
#include <errno.h>
#include <string.h>
#include <sys/types.h>
#include <sys/socket.h>
#include <sys/un.h>
#define SOCK_PATH "my_socket"
int main(void)
{
int s, s2, t, len;
struct sockaddr_un local, remote;
char str[100];
if ((s = socket(AF_UNIX, SOCK_STREAM, 0)) == -1)
{
perror("socket"); exit(1);
```

```
}
local.sun_family = AF_UNIX;
strcpy(local.sun_path, SOCK_PATH);
unlink(local.sun_path);
// remove existing socket
len = strlen(local.sun_path) + sizeof(local.sun_family);
if (bind(s, (struct sockaddr *)&local, len) == -1)
{
 perror("bind");
 exit(1);
}
 if (listen(s, 5) == -1)
 {
 perror("listen");
 exit(1);
 }
for(;;)
{
 int done, n;
 printf("Waiting for a connection...\n");
 t = sizeof(remote);
if ((s2 = accept(s, (struct sockaddr *)&remote, &t)) == -1)
 {
 perror("accept");
 exit(1);
 }
printf("Connected.\n");
 done = 0;
do { n = recv(s2, str, 100, 0);
 if (n > 0){ str[n] = '\0';
 printf("Received : %s\n", str);
}
else if (n <= 0)
 {
```

```
if (n < 0) perror("recv"); done = 1;
}
if (!done) if (send(s2, str, n, 0) < 0)
{
perror("send"); done = 1;
}
}
while (!done);
 close(s2);
}
close(s);
return 0;
}
```

Client code
 Message from the client is echoed by the server
```
#include <stdio.h>
#include <stdlib.h>
#include <errno.h>
#include <string.h>
#include  <sys/types.h>
#include  <sys/socket.h>
#include <sys/un.h>
#define SOCK_PATH "my_socket"
int main(void)
{
 int s, t, len;
struct sockaddr_un remote;
char str[100];
 if ((s = socket(AF_UNIX, SOCK_STREAM, 0)) == -1)
{
perror("socket");
exit(1);
}
```

```c
printf("Trying to connect...\n");
remote.sun_family = AF_UNIX;
strcpy(remote.sun_path, SOCK_PATH);
len = strlen(remote.sun_path) + sizeof(remote.sun_family);
if (connect(s, (struct sockaddr *)&remote, len) == -1)
{
perror("connect");
exit(1);
}
printf("Connected.\n");
while(printf("> "), fgets(str, 100, stdin), !feof(stdin))
{
if (send(s, str, strlen(str), 0) == -1)
{
perror("send");
exit(1);
}
if ((t=recv(s, str, 100, 0)) > 0)
{
str[t] = '\0';
printf("echo> %s", str);
}
Else
{
if (t < 0) perror("recv");
else
printf("Server closed connection\n");
exit(1);

}
}
close(s);
return 0;
}
```

2.1.1.3 Interthread Communications

Inter thread communication is important when you develop an application where two or more threads exchange some information.

Communication between threads is used to :

(a) Share Data

(b) Send a Message

Multiple threads share data to complete their task concurrently. Each thread can perform different processing or the same processing on data streams. The data can be modified, or new data can be created as a result, which in turn is shared. Messages can also be communicated. For example, if an event happens in one thread, this could invoke another event in another thread. Threads may communicate in a peer to peer manner, or the main thread may signal the slave threads. When two processes need to communicate, they use a structure that is external to both processes. When two threads communicate, they typically use structures that are part of the same process to which they both or all belong. Threads cannot communicate with threads outside their process unless you are referring to primary threads of processes. In that case, you refer to them as two processes. Threads within a process can pass values from the data segment of the process or stack segments of each thread. In most cases, the cost of Interprocess Communication is higher than Interthread Communication. The external structures that must be created by the operating system during IPC require more system processing than the structures involved in ITC. The efficiency of ITC mechanisms makes threads a more attractive alternative in many, but not all programming scenarios that require concurrency.

2.1.2 Synchronizing Concurrency

2.1.2.1 Types of Synchronization

There are three major categories of synchronization :

Data : Data synchronization is required to prevent race conditions. It allows concurrent threads/ processes to access a block of memory safely.

Hardware : Hardware synchronization is necessary when several hardware devices are needed to perform a task or group of tasks. It requires communication between tasks and tight control over real-time performance and priority settings.

Task : Task Synchronization is required to prevent race conditions. It enforces preconditions and postconditions of logical processes.

2.1.2.2 Synchronizing Access to Data

Data synchronization is the process of maintaining the consistency and uniformity of data instances across all consuming applications and storing devices. It ensures that the same copy or version of data is used in all devices - from source to destination.

Concurrent access to shared memory, global variables, and files must be synchronized in a multithreaded environment. Data synchronization is needed at the location in a task's code when it attempts to access the block of memory, global variable, or file shared with other concurrently executing processes or threads. This is called the critical section. The critical section can be any block of code that changes the writes or reads to/from a file, closes a file, reads or writes global variables or data structures.

(1) Critical Sections

When a process executes code that manipulates shared data (or resource), we say that the process is in it's critical section (CS) (for that shared data). The execution of critical sections must be mutually exclusive: at any time, only one process is allowed to execute in its critical section (even with multiple CPUs). Then each process must request the permission to enter it's critical section. The section of code implementing this request is called the entry section. The critical section (CS) might be followed by an exit section. The remaining code is the remainder section. The critical section problem is to design a protocol that the processes can use so that their action will not depend on the order in which their execution is interleaved.

Requirements for a valid solution to the critical section problem :

Mutual Exclusion

At any time, at most one process can be in its critical section (CS)

Progress

If no process is executing in its critical section and there exist some processes that wish to enter their critical section, then the selection of the processes that will enter the critical section next cannot be postponed indefinitely.

Bounded Waiting

A bound must exist on the number of times that other processes are allowed to enter their critical sections after a process has made a request to enter its critical section and before that request is granted. Assume that each process executes at a nonzero speed. No assumption concerning relative speed of the N processes.

(1) PRAM Model

In computer science, a **parallel random-access machine** (**PRAM**) is a shared-memory abstract machine. As its name indicates, the PRAM was intended as the parallel-computing analogy to the random-access machine (RAM).

The PRAM model has the following characteristics :

Processors : There are n processors, P1, P2, up to Pn where each is identical to a RAM processor.

Memory : There is a common, global memory available. If processors wish to communicate, they do so via common memory – there is no special communications channel between processors. Sometimes this is called a blackboard. It is typically assumed there are m > n memory locations.

The PRAM model has four algorithms that can be used to access the shared global memory, concurrent read and write algorithms, and exclusive read and write algorithms that work like this :
- Concurrent read algorithms are allowed to read the same piece of memory simultaneously with no data corruption.
- Concurrent write algorithms allow multiple processors to write to the shared memory.
- Exclusive read algorithms are used to ensure that no two processors ever read the same memory location at the same time.
- Exclusive write ensures that no two processors write to the same memory at the same time.

The operation of a synchronous PRAM can result in simultaneous access by multiple processors to the same location in shared memory. There are several variants of our PRAM model, depending on whether such simultaneous access is permitted (concurrent access) or prohibited (exclusive access). As accesses can be reads or writes, we have the following four possibilities:

Exclusive Read Exclusive Write (EREW) : This PRAM variant does not allow any kind of simultaneous access to a single memory location. All correct programs for such a PRAM must insure that no two processors access a common memory location in the same time unit.

Concurrent Read Exclusive Write (CREW) : This PRAM variant allows concurrent reads but not concurrent writes to shared memory locations. All processors concurrently reading a common memory location obtain the same value.

Exclusive Read Concurrent Write (ERCW) : This PRAM variant allows concurrent writes but not concurrent reads to shared memory locations. This variant is generally not considered independently, but is subsumed within the next variant.

Concurrent Read Concurrent Write (CRCW) : This PRAM variant allows both concurrent reads and concurrent writes to shared memory locations. There are several sub-variants within this variant, depending on how concurrent writes are resolved.
- Common CRCW : This model allows concurrent writes if and only if all the processors are attempting to write the same value (which becomes the value stored).
- Arbitrary CRCW : In this model, a value arbitrarily chosen from the values written to the common memory location is stored.
- Priority CRCW : In this model, the value written by the processor with the minimum processor id writing to the common memory location is stored.
- Combining CRCW : In this model, the value stored is a combination (usually by an associative and commutative operator such as or max) of the values written.

(1) Relationships between Cooperating Tasks

There are four basic synchronization relationships between any two tasks in a single process or between any two processes within a single application :

Start - to - start (SS)
Finish - to - start (FS)
Start - to - finish (SF)
Finish - to - finish (FF)

These four basic relationships characterize the coordination of work between threads and processes.

(2) Start - to - Start (SS) Relationship

In a start - to - start synchronization, one task cannot start until another task starts. One task may start before the other but never after.

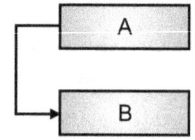

Fig. 2.2 : Start to Start

Task B can't start until Task A starts. They don't have to start at the same time: Task B can begin any time after Task A begins.

(3) Finish - to - Start (FS) Relationship

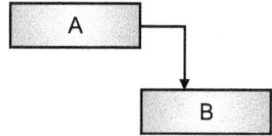

Fig. 2.3 : Finish to Start

In a finish - to - start synchronization, Task B can't start until Task A is done. . This type of relationship is common with parent - child processes. The parent process cannot complete execution of some operation until it spawns a child process or it receives a communication from the child process that it has started its operation. The child process continues to execute once it has signaled the parent or supplied the needed information. The parent process is then free to complete its operation.

(4) Start - to - Finish Relationshi

Until Task B finishes executing or completes a certain operation.

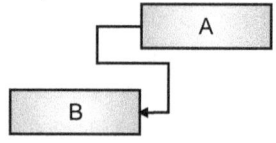

Fig. 2.4 : Start to Finish

Task B can't finish until Task A begins. Task B can finish any time after Task A begins. This type of link is rarely used.

(5) Finish-to-Finish Relationship

A finish - to - finish synchronization relationship means one task cannot finish until another task finishes. Task A cannot finish until Task B finishes. This again can describe the relationship between parent and child processes. The parent process must wait until all its child processes have terminated before it is allowed to terminate. If the parent process terminates before its child processes, those terminated child processes become zombied. The parent process calls a wait() for each of its child processes (like join for threads) or waits for a mutex or condition variable that is broadcast by child threads.

Another example is Master Slave Model.

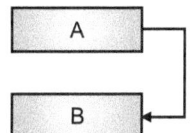

Fig. 2.5 : Finish to Finish Model

Task B can't finish until Task A is done. They don't have to end at the same time: Task B can end any time after Task A ends.

2.1.2.3 Synchronization Mechanisms

The mechanisms can be used to prevent race conditions and deadlocks between multiple tasks by implementing the synchronization access policies we have mentioned and managing critical sections of tasks. In this section, we introduce:

Semaphores and mutexes

Read - write locks

Condition variables

(1) Semaphores

A semaphore is a variable or abstract data type that is used for controlling access, by multiple processes, to a common resource in a parallel programming or a multi user environment. Semaphores are used to coordinate access to a non-sharable resource. Cooperating, or possibly competing, processes use semaphores to determine if a specific resource is available. If a resource is unavailable, by default, the system will place the requesting process in an associated queue. The system will notify the waiting process when the resource is available.

Semaphores are normally of either type binary or counting, depending upon how they are used. A binary semaphore controls a single resource and it is either 0, indicating that the resource is in use, or 1, indicating that the resource is available. A counting semaphore increments and decrements a counter, a non-negative integer to determine if an instance of the controlled resource is currently available.

Basic Semaphore Operations

P() : an atomic operation that waits for semaphore to become positive, then decrement it by 1.

V() : an atomic operation that increments semaphore by 1 and wakes up a waiting thread at P(), if any.

Semaphore Operations are atomic :

Two P() calls cannot decrement the value below zero.

A sleeping thread at P() cannot miss a wakeup from V().

Program :

A semaphore is a protected variable (or abstract data type) which can only be accessed using the following operations :

```
P(s)
Semaphore s;
{
  while (s == 0) ;                      /* wait until s>0 */
  s = s-1;
}

V(s)
Semaphore s;
{
  s = s+1;
}
Init(s, v)
Semaphore s;
Int v;
{
  s = v;
}
```

Semaphore operations can go by other names such as :

P() operation

lock()

wait()

own()

V() operation
unlock()
post()
unown()

The value of the semaphore depends on the type of semaphore it is. There are several types of semaphores.

Posix Semaphores

POSIX semaphores allow processes and threads to synchronize their actions.

Two operations can be performed on semaphores :

sem_post() : increment the semaphore value by one.

sem_wait() : decrement the semaphore value by one.

POSIX semaphores come in two forms :

(a) Named Semaphores

A named semaphore is identified by a name of the form /*somename*; that is, a null-terminated string of up to NAME_MAX-4 (i.e., 251) characters consisting of an initial slash, followed by one or more characters, none of which are slashes. Two processes can operate on the same named semaphore by passing the same name to sem_open().

The sem_open() function creates a new named semaphore or opens an existing named semaphore. After the semaphore has been opened, it can be operated on using sem_post() and sem_wait(). When a process has finished using the semaphore, it can use sem_close() to close the semaphore. When all processes have finished using the semaphore, it can be removed from the system using sem_unlink().

Unnamed semaphores (memory-based semaphores)

An unnamed semaphore does not have a name. Instead the semaphore is placed in a region of memory that is shared between multiple threads (a *thread-shared semaphore*) or processes (a process-shared semaphore). A thread-shared semaphore is placed in an area of memory shared between the threads of a process, for example, a global variable. A process-shared semaphore must be placed in a shared memory region .

Mutex

Mutex-mutual exclusion object**.** In computer programming, a mutex is a program object that allows multiple program threads to share the same resource, such as file access, but not simultaneously.

When a program is started, a mutex is created with a unique name. After this stage, any thread that needs the resource must lock the mutex from other threads while it is using the resource. The mutex is set to unlock when the data is no longer needed or the routine is finished.

Read -Write Locks

A Read Write lock allows concurrent access for read-only operations, while write operations require exclusive access. This means that multiple threads can read the data in parallel but an exclusive lock is needed for writing or modifying data. When a writer is writing the data, readers will be blocked until the writer is finished writing. A common use might be to control access to a data structure in memory that can't be updated atomically and isn't valid until the update is complete.

Read Write Lock Locking Rules

The rules by which a thread is allowed to lock the ReadWriteLock either for reading or writing the guarded resource, are as follows :

Read Lock If no threads have locked the ReadWriteLock for writing, and no thread have requested a write lock (but not yet obtained it).

Thus, multiple threads can lock the lock for reading.

Write Lock If no threads are reading or writing.

Thus, only one thread at a time can lock the lock for writing.

Program that shows how to create a Read Write Lock and how to lock it for reading and writing :

```
ReadWriteLock readWriteLock = new ReentrantReadWriteLock();


readWriteLock.readLock().lock();

   // multiple readers can enter this section
   // if not locked for writing, and not writers waiting
   // to lock for writing.

readWriteLock.readLock().unlock();

readWriteLock.writeLock().lock();

   // only one writer can enter this section,
   // and only if no threads are currently reading.

readWriteLock.writeLock().unlock();
```

(1) Condition Variables

Synchronization mechanisms need more than just mutual exclusion; also need a way to wait for another thread to do something (e.g., wait for a character to be added to the buffer)

Condition Variables : used to wait for a particular condition to become true (e.g. characters in buffer).

wait(condition, lock): release lock, put thread to sleep until condition is signaled; when thread wakes up again, re-acquire lock before returning.

signal(condition, lock): if any threads are waiting on condition, wake up one of them. Caller must hold lock, which must be the same as the lock used in the wait call.

broadcast(condition, lock): same as signal, except wake up all waiting threads.

Note : after signal, signaling thread keeps lock, waking thread goes on the queue waiting for the lock.

Warning : when a thread wakes up after condition_wait there is no guarantee that the desired condition still exists: another thread might have snuck in.

Producer/Consumer program using condition variables :

```
char buffer[SIZE];
int count = 0, head = 0, tail = 0;
struct lock l;
struct condition notEmpty;
struct condition notFull;

lock_init(&l);
condition_init(&notEmpty);
condition_init(&notFull);

void put(char c) {
   lock_acquire(&l);
   while (count == SIZE) {
      condition_wait(&notFull, &l);
   }
   count++;
   buffer[head] = c;
   head++;
   if (head == SIZE) {
      head = 0;
   }
   condition_signal(&notEmpty, &l);
   lock_release(&l);
}
```

```
char get() {
    char c;
    lock_acquire(&l);
    while (count == 0) {
        condition_wait(&notEmpty, &l);
    }
    count--;
    c = buffer[tail];
    tail++;
    if (tail == SIZE) {
        tail = 0;
    }
    condition_signal(&notFull, &l);
    lock_release(&l);
    return c;
}
```

QUESTIONS

1. How communication and synchronization take place between different processes and threads ?
2. Write short note on Inter Process Communication.
3. Explain the mechanism of pipes – communication channel with suitable diagram.
4. What are Inter Thread Communication ?
5. Explain in detail synchronizing concurrency.
6. Write short note on relationship between co-operating tasks. Draw suitable diagram.
7. Explain various synchronization mechanisms.
8. Explain different thread strategy approaches.
9. Write short note on shared memory.
10. What is concurrent lisp ? Explain different lisp languages that support concurrency.
11. What is Cl-UUDA ? explain with suitable example.
12. What is Cl-GPU ?
13. Write short note on threads in JAVA.
14. What is JAVA locking ?
15. Write short note on deadlock.

UNIT - III
PARALLEL ARCHITECTURES AND PROGRAMMING PRINCIPLES

3.1 INTRODUCTION

- Parallel processing technologies are available everywhere in the computing domain. Game computers and standard PCs from workstations to supercomputers are totally influenced by these parallel processing technologies.
- The main reason for this trend is the parallelism that enables a substantial increase in processing power using standard technologies. Parallel processing has emerged as an area with the potential of providing satisfactory ways of meeting real-time computation requirements in various applications and the pursuit for speed.
- Cost of using parallel processing technologies is much lesser than specialized high-performance hardware. Today the processing capacity of a desktop PC with a multi-core processor is much more than the compute power of a supercomputer of two decades ago almost at the same cost. The utilization of such powerful equipment requires suitable software. This software need is greatly driven by the development of appropriate parallel algorithms and the development of system and application software that can utilize the advantages of parallel hardware. Although much progress has been made in the areas of parallel architectures, algorithm and software design, major problems still remain to be addressed.
- With the fast growth in the number of multi-core processors for PCs there is an increasing need for methods and tools to support the development of software to effectively and efficiently utilize parallel structures. Single processor supercomputers have achieved great speeds in computation. Still this trend will come to an end, because there are physical and architectural bounds, which limit the computational power that can be achieved with a single processor system. Parallel computing in the form of internally linked processors, was the main form of parallelism. Advances in computer networks have created a new type of parallelism in the form of networked autonomous computers.
- Instead of putting everything in a single box and tightly couple processors to memory, the Internet achieved a kind of parallelism by loosely connecting everything outside of the box. To get the most out of a computer system with internal or external parallelism, designers and software developers must understand the interaction between hardware and software parts of the system.

3.2 Introduction To Graphics Processing Units (GPUs)

- Graphics processing units (GPUs) are devices present in most modern PCs. They provide a number of basic graphics related operations to the CPU, such as rendering an image in memory and then displaying that image onto the screen. A GPU will typically process a complex set of shapes such as polygons, a map of the scene to be rendered. It then applies textures to the polygons and then performs shading and lighting calculations.
- One of the important steps in GPUs was the development of programmable shaders. Programmable shaders are sweet and short programs that GPU ran to calculate different effects. This was the first evolution of General Purpose Graphical Processor Unit (GPGPU) programming, in that the design had taken its first steps in moving away from fixed function units.
- The shaders applied the various graphical operations in a hugely parallel manner, giving huge throughput of computing power.
- Some researchers made use of GPU technology to try and speed up general-purpose computing. This led to the development of a number of initiatives, all of which were aimed at making the GPU a real programmable device in the same way as the CPU. Unfortunately, each had its own advantages and problems. None were particularly easy to learn or program in and were never taught to people in large numbers. In short, there was never a large group of programmers or interested programmers in this hard-to-learn technology.
- CUDA has for the first time managed to do, and at the same time provided programmers with a truly general-purpose language for GPUs.

3.2.1 The Death of The Single-Core Solution

- Limited clock rate limit of around 4 GHz is one of the major problems faced by modern processors.
- Modern processors generate too much heat for the current technology and require special and expensive cooling solutions. This is because as we increase the clock rate, the power consumption rises. In fact, the power consumption of a CPU is approximately the cube of its clock rate (for fix voltage).
- Also when you increase the heat generated by the CPU, for the same clock rate, the power consumption also increases due to the properties of the silicon. This conversion of power into heat is a complete waste of energy. This increasingly inefficient use of power eventually means you are unable to either power or cool the processor sufficiently and you reach the thermal limits of the device.
- To overcome the above mentioned disadvantages the two main PC processor manufacturers, Intel and AMD came up with a different approach. They have focused on adding cores to processors, rather than continuously trying to increase CPU clock rates

and/or extract more instructions per clock through instruction-level parallelism. We have dual, tri, quad, hex, 8, 12, and soon even 16 and 32 cores and so on. This approach has impressed every processor manufacturer. The Fermi GPU is effectively already a 16-core device in CPU terms.

- There is a big problem with this approach. It requires programmers to switch from their traditional serial, single-thread approach, to dealing with multiple threads all executing at once. Now the programmer has to think about two, four, six, or eight program threads and how they interact and communicate with one another. When dual-core CPUs arrived, it was fairly easy, in that there were usually some background tasks being done that could be offloaded onto a second core. When quad-core CPUs arrived, not many programs were changed to support it. They just carried on being sold as single-thread applications. Although gaming industry is expected to use most technology, it didn't really move to quad-core programming very quickly. In some ways the processor manufacturers are to blame for this, because the single-core application runs just fine on one-quarter of the quad-core device. Some devices even increase the clock rate dynamically when only one core is active, encouraging programmers to be lazy and not make use of the available hardware.

- There are economic reasons too. The software development companies need to get the product to market as soon as possible. Developing a better quad-core solution is all well and good, but not if the market is being grabbed by a competitor who got there first. As manufacturers still continue to make single- and dual-core devices, the market naturally settles on the lowest configuration, with the widest scope for sales. Until the time that quad-core CPUs are the minimum produced, market forces work against the move to multi-core programming in the CPU market.

3.3 NVIDIA AND CUDA

- Refer Fig. 3.1 for relative computational power in GPUs and CPUs. We will able to see divergence of CPU and GPU computational power until 2009 when we see the computing power of crossing GPU 1000 gigaflops or 1 teraflop barrier. At this point we were moving from the G80 hardware to the G200 and then in 2010 to the Fermi evolution. This is driven by the introduction of massively parallel hardware. The G80 is a 128 CUDA core device, the G200 is a 256 CUDA core device, and the Fermi is a 512 CUDA core device.

- NVIDIA GPUs make a jump of 300 gigaflops from the G200 architecture to the Fermi architecture, nearly a 30% improvement in throughput. By comparison, Intels fly from their core 2 architecture to the Nehalem architecture sees only a minor improvement. Traditional CPUs aimed at serial code execution and are extremely good at it. They contain special hardware such as branch prediction units, multiple caches, etc., all of which target serial code execution. The GPUs are not designed for this serial execution flow and only achieve their peak performance when fully utilized in a parallel manner. In 2007, NVIDIA saw an opportunity to bring GPUs into the mainstream by adding an easy-to use programming interface known as Compute Unified Device Architecture (CUDA). This opened up the possibility to program GPUs without having to learn complex shader languages, or to think only in terms of graphics primitives.

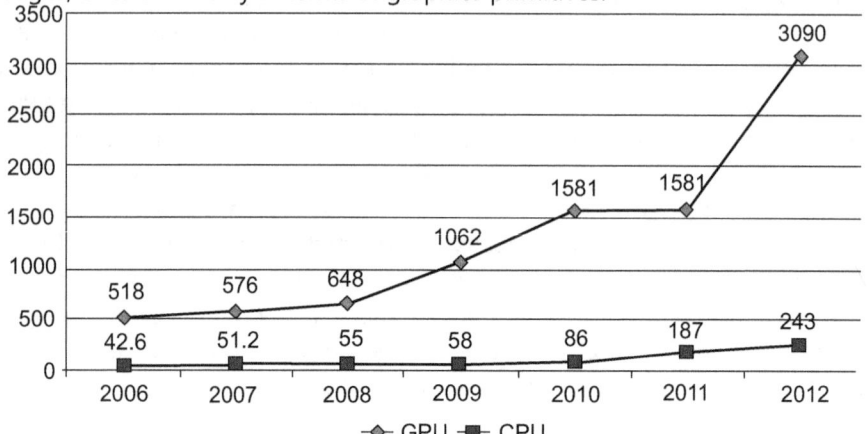

Fig. 3.1 : Relative Peak Performance of CPU and GPU

- CUDA is an extension to the C language that allows GPU code to be written in regular C. The code is either targeted for the host processor (the CPU) or targeted at the device processor (the GPU). The host processor spawns multithread tasks (or kernels as they are known in CUDA) onto the GPU device.
- The GPU has its own internal scheduler that will then allocate the kernels to whatever GPU hardware is present. Number of Streaming Multiprocessors (SMs) is directly proportional to speed of execution. Provided there is enough parallelism in the task, as the number of SMs in the GPU grows, there is proportional increase in speed of program execution. Again question arises is what percentage of the code can be run in parallel. The maximum speedup possible is limited by the amount of serial code. If you have an infinite amount of processing power and could do the parallel tasks in zero time, you would still be left with the time from the serial code part. Therefore, we have to consider at the start if we can indeed parallelize a significant amount of the workload.
- NVIDIA is committed to providing support to CUDA.
- Given that the number of CUDA-enabled GPUs now number in the millions, there is a huge market out there waiting for CUDA-enabled applications.
- Along with the introduction of CUDA came the Tesla series of cards. These cards are not graphics cards. They are dedicated compute cards aimed at scientific computing. These cards can either be installed in a regular desktop PC or in dedicated server racks. NVIDIA provides such system which can provide up to 30 times the power of a conventional cluster. CUDA and GPUs are reshaping the world of high performance computing.

3.3.1 GPU Hardware

- The NVIDIA G80 series processor design is similar to both the Connection Machine and IBMs Cell processor. Each graphics card consists of a number of Streaming multiprocessors (SMs). To each SM is attached eight or more SPs (Stream Processors). The original 9800 GTX card has eight SMs, giving a total of 128 SPs.
- The GPU cards can broadly be considered as accelerator or coprocessor cards. A GPU card, currently, must operate in conjunction with a CPU-based host. In this regard it follows very much the approach of the Cell processor with the regular serial core and N SIMDSPE cores.
- Each GPU device contains a set of SMs, each of which contain a set of SPs or CUDA cores. The SPs execute work as parallel sets of up to 32 units. They eliminate a lot of the complex circuitry needed on CPUs to achieve high-speed serial execution through instruction-level parallelism. They replace this with a programmer-specified explicit parallelism model, allowing more compute capacity to be squeezed onto the same area of silicon.
- The overall throughput of GPUs is largely determined by the number of SPs present, the bandwidth to the global memory, and how well the programmer makes use of the parallel architecture he or she is working with. Refer table 3.1 for the list of current NVIDIA GPU cards.
- The correct choice of board for a given application is determined by a balance between memory and GPU processing power needed for a given application. Cards mention in the table : such as 9800 GX2, 295, 590, 690, and K10 cards are actually dual cards, so to make full use of these they need to be programmed as two devices not one. All the numbers indicated in the Fig. 3.1 are for single-precision (32-bit) floating-point performance, not double-precision (64-bit) precision.
- Tesla cards have doubled the number of double-precision units so this achieves significantly better double-precision throughput.
- As the generations have evolved, the power consumption, clock rate per SM has come down. However, the overall power consumption has increased considerably and this is one of the key considerations in any multi-GPU-based solution.
- Typically, we see dual-GPU-based cards (9800 GX2, 295, 590, 690) having marginally lower power consumption figures than the equivalent two single cards due to the use of shared circuitry and/or reduced clock frequencies.
- NVIDIA provides various racks containing two to four Tesla cards connected on a shared PCI-E bus for high-density computing.

Table 3.1 : Series of NVIDIA GPU Cards

GPU	Series Device	Number of SPs	Max Memory	GFlops (FMAD)	Bandwidth (GB/s)	Power (Watts)
9800 GT	G92	96	2GB	504	57	125
9800 GTX	G92	128	2GB	648	70	140
9800 GX2	G92	256	1GB	1152	2 x 64	197
260	G200	216	2GB	804	110	182
285	G200	240	2GB	1062	159	204
295	G200	480	1.8GB	1788	2 x 110	289
470	GF100	448	1.2GB	1088	134	215
480	GF100	448	1.5GB	1344	177	250
580	GF110	512	1.5GB	1581	152	244
590	GF110	1024	3GB	2488	2 x 164	365
680	GK104	1536	2GB	3090	192	195
690	GK104	3072	4GB	5620	2 x 192	300
Tesla C870	G80	128	1.5GB	518	77	171
Tesla C1060	G200	240	4GB	933	102	188
Tesla C2070	GF100	448	6GB	1288	144	247
Tesla K10	GK104	3072	8GB	5184	2 x 160	250

- The great thing about CUDA is that, despite all the variability in hardware, programs written for the original CUDA devices can run on today's CUDA devices. The CUDA compilation model applies the principle as used in Java runtime compilation of a virtual instruction set. This allows modern GPUs to execute code from even the oldest generation GPUs. In many cases they benefit significantly from the original programmer reworking the program for the features of the newer GPUs.

3.4 ALTERNATIVES TO CUDA

In this subsection we will see details of OpenCL and DirectCompute which are considered as alternatives of CUDA.

3.4.1 OpenCL

- AMD's product range is as impressive as the NVIDIA range in terms of raw computer power. However, AMD's entry in stream computing technology to the marketplace is

- long time after NVIDIA brought out CUDA. As a consequence, NVIDA has far more applications available for CUDA than AMD/ATI does for its competing stream technology. CUDA is currently only officially executable on NVIDIA hardware.
- While NVIDIA has a substantial chunk of the GPU market, its competitors also hold a considerable market share. Considering this fact people should be aware there are alternatives to CUDA, which support both NVIDIA's and others' hardware.
- OpenCL is an open and royalty-free standard supported by NVIDIA, AMD, and others. The OpenCL trademark is owned by Apple. It sets out an open standard that allows the use of computing devices. A compute device can be a GPU, CPU, or other specialist device for which an OpenCL driver exists. As of 2012, OpenCL supports all major brands of GPU devices, including CPUs with at least SSE3 support.
- As the fundamental concepts of CUDA and OpenCL are quite similar, anyone who is familiar with CUDA can pick up OpenCL relatively easily.
- However, OpenCL is more complex to use than CUDA because much of the work the CUDA runtime API does for the programmer needs to be explicitly performed in OpenCL.

3.4.2 DirectCompute

- DirectCompute is Microsoft's alternative to CUDA and OpenCL. It is a proprietary product linked to the Windows operating system, and in particular, the DirectX 11 API. The DirectX API was a huge dive forward for any of those who remember programming video cards before it. It meant the developers had to learn only one library API to program all graphics cards, rather than write or license drivers for each major video card manufacturer.
- DirectX 11 is the latest standard and supported under Windows 7. With Microsoft's name behind the standard, you might expect to see some quite rapid adoption among the developer community. This is especially the case with developers already familiar with DirectX APIs. If you are familiar with CUDA and DirectCompute, then it is quite an easy task to port a CUDA application over to DirectCompute.
- Microsoft also set to launch C++ AMP, an additional set of standard template libraries (STLs), which may appeal more to programmers already familiar with C++ style STLs.

3.5 CPU Alternatives

The main parallel processing languages extensions are MPI, OpenMP, and pthreads if you are developing for Linux. For Windows there is the Windows threading model and OpenMP.

3.5.1 Message Passing Interface

MPI (Message Passing Interface) is perhaps the most widely known messaging interface. It is process-based and generally found in large computing environment. It requires an administrator to configure the installation correctly and is best suited to controlled environments. Parallelism is expressed by distributing hundreds of processes over a cluster of nodes and explicitly exchanging messages, typically over high-speed network-based communication links (Ethernet or InfiniBand).

3.5.2 Open Multi-Processing (OpenMP)

OpenMP (Open Multi-Processing) is a system designed for parallelism within a node or computer system. It works entirely differently, in that the programmer specifies various parallel directives through compiler entities. It is the compiler that attempts to automatically split the problem into N parts, according to the number of available processor cores. OpenMP support is in-built into many compilers, including the NVCC compiler used for CUDA. OpenMP tends to hit problems with scaling due to the underlying CPU architecture. Often the memory bandwidth in the CPU is just not large enough for all the cores continuously streaming data to or from memory.

3.5.3 Pthreads

Pthreads is a library that is used significantly for multithread applications on Linux. As with OpenMP, pthreads uses threads and not processes as it is designed for parallelism within a single node. However, unlike OpenMP, the programmer is responsible for thread management and synchronization. This provides more flexibility and consequently better performance for well-written programs.

3.5.4 ZeroMQ

ZeroMQ (0MQ) is a simple library that supports thread, process, and network-based communications models with a single cross platform API. It is also available on both Linux and Windows platforms. It's designed for distributed computing, so the connections are dynamic and nodes fail gracefully.

3.5.5 Hadoop

Hadoop is an open-source version of Google's MapReduce framework. It's aimed primarily at the Linux platform. The concept is that you take a huge dataset and break (or map) it into a number of chunks. However, instead of sending the data to the node, the dataset is already split over hundreds or thousands of nodes using a parallel file system. Thus, the program known as the reduce step is sent to the node that contains the data. The output is written to the local node and remains there. Subsequent MapReduce programs take the previous output and again transform it in some way. As data is in fact mirrored to multiple nodes, this allows for a highly fault-tolerant as well as high-throughput system.

3.5.6 Directives and Libraries

There are a number of compiler vendors that support the recently declared OpenACC set of compiler directives for GPUs. These, in essence, replicate the approach of OpenMP, in that the programmer inserts a number of compiler directives marking regions as "to be executed on the GPU." The compiler then does the work of moving data to or from the GPU, invoking kernels, etc. As with the use of pthreads over OpenMP, with the lower level of control pthreads provides, you can achieve higher performance. This extra level of control comes with a much higher level of required programming knowledge, a higher risk of errors, and the consequential time impact that may have on a development schedule. Currently, OpenACC requires directives to specify what areas of code should be run on the GPU, but also in which type of memory data should exist. NVIDIA claims you can get speedup of 5x using such directives. It's a good solution for those programmers who need to get something working quickly. It's also great for those people for whom programming is a secondary consideration who just want the answer to their problem in a reasonable timeframe.

The use of libraries is also another key area where you can obtain some serious productivity gains, as well as execution time speedups. Libraries like SDK provide common functions implemented in a very efficient way. Libraries like CUBLAS are some of the best around for linear algebra. Libraries exist for many well-known applications such as Matlab. Language bindings exist for Python, Perl, Java, and many others. CUDA can even be integrated with Excel.

3.6 Understanding Parallelism with GPUs

3.6.1 Conventional Serial Programming

- Most programmers developed applications in a simple serial fashion. This is because writing programs serially is quite easy task as compared to writing programs in parallel.
- Parallel Programming is quite large domain. Actually there was no large-scale market need for parallel hardware and, as a consequence of this there is absence of significant numbers of parallel programmers. Every year or two the various CPU vendors would bring out a new processor generation that executed code faster than the previous generation, thereby continuing with serial code. Parallel programs by comparison were often linked closely to the hardware. Their goal was to achieve faster performance and often that was at the cost of portability.
- Periodically many revolutions take place and new architectures require a complete rewrite of all code. If your knowledge as a programmer was concentrated around processor X, it was valuable in the marketplace only so long as processor X was in use. Therefore, it made a lot more commercial sense to learn to program x86-type architecture than some unusual parallel architecture that would only be around for a few years.
- However couple of standards such as the OpenMP standard that addresses parallelism within a single node and is designed for shared memory machines that contain multi core processors. It does not have any concept of anything outside a single node or box.

- Thus you are limited to the context that fit within a single box in terms of processing power, memory capacity, and storage space. Programming, however, is relatively easy as most of the low-level threading code is taken care of for you by OpenMP.
- The MPI (Message Passing Interface) standard addresses parallelism between nodes and is aimed at clusters of machines within well-defined networks. It is often used in supercomputer installations where there may be many thousands of individual nodes. Each node holds a small section of the problem. Thus, common resources such as CPU, cache, memory, storage, etc are multiplied by the number of nodes in the network. Inter node communication is usually the dominating factor determining the maximum speed in any cluster-based solution.
- Both OpenMP and MPI can be used together to exploit parallelism within nodes as well as across a network of machines. However, the APIs and the approaches used are entirely different, meaning they are often not used together. The OpenMP directives allow the programmer to take a high-level view of parallelism via specifying parallel regions. MPI on the other hand uses an explicit interprocess communication model making the programmer do a lot more work.
- Programmers are often disliked to learn one API when they have spent significant amount of time to become familiar with another. Thus, problems that fit within one computer are often implemented with OpenMP solutions, whereas really large problems are implemented with cluster-based solutions such as MPI.
- CUDA, the GPU programming language can be used in conjunction with both OpenMP and MPI. There is also an OpenMP-like directive version of CUDA - OpenACC that may be somewhat easier for those familiar with OpenMP to pick up.
- While switching from serial programming to parallel programming technology, programmers must start from introduction of multi core CPUs. The primary use of multi core CPUs was for OS-based parallelism.
- Almost all desktops today have either a dual or quad-core processor. Thus, programmers started using threads to allow the multiple cores on the CPU to be exploited.
- A thread is a separate execution flow within a program that may move away and come together as and when required with the main execution flow. Typically, CPU programs will have no more than twice the number of threads active than the number of physical processor cores. As with single-core processors, typically each OS task is time-sliced, given a small amount of time in turn, to give the appearance of running more tasks than there are physical CPU cores.
- However, as the number of threads grows, this becomes more obvious to the end user. In the background the OS is having to context switch (swap in and out a set of registers) every time it needs to switch between tasks. As context switching is an expensive operation, typically thousands of cycles, CPU applications tend to have a fairly low number of threads compared with GPUs.

3.6.2 Problems with Serial and Parallel Computing

- Threads lead programmer with many of the issues of parallel programming, such as sharing resources. Typically, this is done with a semaphore, which is simply a lock. Whoever has the lock can use the resource and everyone else has to wait for the user of the lock to release it. As long as there is only a single lock, everything works fine. Problems occur when there are two or more locks that must be shared by the same threads. In such situations, thread 0 grabs lock 0, while thread 1 grabs lock 1. Thread 0 now tries to grab lock 1, while thread 1 tries to grab lock 0. As the locks become unavailable, both thread 0 and thread 1 sleep until the lock becomes available. As neither thread ever releases the one lock they already own, all threads wait forever. This is known as a deadlock, and it is something that can and will happen without proper design. With any sort of locking system, all parties that need a resource must behave correctly. That is, they must request the lock, wait if necessary, and, only when they have the lock, perform the operation. This relies on the programmer to identify shared resources and specifically put in place mechanisms to coordinate updates by multiple threads.
- The alternative to threads is processes. These are somewhat heavier in terms of OS domain in that both code and data contexts must be maintained by the OS. A thread by contrast needs to only maintain a code context which includes the program/instruction counter and a set of registers and threads share the same data space.
- Both threads and processes may be executing entirely different sections of a program at any point in time. Processes by default operate in an independent memory area. This usually is enough to ensure one process is unable to affect the data of other processes.
- Data consequently has to be transferred by formally passing messages to or from processes. In many respects the threading model sits well with OpenMP, while the process model sits well with MPI. In terms of GPUs, they map to a combination of both approaches. CUDA uses a grid of blocks. This can be thought of as a queue (or a grid) of processes (blocks) with no interprocess communication.

3.6.3 Parallelism with GPUs

- The first aspect of concurrency is to think about the particular problem, without considering the details of implementation, and think of what aspects of it could run in parallel. Problems like matrix multiplication where knowledge about surrounding elements is required can be implemented extremely well on GPUs and are easy to code.
- If the problem requires the knowledge about the value of its surrounding neighbors then the speedup will ultimately be limited. In such cases, throwing more processors at the problem will work to that point. At this point the computation slows down due to the processors (or threads) spending more time sharing data than doing any useful work. The point at which you strike this will depend largely on the amount and cost of the communication overhead.

- CUDA is ideal for an embarrassingly parallel problem, where little or no inter thread or inter block communication is required. It supports inter thread communication with explicit primitives using on chip resources. Inter block communication is, however, only supported by invoking multiple kernels in series, communicating between kernel runs using off-chip global memory. It can also be performed in a somewhat restricted way through atomic operations to or from global memory.
- CUDA splits problems into grids of blocks, each containing multiple threads. The blocks may run in any order. Only a subset of the blocks will ever execute at any one point in time.
- A block must execute from start to completion and may be run on one of N SMs (symmetrical multiprocessors). Blocks are allocated from the grid of blocks to any SM that has free slots. Initially this is done on a round-robin basis so each SM gets an equal distribution of blocks. For most kernels, the number of blocks needs to be in the order of eight or more times the number of physical SMs on the GPU.
- A typical GPU has on the order of 24 K active threads. On Fermi GPUs you can define 65,535 x 65,535 x 1536 threads in total, 24 K of which are active at any time. This is usually enough to cover most problems within a single node.

3.7 CUDA Hardware Overview

- Compute Unified Device Architecture (CUDA) is a scalable parallel programming model and a software environment for parallel computing.
- CUDA is parallel computing platform and programming model invented by NVIDIA.
- It enables drastic increases in computing performance by utilizing the power of graphics processing unit (GPU). With CUDA it is possible to send C, C++ and FORTRAN code straight forward to GPU, no assembly language is required.
- Using high-level languages, GPU accelerated applications run the sequential part of their workload on the CPU, which is optimized for single-threaded performance while accelerating parallel processing on the GPU. This is called "GPU computing."
- GPU computing is possible because today's GPU does much more than render graphics : It sizzles with a teraflop of floating point performance and crunches application tasks designed for anything from finance to medicine.
- Single Instruction Multiple Data (SIMD) architecture works well when similar operation is applied to a large dataset. It does not work well for heterogeneous serial-parallel programming.
- CUDA is small extension to familiar C, C++ environment that provides a small amount of additional syntax to C or C++ which allows parallel "kernels" to be run on the device.

3.7.1 CUDA Physical Architecture

- CUDA architecture exposes GPU for general purpose computing.
- The architecture is built around Streaming Multiprocessors (SMs). Each SM has 8 processing cores. These 8 cores can run simultaneously. Refer Fig. 3.2

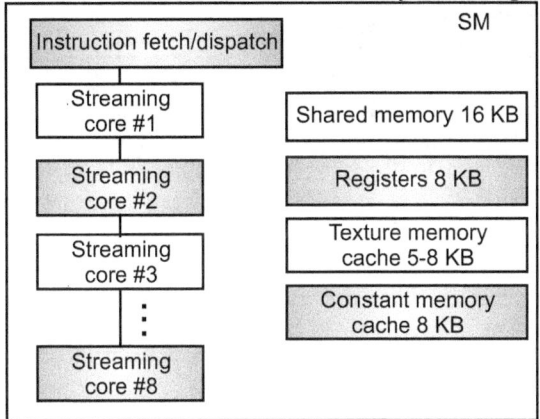

Fig. 3.2 : Device Architecture : Streaming Multiprocessor

- Each core executes identical instruction set. SM is responsible for scheduling instructions across cores with 0 overhead.
- Each thread is mapped to one SM. Threads are managed in groups of 32 – warps (basically, a SIMD group). That means up to 32 threads may be scheduled at a time. But maximum 24 wraps are active in 1 SM. Warp elements free to branch, though device will then serialize. Refer Fig. 3.3
- In CUDA thread level memory sharing is supported via Shared Memory.
- Register memory is local to thread, and it is divided amongst all blocks on SM.
- Computing capability of CUDA is given as follows :
  a. 13 nodes
  b. 4 Tesla S1070 Units / Node
  c. 240 Streaming Processors / S1070
  d. 12,480 total CUDA cores
- CUDA can scale to 100's of cores and 1000's of parallel threads.
- CUDA lets the programmers to focus on parallel algorithms and not on the mechanisms of parallel computing language.
- CUDA enables heterogeneous systems (CPU+GPU) for computing purpose. CPU and GPU are separate processing devices with separate DRAMs.
- GPU is a specialized processor that addresses the demands of real time high resolution 3D graphics compute intensive tasks.

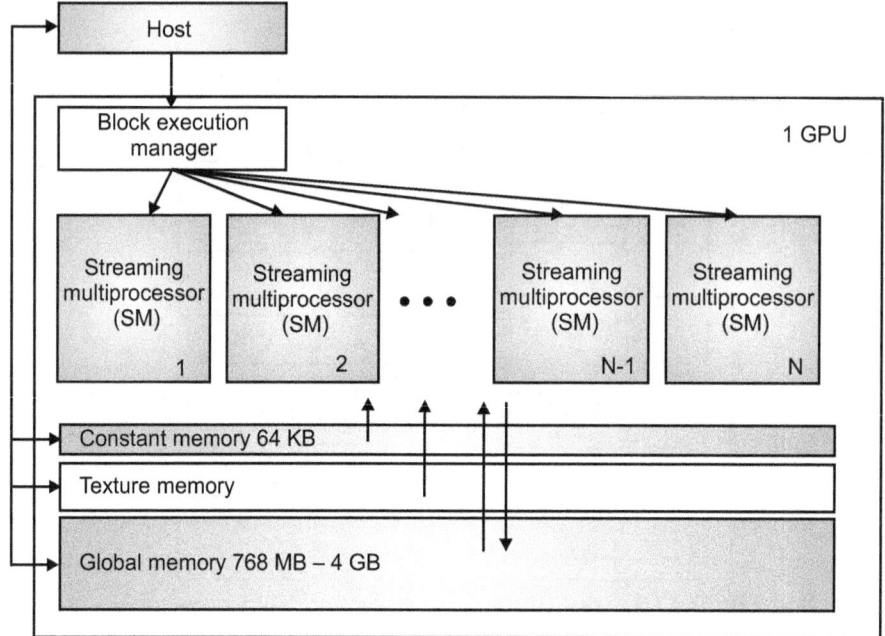

Fig. 3.3 : Role of Streaming Multiprocessors in Scheduling Instructions

- GPUs have transformed into highly parallel multi core systems allowing very efficient manipulation of large blocks of data.
- This design is more effective than general purpose CPUs for algorithms where processing of large blocks of data is done in parallel.

3.8 Parallel Computing

3.8.1 Serial Computing

- Traditionally almost all the software are written for serial computation.
- In serial computation a problem is divided in-to a discrete series of instructions.
- Execution of Instructions is sequential i.e. one after another.
- Instructions are executed on a single processor.
- At any moment in time a single instruction can be executed.
- Sequential computers are based on the model presented by John von Neumann
- Performance of the such serial computing model is limited by :
    1. Speed of information exchange between
    2. Memory and CPU
    3. Execution rate of instructions

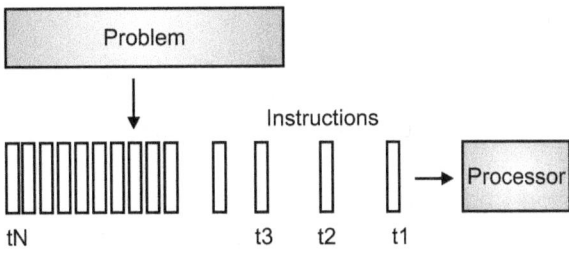

Fig. 3.4 : Serial Computation

3.8.2 Parallel Computing

- Computer architects have always tried hard to increase the performance of their computer architectures. Parallelism is the important reason for the high performance computing. Single-processor supercomputers have achieved speed in computation and have been pushing hardware technology to the physical limit of chip manufacturing. However, this trend will soon come to an end, because there are physical and architectural bounds that limit the computational power that can be achieved with a single-processor system.
- Parallel computing is the simultaneous use of multiple compute resources to solve a computational problem. Like sequential computing, in parallel computing also problem is divided into distinct parts that can be solved in parallel. Each part is further divided down to a sequence of instructions. Different processors are used to simultaneously execute Instructions from each part.
- Control/coordination mechanism is used between different processors to solve the distinct parts of the problem in parallel.

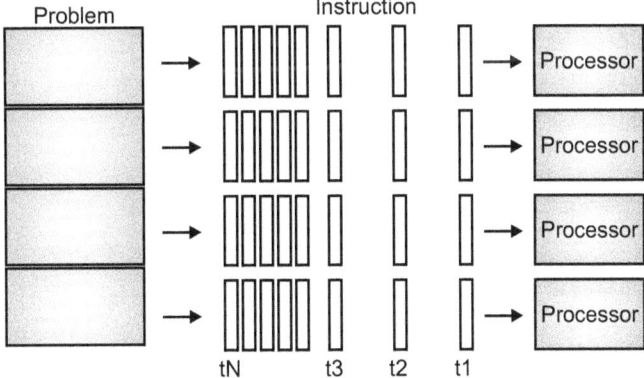

Fig. 3.5 : Parallel Computation

- The computational problem should be divided into distinct part of work which can be worked out simultaneously. At any moment in time multiple program instructions are executed. In parallel computing multiple compute resources are used to solve problem in less time.

- The compute resources are typically :
  - A single computer having multiple processors/cores.
  - Number of computers with multiple processors/cores connected by a network.
- Parallel processors are computer systems consisting of multiple processing units connected via some interconnection network plus the software needed to make the processing units work together. There are two major factors used to categorize such systems : the processing units themselves, and the interconnection network that ties them together. The processing units can communicate and interact with each other using either shared memory or message passing methods. The interconnection network for shared memory systems can be classified as bus-based versus switch-based.
- In message passing systems, the interconnection network is divided into static and dynamic. Static connections have a fixed topology that does not change while programs are running. Dynamic connections create links as the program executes.
- The main argument for using multiprocessors is to create powerful computers by simply connecting multiple processors. A multiprocessor is expected to reach faster speed than the fastest single-processor system.
- In addition, a multiprocessor consisting of a number of single processors is expected to be more cost-effective than building a high-performance single processor. Another advantage of a multiprocessor is fault tolerance. If a processor fails, the remaining processors should be able to provide continued service, albeit with degraded performance.

3.8.3 Parallel Computers

- From a hardware perspective nearly all stand-alone computers are parallel today.
- They have several functional units (L1 cache, L2 cache, branch, prefetch, decode, floating-point, graphics processing (GPU), integer, etc.)
- Parallel computers have several execution units/cores. They also have several hardware threads.
- Networks connect multiple stand-alone computers (nodes) to make larger parallel computer clusters.

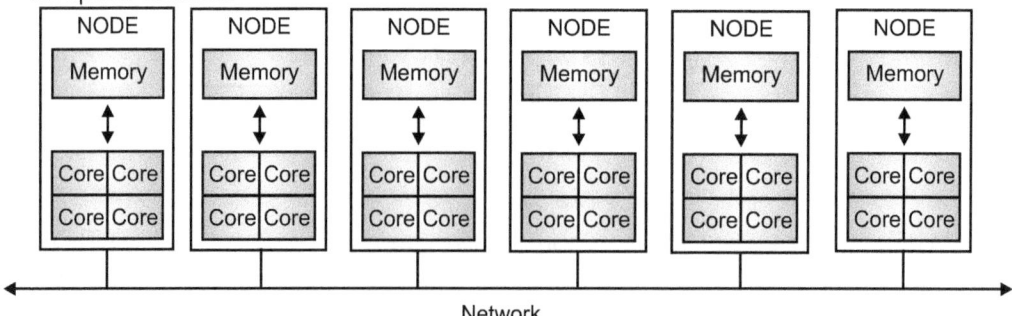

Fig. 3.6 : Parallel Computers

3.8.4 Need of Parallel Computing

- The Real World data is Massively Parallel. These problems require more computing power than provided by serial computers. Parallel computing provides cost effective solutions by adding more number of computers and sharing the workload among number of computers them. The need for parallel computers originates from the need to build faster machines.
- The increased computing power and the decreased cost, changes one's thinking in terms of the machine's use and predicts new applications. Problems requiring large scale computing (in terms of the memory and the computing speed) are numerous. Most considerable among them are large sized problems in optimization, planning, scheduling, network flows, field problems, artificial intelligence requiring logical deductions and search. These problems become non computable when the size of the problem becomes too large to fit into the computing power (the memory and the speed) of the available machines. Parallel computing is suitable for understanding, modeling and solving complex problems.
- Main reasons of using parallel computing are :
  1. It is cost effective.
  2. It efficiently solves complex problems by utilizing the power of multiple processors. Problems like database processing millions of transactions per second can be solved efficiently.

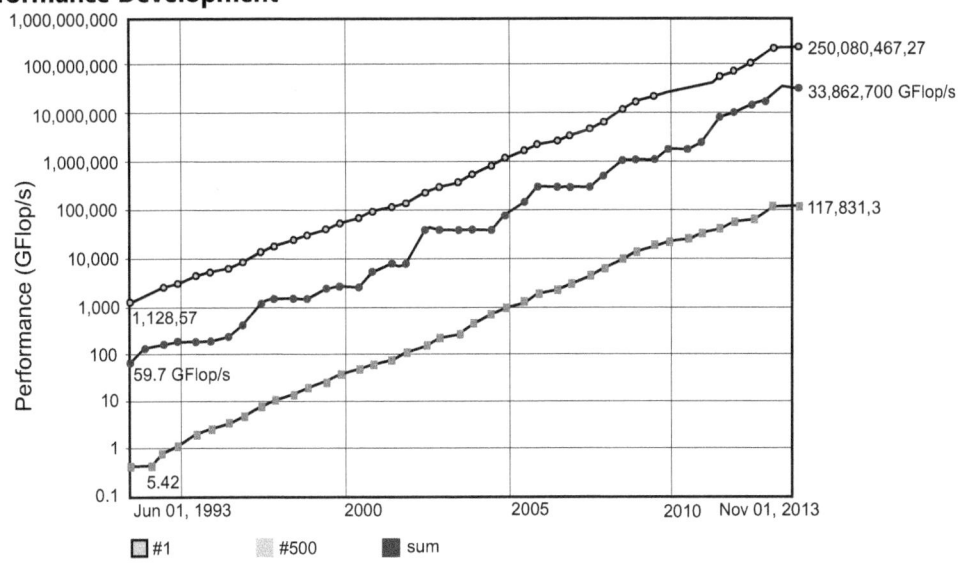

Fig. 3.7 : Exponential Growth of Supercomputing Power

  3. Multiple compute resources provide concurrency.

4. Compute resources on Internet can be used when local compute resources are not sufficient to solve given Problem.
5. Now a day's even laptops have parallel architecture, hence parallel software written for parallel hardware can be effectively utilized.

3.8.5 Uses of Parallel Computing

- Parallel Computing is used for massively parallel application.
- It is used in Science and engineering application areas like electrical and mechanical engineering, genetics, biomedical, computer science, defense and weapons etc.
- Parallel computing is used in Industrial and commercial applications areas finance and management, advance graphics and virtual reality in entertainment industry etc.

3.9 PARALLEL ARCHITECTURE AND CLASSIFICATION

- Parallel processing meets the real-time computation requirements such as speed.
- Various forms of parallel architectures have developed and worldwide research is being done to discover new architectures that can perform better than current architectures.
- The primary goal is to achieve speed. Other factors those which are considered in developing a new architecture are the internal circuitry of processors or PEs, number of PEs, arrangement of PEs and memory modules in an architecture, the communication mechanism among the PEs and between the PEs and memory modules, number of instruction and data streams, nature of memory connections with the PEs, nature and types of interconnection among the PEs, and program overlapping.
- The internal circuitry of PEs plays a very important role in designing parallel architecture.
- To enhance the overall performance of the architecture, few parallel architecture are designed with small number of PEs of complex internal circuitry while the other architectures are designed with a substantial number of PEs of simple internal circuitry to gain the desired performance.
- Adding more PEs enhances the performance of architecture .This is possible only up to a certain limit, as adding more PEs to the architecture causes more communication overhead which may not be cost effective after a certain limit.
- In the design of a parallel architecture arrangement of processors is also important. Various types of interconnection strategies, such as static and dynamic can be used for arrangement of processors in different forms.
- In a static form, the format of the architecture remains fixed and is not expandable by adding more processors.
- In a dynamic format more processors can be added under system control to meet a particular requirement.
- The communication mechanism among PEs in some architectures is straight forward, while in others the Communication scheme is complicated and requires extra effort and circuitry.

- The arrangement of memory modules in architecture is also vital and it adds to the development of varied forms of parallel architectures.
- The memory arrangement in some architectures is global, i.e., all PEs use a common memory or memory modules, which helps to establish communication among the processors, while others have memory modules associated with individual PEs and communication is established via messages passing among the PEs.
- Some forms of parallel architecture have evolved on the basis of the methodology an algorithm is implemented. Example is pipeline architecture.
- Special forms of parallel architectures are developed by merging the characteristics of various forms of existing parallel architectures.
- Efforts have been made to develop application-specific parallel architectures. For example, vector parallel architectures have been developed to execute vector intensive algorithms, DSP devices have been designed for efficient implementation of signal processing, e.g. digital filtering algorithms.
- Research and development in parallel computing is a ongoing process, and therefore it is expected to have various forms of parallel architectures in future.
- Parallel processing meets the real-time computation requirements such as speed in various applications.
- Various forms of parallel architectures have developed and worldwide research is being done to discover new architectures that can perform better than current architectures.
- The primary goal is to achieve speed .Other factors those which are considered in developing a new architecture are the internal circuitry of processors or processing elements (PEs), number of PEs, arrangement of PEs and memory modules in an architecture, the communication mechanism among the PEs and between the PEs and memory modules, number of instruction and data streams, nature of memory connections with the PEs, nature and types of interconnection among the PEs, and program overlapping.
- The internal circuitry of PEs plays a very important role in designing parallel architecture.
- To enhance the overall performance of the architecture, few parallel architecture are designed with small number of PEs of complex internal circuitry while the other architectures are designed with a substantial number of PEs of simple internal circuitry to gain the desired performance.
- Adding more PEs enhances the performance of architecture .This is possible only up to a certain limit, as adding more PEs to the architecture causes more communication overhead which may not be cost effective after a certain limit.
- In the design of a parallel architecture arrangement of processors is also important. Various types of interconnection strategies, such as static and dynamic can be used for arrangement of processors in different forms. In a static form, the format of the architecture remains fixed and is not expandable by adding more processors.

- In a dynamic format more processors can be added under system control to meet a particular requirement.
- The communication mechanism among PEs in some architectures is straightforward, while in others the

Communication scheme is complicated and requires extra effort and circuitry.
- The arrangement of memory modules in architecture is also vital and it adds to the development of varied forms of parallel architectures.
- The memory arrangement in some architectures is global, i.e., all PEs use a common memory or memory modules, which helps to establish communication among the processors, while others have memory modules associated with individual PEs and communication is established via messages passing among the PEs.
- Some forms of parallel architecture have evolved on the basis of the methodology an algorithm is implemented. Example is pipeline architecture.
- Special forms of parallel architectures are developed by merging the characteristics of various forms of existing parallel architectures.
- Efforts have been made to develop application-specific parallel architectures. For example, vector parallel architectures have been developed to execute vector intensive algorithms, DSP devices have been designed for efficient implementation of signal processing, e.g. digital filtering algorithms.
- Research and development in parallel computing is a ongoing process, and therefore it is expected to have various forms of parallel architectures in future.
- Every parallel processor has its own characteristics, advantages, disadvantages and suitability in certain application areas.

A brief introduction to various architectures is given below :

3.9.1 Pipelined Architectures

- Pipelined architecture is one of the simplest and most successful architecture.
- A complex procedure is broken down into stages and all stages take one unit of time to execute.
- Each stage of instruction can be is performed by individual parts of processor circuitry i.e. they can be in parallel.
- The instruction can be broken down as instruction fetch, decode, operand fetch and execute instruction. These stages are done in pipeline.
- Pipelining keeps every portions of processor busy with some instruction.
- Pipelined architectures are mostly followed by high performance computers.
- Hence due to pipelining of instructions higher speedup of instruction execution is achieved as much instruction can be executed at same time.
- The manufacturing assembly line is an example which implements pipelining.

- An assembly line builds many vehicles at once, rather than waiting until one vehicle has moved through the line before taking the next one.
- The computer's cycle time in pipelining is the time of the slowest step, and ideally one instruction is complete in every cycle.
- Pipelined architectures are based on serialization or queue concept. Tasks to be executed are stored in queue and will be processed in order.

Instruction 1 Fetch ------> Decode -----> Execute -----> Writeback
Instruction 2 Fetch ------> Decode -----> Execute -----> Writeback
Instruction 3 Fetch -------> Decode -----> Execute -----> Writeback
Instruction 4 Fetch -------> Decode -----> Execute -----> Writeback time ----->

Time

Fig 3.8 : Parallel Executions of Instructions in a Pipelined Processor

Multiple Pipelines
- Multiple pipeline architecture can be defined as a type of parallel architecture, formed using more than single independent pipeline in parallel.
- This architecture is a combination of pipeline and MIMD architectures.

Multiple SIMD
- Multiple SIMD is a specific type of MIMD-SIMD architecture.
- It can be defined as an MIMD type connection of a number of independent SIMD architectures.
- There are a number of control units for these architectures, each of which controls a subset of the PEs

3.9.2 Synchronous Multiprocessors / Array Processor

- Synchronous multiprocessor or array processor is a general purpose computer architecture based on single instruction multiple data (SIMD) mechanism.
- Array processor is processor that has an architecture especially designed for processing arrays of numbers. The architecture includes a number of processors (For example 64 by 64) working simultaneously, each handling one element of the array, so that a single operation can apply to all elements of the array in parallel.
- To obtain the same effect in a conventional processor, the operation must be applied to each element of the array sequentially and so consequently much more slowly.
- An array processor can be built as a self-contained unit attached to a main computer through an I/O port or internal bus, or it can be a distributed array processor where the processing elements are distributed throughout, and closely linked to, a section of the computer's memory.

- An array processing unit is basically a processing element which executes the instructions on the data which is present in their own memory called as local memory.

The three major components of an array structure are
- Array units
- Memory
- Interconnection between Array Unit and Memory

Two ways in which the components can be organized
1. An array processor in which memory is shared between the array elements. Example is Burroughs Scientific Processor (BSP)
2. An array processor in which all memory is distributed amongst the array elements. Example is ILLIAC IV machine

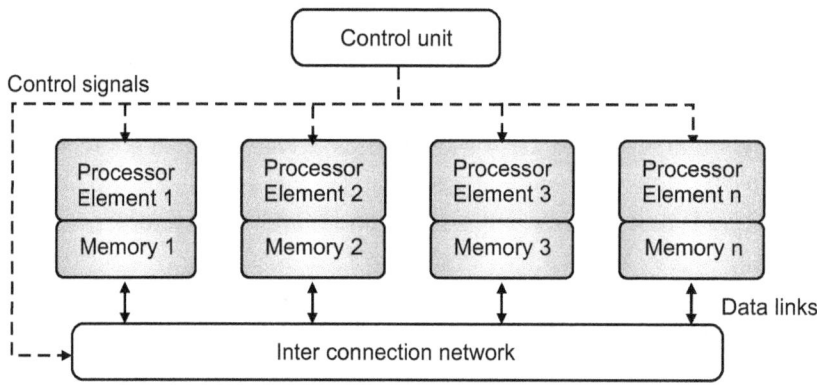

Fig. 3.9 : Array Processor with Distributed Memory

3.9.3 Shared Memory Multiprocessor Architecture

- In a shared memory multiprocessor multiple processors share a common memory consisting of single or several memory modules.
- All the processors see the shared memory as a single address space and they have equal access to this memory
- The memory modules store data as well as is used to set up communication among the processors by some bus arrangement.
- Shared memory system handles inter-processor communication by allowing all processors to see data written by any processor.
- Communication is set up through memory access instructions. Processors exchange messages between them by one processor writing data into the shared memory and another reading that data from the memory.
- Message-passing systems communicate through explicit messages.
- Threads in different processors can use the same virtual address space.

- Communication is done through shared memory variables.
- The executable programming codes are stored in the memory for each processor to execute.
- The data related to each program is also stored in this memory.
- Each program can gain access to all data sets present in the memory if necessary.
- Shared memory modules are responsible for handling the communication between the processors.
- The architecture suffers from a bottleneck problem when a number of processors try to access the global memory at the same time. It limits the scalability of the system.
- Synchronization is needed between communicating processors. Semaphore, monitors, hardware locks are used to regulate access to shared memory.
- Two common organizations of shared memory multiprocessor architecture are as follows:

1. **Physically centralized memory, uniform memory access (UMA)**
    - → Equal latency to all memory.
    - → Simple software, doesn't matter where you put data.
    - → Lower peak performance.
    - → Bus-based UMAs common also called symmetric multi-processors (SMP).
2. **Physically distributed memory, non-uniform memory access (NUMA)**
    - → Faster to local memory.
    - → More complex software: where you put data matters.
    - → Higher peak performance: assuming proper data placement.

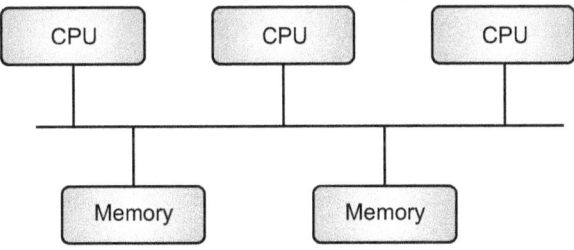

Fig. 3.10 : Shared Memory Multiprocessor

3.9.4 Conventional Multiprocessors

- A multiprocessor is a computer system having two or more processing units (multiple processors) each sharing main memory and peripherals, in order to simultaneously process programs.
- The processors may share "some or all of the system's memory and I/O facilities". Such systems are called as tightly coupled system.
- Multiprocessing is the use two or more central processing units (CPUs) within a single computer system. The term also refers to the ability of a system to support more than one processor and/or the ability to allocate tasks between them.

- At the operating system level, multiprocessing is sometimes used to refer to the execution of multiple concurrent processes in a system as opposed to a single process at any one instant. Multiprocessing however means true parallel execution of multiple processes using more than one processor.
- Multiprocessing doesn't necessarily mean that a single process or task uses more than one processor simultaneously. The term parallel processing is generally used to denote that scenario. According to Michael Flynn has defined these multiprocessors as MIMD machines. As they are normally interpreted to be tightly coupled (share memory), multiprocessors machines also contains message passing multicomputer systems.
- In multiprocessor system number of CPUs and memory units are connected by some interconnection mechanism such as bus to improve the throughput and response time of the system.
- With multiprocessor system, large computing problem is divided into smaller tasks and each CPU operated independently on the task given to it. This enables the computation to be performed in parallel.
- This also reduces the total execution time of computation problem.
- Multiprocessor system works well for the computation problem having low communication and synchronization requirement.
- From the communication point of view conventional multiprocessor are divided into following four architectures :
  1. Shared memory multiprocessor
  2. Multiprocessor architecture based on message passing
  3. Hybrid multiprocessor architecture
  4. Cluster based architecture
- Shared memory multiprocessors are very common. Number of processors attached be some interconnection mechanism operate in parallel. Scalability of shared memory multiprocessors is limited because of the limited bandwidth of the interconnection entity.
- In multiprocessor architecture based on message passing processing elements can interact with each other using the interconnection mechanism. Unlike shared memory this architecture can have any number of processing elements. However the communication is more in this case.
- Hybrid multiprocessor architecture is the combination of both shared memory architecture and multiprocessor architecture based on message passing.
- In cluster based architecture multiple processors are connected to each other by some networking mechanism.

Processor Symmetry

- In a multiprocessing system, all CPUs may be equal, or some may be reserved for special purposes. A combination of hardware and operating system software design considerations determine the symmetry in a given system.
- For example, hardware or software considerations may require that only one particular CPU respond to all hardware interrupts, whereas all other work in the system may be distributed equally among CPUs; or execution of kernel-mode code may be restricted to only one particular CPU, whereas user-mode code may be executed in any combination of processors. Multiprocessing systems are often easier to design if such restrictions are imposed, but they tend to be less efficient than systems in which all CPUs are utilized.
- Systems that treat all CPUs equally are called symmetric multiprocessing (SMP) systems. In systems where all CPUs are not equal, system resources may be divided in a number of ways, including asymmetric multiprocessing (ASMP), non-uniform memory access (NUMA) multiprocessing, and clustered multiprocessing.

3.9.5 Data Flow Computers

Dataflow architecture is a computer architecture that directly contrasts the traditional von Neumann architecture or control flow architecture. Dataflow architectures do not have a program counter, or (at least conceptually) the execution of instructions is determined based on the availability of input arguments to the instructions.

The basic idea of data flow computers is that data flow through an arrangement of Computational modules whose structure parallels the flow of dependencies within the algorithm being performed. All algorithms can be expressed within data flow paradigm. A data flow graph is used to describe data flow system. A data flow system is made of computation modules, message-passing links, communication packets called as tokens contains result.

A module performs computations on its input data to produce output data. A processing module is represented by rectangular box and decision module is represented by diamond-shape box. A path is a directed connection from an output of source module to input of destination module.

Data flow architecture is implemented in specialized hardware such as in digital signal processing, network routing, graphics processing, telemetry, and more recently in data warehousing. It is also very relevant in many software architectures today including database engine designs and parallel computing frameworks.

Instructions and their data dependencies proved to be too fine-grained to be effectively istributed in a large network. That is, the time for the instructions and tagged results to travel through a large connection network was longer than the time to actually do the computations.

Static and Dynamic Dataflow Machines

Designs that use conventional memory addresses as data dependency tags are called static dataflow machines. These machines did not allow multiple instances of the same routines to be executed simultaneously because the simple tags could not differentiate between them.

Designs that use content-addressable memory (CAM) are called dynamic dataflow machines. They use tags in memory to facilitate parallelism.

Programs

Programs are loaded into the CAM of a dynamic dataflow computer. When all of the tagged operands of an instruction become available (that is, output from previous instructions and/or user input), the instruction is marked as ready for execution by an execution unit. This is known as activating or firing the instruction. Once an instruction is completed by an execution unit, its output data is stored (with its tag) in the CAM. Any instructions that are dependent upon this particular datum (identified by its tag value) are then marked as ready for execution. In this way, subsequent instructions are executed in proper order, avoiding race conditions. This order may differ from the sequential order envisioned by the human programmer, the programmed order.

Instructions

An instruction, along with its required data operands, is transmitted to an execution unit as a packet, also called an instruction token. Similarly, output data is transmitted back to the CAM as a data token. The packets of instructions and results allows for parallel execution of ready instructions on a large scale. Dataflow networks deliver the instruction tokens to the execution units and return the data tokens to the CAM. In contrast to the conventional von Neumann architecture, data tokens are not permanently stored in memory; rather they are transient messages that only exist when in transit to the instruction storage.

Data Flow Languages

Main characteristic of data flow language is single assignment rule. A variable appear on left side of assignment only once within area of program in which it is active.

Example of Data Flow Language are :

- Value Algorithmic Language (VAL).
- Irvine Dataflow language (Id).
- Stream and Iteration in a Single-Assignment Language (SISAL).

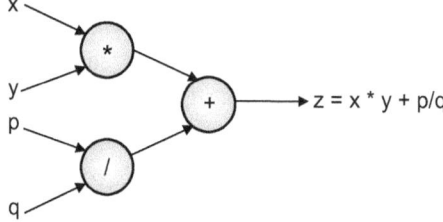

Fig. 3.11 : Data Flow Example

A dataflow program is compiled into a dataflow graph which consists of nodes representing instructions and arcs representing dependencies among the instruction. Data moves along the arcs in form of tokens. The flow of tokens enables some nodes and fires them.

3.9.6 Systolic Architectures

- Systolic computers are generalization of pipelined array architecture.
- Systolic systems consists of an array of PE (Processing Elements)
- Processors are called cells.
- Each cell is connected to a small number of nearest neighbors in a mesh like topology.
- Each cell performs a sequence of operations on data that flows between them.
- Generally the operations will be the same in each cell, each cell performs an operation or small.
- Number of operations on a data item and then passes it to its neighbor.
- Systolic arrays compute in "lock-step" with each cell (processor) undertaking alternate.

Compute/Communicate Phases

- Systolic computers are a new class of pipelined array architecture. Systolic approach can speed up a compute-bound computation in a relatively simple and inexpensive manner.
- A systolic array in particular achieves higher computation throughput without increasing memory bandwidth
- Systolic computers can be used for both pipelining and parallel computation

Systolic arrays can be used for Matrix Inversion and Decomposition, Polynomial Evaluation, Convolution, Image Processing, Artificial neural networks etc.

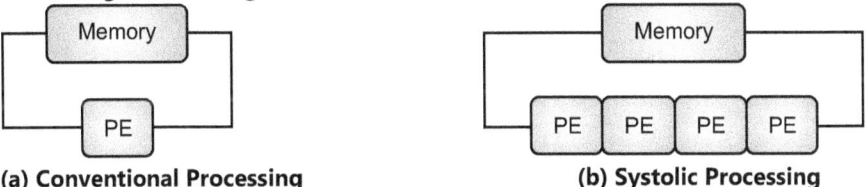

(a) Conventional Processing   (b) Systolic Processing

Fig 3.12 : Conventional Processing vs. Systolic Processing

3.9.7 Neural Network

- Artificial neural network (ANN) is a machine learning approach that models human brain and consists of a number of artificial neurons.
- Neuron in ANNs tends to have fewer connections than biological neurons.
- Each neuron in ANN receives a number of inputs.
- An activation function is applied to these inputs which results in activation level of neuron (output value of the neuron).
- Knowledge about the learning task is given in the form of examples called training examples.

- An Artificial Neural Network is specified by:
- ➢ Neuron model: The information processing unit of the NN.
- ➢ Architecture: a set of neurons and links connecting neurons. Each link has a weight.
- ➢ Learning algorithm: Used for training the NN by modifying the weights in order to model a particular learning task correctly on the training examples.
- Neural Network should behave correctly on new instances of the learning task.
- The simplest kind of neural network is a single-layer perceptron network, which consists of a single layer of output nodes; the inputs are fed directly to the outputs via a series of weights. In this way it can be considered the simplest kind of feed-forward network. The sum of the products of the weights and the inputs is calculated in each node, and if the value is above some threshold (typically 0) the neuron fires and takes the activated value (typically 1); otherwise it takes the deactivated value (typically -1).
- Neurons with this kind of activation function are also called artificial neurons or linear threshold units. A perceptron can be created using any values for the activated and deactivated states as long as the threshold value lies between the two. Most perceptrons have outputs of 1 or -1 with a threshold of 0 and such networks can be trained more quickly than networks created from nodes with different activation and deactivation values.
- Perceptrons can be trained by a simple learning algorithm that is usually called the delta rule. It calculates the errors between calculated output and sample output data, and uses this to create an adjustment to the weights, thus implementing a form of gradient descent.

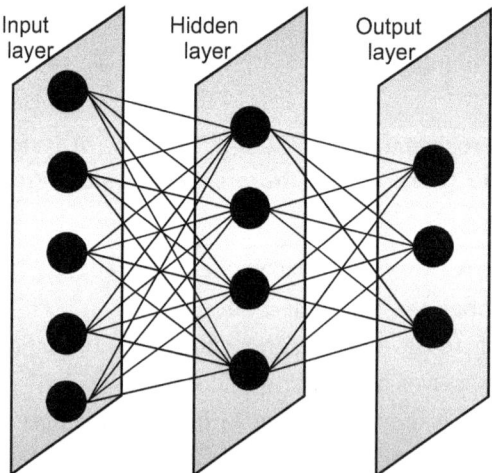

Fig. 3.13 : Neural Network

The figure 3.13 is representative of this typical network architecture comprising of
- A set of input nodes.
- One or more layers of hidden nodes.
- A set of output nodes.

The input nodes receive information and could equate to a sensory organ in the biological model. However, the input information could also be in the form of a digitized picture, which the neural net is required to analyze. This information is then passed through the network, where connection strengths, inhibition/excitation conditions, and transfer functions determine the results passed on to the next node. Each node in turn sums the inputs received and determines the output result to be passed along to the next nodes in the network. If a network is properly trained, this output should reflect the input in some meaningful way and trigger an appropriate response. Of course, the neural net must acquire the knowledge to interpret the information it receives in order to have meaning. In this respect, the connection strengths effectively store this knowledge in the neural net's own architecture. Therefore, the process of 'learning' in neural nets is primarily a process of adjusting the connection strengths. While the learning process in these terms might appear fairly straightforward, in practice it is the key issue to neural nets taking the next step. The neural networks provide a non-algorithmic approach to cognitive tasks in which the connections represented by weights are modified using models from adaptive systems theory. The research in these application areas have not yet produced computational models to give the desired performance. Actually these are recognized as highly complex tasks. The neural network model uses the neural system to provide the analog of the brain by using artificial neurons and their dense connections having weights to store and process the knowledge and carry out the cognitive tasks.

3.10 CLASSIFICATIONS

A large number of parallel architectures are available today. Developing a classification system for parallel architectures is very difficult job. Many of the parallel architectures share their properties.
1. Classification of parallel architectures based instruction and data stream by Flynn.
2. Classification of parallel architectures based on memory arrangement and communication among processing elements.
3. Classification of parallel architectures based on interconnections among processing elements and memory modules.
4. Classification of parallel architectures based on characteristics of processing elements.
5. Special types of parallel architectures.
6. Shore's Classification.
7. Feng's Classification.
8. Handler's Classification.

3.10.1 Classification of Parallel Architectures by Flynn

According to Flynn parallel processors can be classified based on the simultaneous instruction and data streams during program execution. During program execution instruction and data streams play a major role. Refer figure 3.14. During program execution the processing elements fetches instructions and data from the main memory, processes the data as per the instructions and sends the results to the main memory after processing has been completed. Instruction stream is set of instructions, which flows from the main memory to the processing element, and data stream is a collection of data which flows from the processing element to main memory and vice versa. Based on these instruction stream and data stream, Flynn classified computer architecture into four major classes, which are described below.

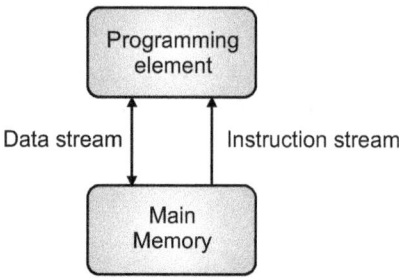

Fig 3.14 : Instruction Stream and Data Stream

Single-Instruction Single-Data Stream(SISD)

The first computer architecture Von Neumann computer falls under the category of single-instruction single-data (SISD) stream. Von Neumann architecture is based on serial execution technique. That means instructions are executed one after another. Refer fig. 3.15. Single-instruction-single-data stream architecture is represented in fig 3.16 using instruction and data flow. The SISD computer architecture have a central processing unit (CPU), memory unit and input/output (I/O) devices. The CPU consists of arithmetic and logic unit (ALU) to perform arithmetic and logical operations, control unit (CU) to perform control operations and registers to store small amounts of data. SISD computers are sequential computers. It is not possible to perform parallel operations on SISD computers.

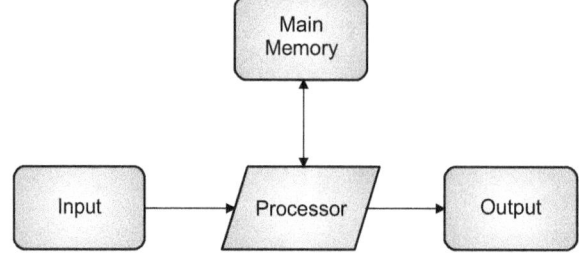

Fig. 3.15 : Von Neumann Computer Architecture

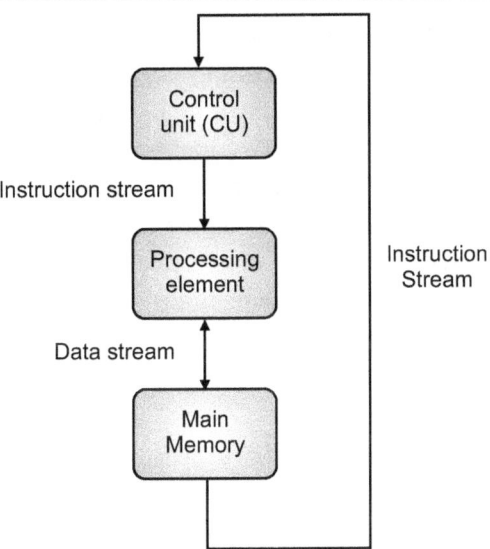

Fig. 3.16 : SISD Architecture with Instruction and Data Flow

Single-instruction Multiple-data Stream (SIMD)

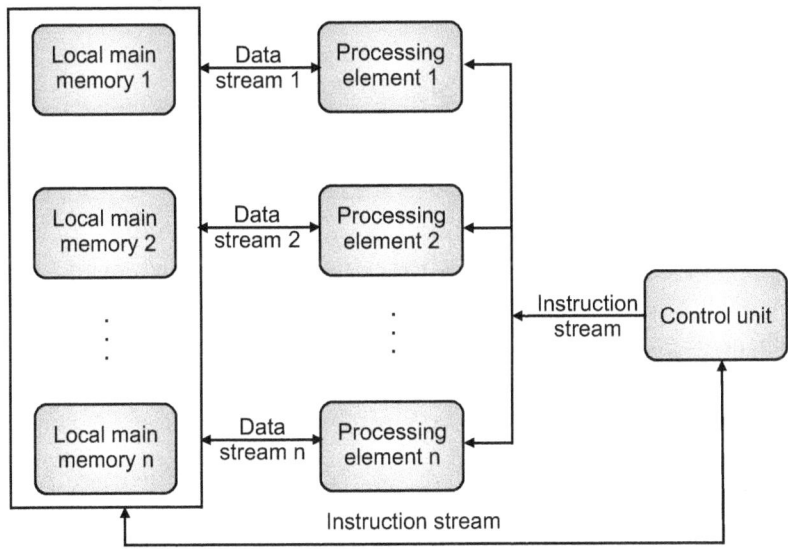

Fig. 3.17 : SIMD Computer Architecture

In figure 3.17 the general structure of a single-instruction multiple-data (SIMD) parallel architecture is shown. SIMD parallel architecture has a single instruction stream so that it can process multiple-data stream. In SIMD architecture a single program control unit controls multiple execution units i.e. processing elements. Each processing element has a local memory. These processing elements will work only on the data that has been stored on their respective local memory. Each processing element executes the same instruction issued by the control unit on its local data. The processing elements are capable of communicating with each other as and when required. This communication is possible because the local memories of the entire processing elements can treated as single shared memory. SIMD architectures are good for problems where the same operation is executed on a number of different data i.e. multiple data streams, for example image processing. Some other suitable applications of SIMD architectures include matrix operations and sorting. Programming is quite simple and straightforward for this architecture.

SIMD architecture could be divided into two subclasses according to the interconnections between the processing elements. These two subclasses are vector architecture and array architecture.

SIMD vector architecture is shown in figure 3.18. In SIMD vector architecture processing elements are connected to each other via special data links. These links are used to perform simple data exchange operations like shifts and rotations. All the processing elements are connected to the central control unit to obtain the instructions to be executed.

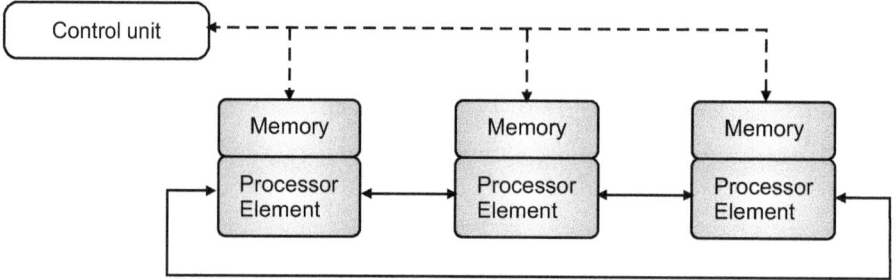

Fig. 3.18 : SIMD Vector Architecture

Array architecture is often referred by the term SIMD architecture. Unlike vector architecture, processing elements in array architecture are connected by interconnecting network. A general form of array structure is shown in Figure 3.19, where a two dimensional arrangement of processing elements executes instructions issued from the control processor.

From the Fig 3.19 it is clear that each processing element is connected to its four neighbours. The main purpose behind this connection is to exchange the data among each other. This is because of all processing elements are capable of exchanging values with each of their neighbours. Each processing element has a few registers and some local memory so that they can easily store data. Each processing element is also having a special register called a network register. This network register is responsible for the movement of values to and from its neighbours. Each processing element also contains an Arithmetic Logic Unit (ALU) to execute arithmetic instructions issued from the control processor.

The central processor is capable of submitting an instruction (to all processing elements) to shift the values in the network registers one step up, one step down, one step left or one step right. Array architecture is very powerful and it is specially designed problems that can be expressed in matrix or vector format.

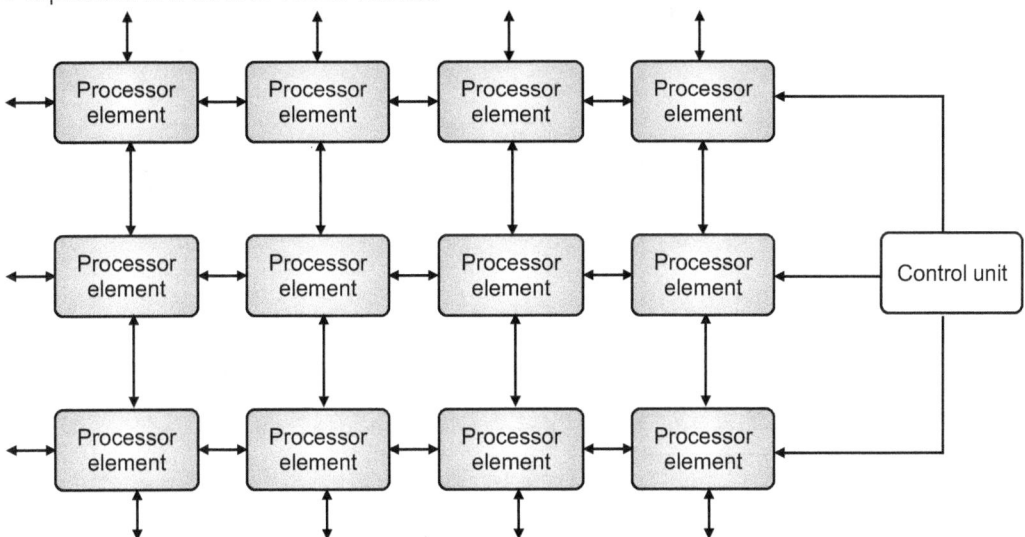

Fig. 3.19 : SIMD Array Architecture

Both array and vector architectures are specialized machines. They are mainly designed to solve numerical problems that have large numbers of vector and/or matrix elements. The basic difference between vector and array architectures is that high-performance is achieved in vector architecture by taking the advantage of a pipelining mechanism whereas in array architecture a large number of processing elements are connected to four neighbours to accelerate the performance. None of these architectures is well suited to enhance the performance of general computation.

Multiple-instruction Single-data Stream (MISD)

The general structure of multiple-instruction single-data stream (MISD) architecture is shown in figure 3.20. As the name implies this architecture has multiple instruction stream and single data stream. This architecture has not evolved significantly and hence, there are not many examples of this architecture However pipeline computers – usually treated as major class of parallel architectures can be considered as MISD architecture. MISD computers can be useful in applications of a specialized nature. A typical example of one such specialized application is robot vision.

An MISD machine can quickly carry out a classification task by assigning each of its processors a different class of objects and after receiving what the robot sees each processor may carry out tests to determine whether the given object belongs to its class or not.

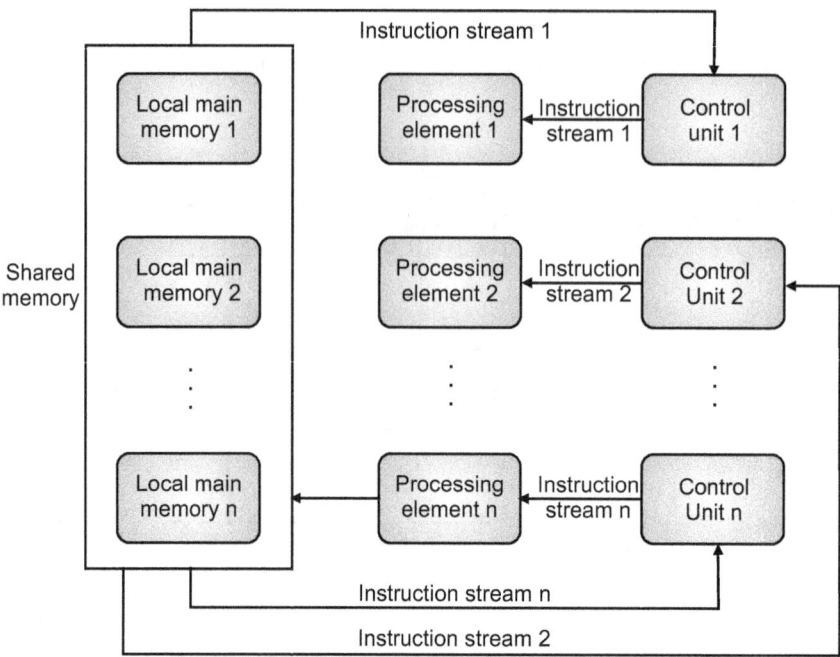

Fig. 3.20 : MISD Computer Architecture

Multiple-instruction Multiple-data Stream (MIMD)

Figure 3.21 shows the general structure of multiple-instruction multiple-data (MIMD) stream architecture. This architecture is the most common and widely used form of parallel architectures. MIMD architecture has several processing elements, each of these processing elements is capable of executing independent instruction streams on independent data streams.

The processing elements in the MIMD architecture typically share resources such as communication facilities, I/O devices, program libraries and databases. Since there are many processing elements, it is necessary to have a common entity that can monitor and control the processing elements. Common operating system is there to control the processing elements. The multiple processing elements in the system improve performance and increase reliability. Performance increases due to the fact that computational load is shared by the processing elements in the system. So load balancing is one of the major advantages of MIMD computer architecture. Theoretically, if there are m processing elements in the system, the performance will raise by m times in comparison to a single processing element based system. System reliability is increased by the fact that failure of one processing element in the system does not cause failure of the whole system. There is no single point of failure in MIMD architecture.

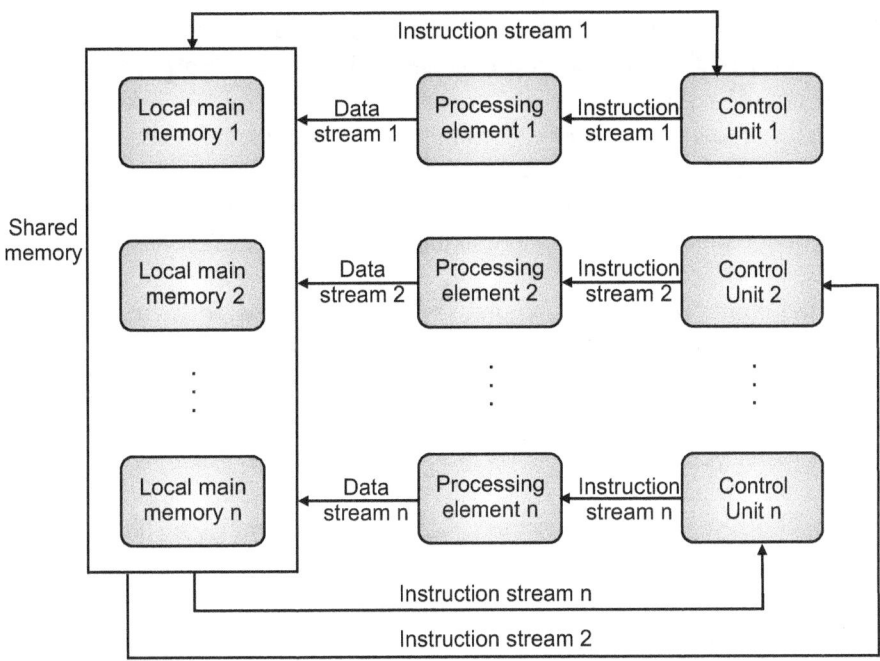

Fig. 3.21 : MIMD Computer Architecture

3.10.2 Classification of Parallel Architectures Based On Memory Arrangement and Communication Among Processing Elements

Memory arrangement and communication between processing elements are two important concepts by which parallel architectures can be divided into two important classes. These are: shared memory and message passing or distributed memory. In fact, these architectures are the form of MIMD parallel architecture. Shared memory and distributed memory architectures are also called tightly coupled and loosely coupled architectures respectively. Each type of architecture has its own advantages and disadvantages.

Shared Memory Multiprocessor

In a shared memory multiprocessor multiple processors are present. These multiple processors share a common memory unit. This common memory unit is either a single large memory module or several memory modules. All the processors have the same access to these memory modules and these memory modules are seen as a single memory module by all the processors. The memory modules can be store the data. This common memory module known as shared memory is also used for carrying out communication between the processors via some bus arrangement. Communication is established through memory access instructions, commonly referred as read-write operations. That is, processors exchange messages between one another by one processor writing data into the shared memory and another reading that data from the shared memory. Programming this architecture is very straightforward and interesting. The executable programming modules are stored in the memory so that each processor can execute it. The data related to each program is also stored in this memory. Each program can gain access to all data sets present in the memory as and when required. The executable programming modules and shared data for the processor can be created and managed in different ways by designing parallel programming language or using existing sequential languages such as C/C++. There is no direct processor-to-processor communication involved in this overall programming process. However all the communication is handled mainly by the shared memory. Access to this common memory module-shared memory can easily be controlled through an appropriate programming mechanism such as multitasking.

Disadvantage of this architecture is bottleneck problem. The problem arises when a number of processors attempt to access the shared memory at the same time. This bottleneck problem limits the scalability of the system. A solution to this problem is to have some form of hierarchical or distributed memory structure (for shared memory) such that processors can access physically nearby memory locations faster than distant memory locations. This is called non-uniform memory access (NUMA). Figure 3.22 shows a general form of shared memory multiprocessor architecture.

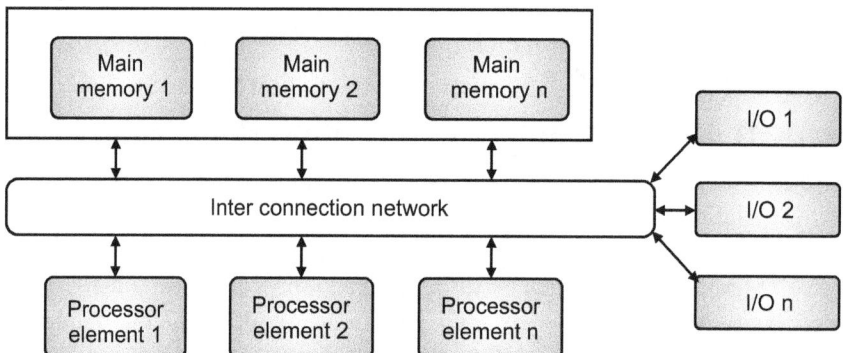

Fig. 3.22 : Shared Memory Multiprocessor Architecture

Shared memory multiprocessors are classified as uniform memory access (UMA) architecture and non-uniform memory access (NUMA) architecture. As the name implies, the memory access time to the different parts of the memory are almost the same in the case of UMA architectures. UMA architectures are also called symmetric multiprocessors. UMA architecture consists of two or more processors with common characteristics. The processors share the same main memory and I/O facilities. These processors are interconnected by some form of bus-based interconnection scheme such that the memory access time is approximately the same for all processors. All processors can perform the same functions under control of an integrated operating system, which provides interaction between processors and their programs at the job, task, file and data element levels.

In the case of NUMA architectures the memory access time of processors differs depending on location of the main memory which is accessed. A subdivision NUMA system is cache coherent NUMA (CC-NUMA) where cache coherence is maintained among the caches of various processors. The main advantage of a CC-NUMA system is that it can deliver effective performance at higher levels of parallelism than UMA architecture.

Message Passing Multicomputer

Distributed memory architecture is different from shared memory architecture in that each unit of this architecture is a complete computer building block. Each unit is known as complete computer building block because it is equipped with processor, memory and I/O system. A processor can access the memory, which is directly attached to it. Communication among the processors is established in the form of I/O operations through message signals and bus networks. For example, if a processor needs data from another processor it sends a signal to that processor through an interconnected bus network and demands the required data. The remote processor then responds accordingly. Certainly, access to local memory is faster than access to remote processors. Most importantly, the larger the physical distance to the remote processor, the longer time will be required to access the remote data. Message passing multiprocessor architecture suffers from the drawback of requiring direct communication between processors, In message passing multiprocessor architecture there is no bottleneck problem as it is there in shared memory multiprocessor.

The performance of distributed memory architecture largely depends on the way by which processors are connected to each other. It is not a good practice to connect each processor to the remaining processors in the system through independent cables. This mechanism will work for a very low number of processors but becomes nearly impossible as the number of processors in the system increases. Numbers of solutions have been proposed to overcome the above mention problem over some years. The most common solution among them is to use specialized bus networks to connect all the processors in the system so that each processor can communicate with any other processor attached to the system.

3.10.3 Classification of Parallel Architectures Based on Interconnections Between Processing Elements and Memory Modules

Parallel architectures can also be classified based on interconnecting network arrangements used for communication between the various processing elements present in the respective architecture. In fact, this classification is very similar to MIMD architectures. This is because the architecture also contains multiple PEs and memory modules as MIMD architecture. The various interconnecting communication networks used for establishing communication among the processing elements of a parallel architecture are: linear, shared single bus, shared multiple bus, crossbar, ring, mesh, star, tree, hypercube and complete graph.

Among these interconnecting networks, linear, mesh, ring, star, tree, hypercube and complete graph are static interconnection communication structures. Static communication structures are not reconfigurable. Shared single bus, shared multiple bus and crossbar are dynamic interconnection communication structures as they are reconfigurable under system control.

Linear Network

Linear network falls under the category of static interconnection communication structure. A number of nodes are connected through buses in a linear format to form a network of nodes in serial fashion. As shown in figure 3.23. Every node, except the nodes at the two ends, in this configuration is directly connected to two other nodes. Thus, to connect n nodes in this configuration $n-1$ buses are required and the maximum distance between all the nodes in the system is $n-1$.

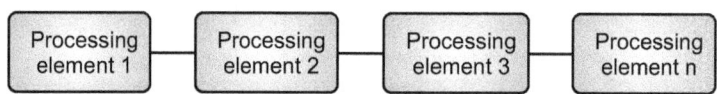

Fig. 3.23 : Linear Network

Single Shared Bus Network

The single shared bus network falls under the category of dynamic interconnection communication structure. This single shared bus network is shown in figure 3.24. It is widely used in parallel architectures. A number of processing elements and memory units are connected to a single bus. Communication is established among the processing elements and memory units connected to this single bus. The operation of the single bus interconnection structure is explained as follows :

1. A processor issues a read request to required memory location.

2. This processor holds the bus until it receives the required data from the memory module. Note that this will require some time for the memory module to access the data from the appropriate location.

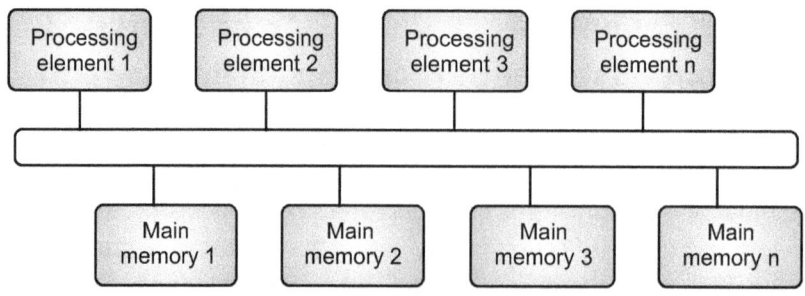

Fig. 3.24 : Single Shared Bus Network

The transferring mechanism also will need some time and any other request from the processor (excluding the processor which has issued a request which is in progress) will not be entertained until the current transfer is completed. This means the bus will remain idle for a certain amount of time that can be as high as two-thirds of the total time required for the transfer. A solution to this problem is given by split transfer protocol scheme. With this mechanism the bus can issue a number of requests from different processors to different memory modules. In this case after transferring the address of the first request the bus starts the transfer of the next request so that two requests are executed in parallel. If none of the two requests has completed, the bus can issue a third request. When the first memory module completes its access cycle, the bus is used to send the data to the destination processor. As another module completes its access cycle the data is transferred using the bus, and the process continues. The split transfer protocol increases the performance of the bus at the cost of complexity. The complexity increases due to maintaining synchronization and coordination among the requests, processors and memory modules.

One of the limitations of single bus interconnection is its scalability. This means it is not possible to connect a large number of processors and memory modules to a bus. The number of modules to be connected with the bus could be increased by using a wider bus with increased bandwidth.

Multiple Shared Bus Network

Limited scalability is the major problem faced by single shared bus network. This network cannot cope with large numbers of processing elements and memory units. This limited scalability problem will be overcome by using multiple shared bus networks. Multiple shared bus network falls under the category of dynamic interconnection communication structure. The structure of a multiple shared bus network is shown in figure 3.25. In multiple shared bus network each processor and memory are connected to one or more of the available buses, each of which possesses all the characteristics of an independent system bus. Besides reducing the communication load per bus, a degree of fault tolerance is provided, since the system can be designed to continue operation, possibly with reduced performance, if an individual bus fails. So there is no single point of failure as in single shared bus network.

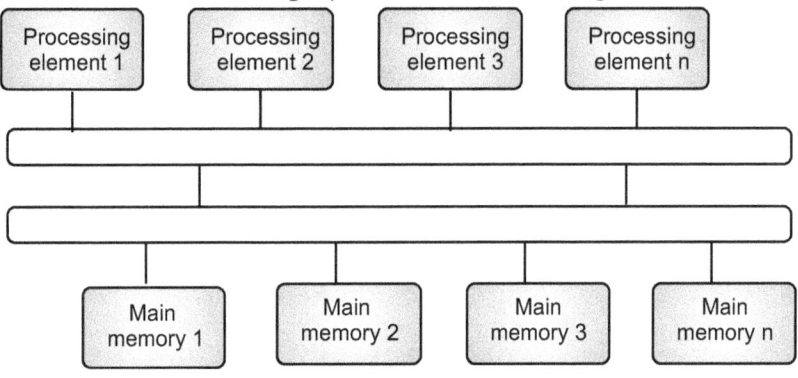

Fig. 3.25 : Multiple Shared Buses Network

Crossbar Interconnection Network

The structure of crossbar architecture is shown in figure 3.26. This architecture falls under the category of dynamic interconnection communication structure. In this architecture, all the processing elements and memory modules are interconnected through a multi bus crossbar network system where subscript m denotes the 'm' number of processing elements and n denotes the 'n' number of main memory modules. The crossbar architecture becomes very complicated as the number of memory modules and processing elements increases.

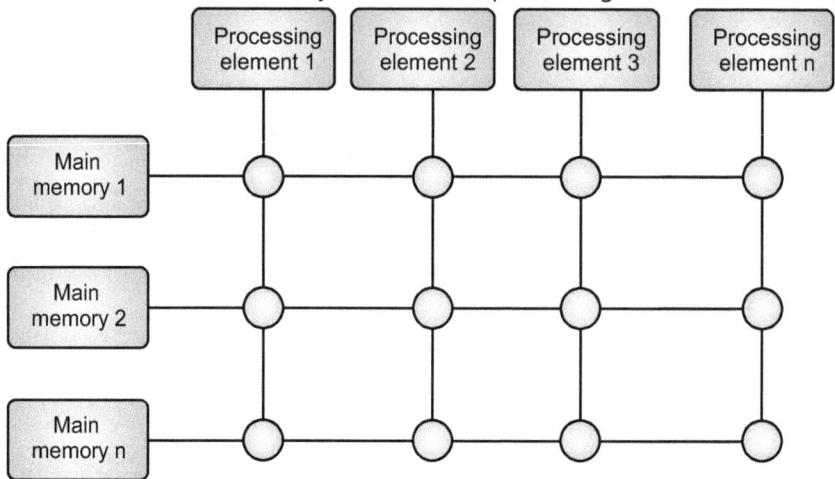

Fig. 3.26 : Crossbar Interconnection Network

Star Interconnection Network

The structure of star interconnection network is shown in figure 3.27. Star interconnection network is one of the simplest interconnection networks. In this configuration $n-1$ buses are required for connecting n nodes and the maximum inter node distance is n-2. A node in this structure can communicate with any other node with the help of the node in the centre.

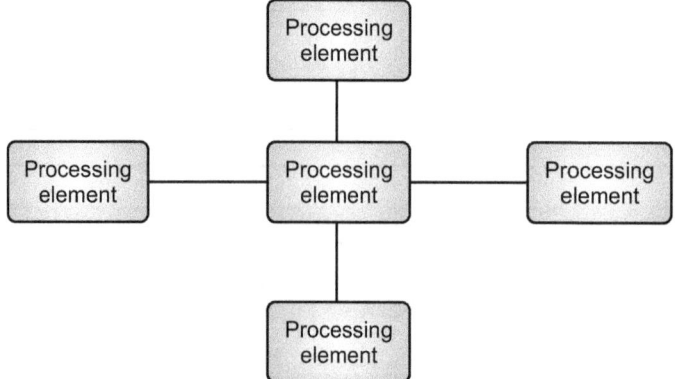

Fig. 3.27 : Star Interconnection Network

Ring Interconnection Network

The structure ring interconnection network is shown in figure 3.28. It is also one of the simplest interconnection topologies. Ring interconnection network is very easy to implement. In the case of ring interconnection n buses are required to connect n nodes and the maximum internodes distance is $n/2$. Rings can be used as building blocks to form other interconnection structures such as mesh, hypercube and tree. A ring-based two stage tree structure is shown in figure 3.29. However, the highest-level ring could be a bottleneck for traffic in this case.

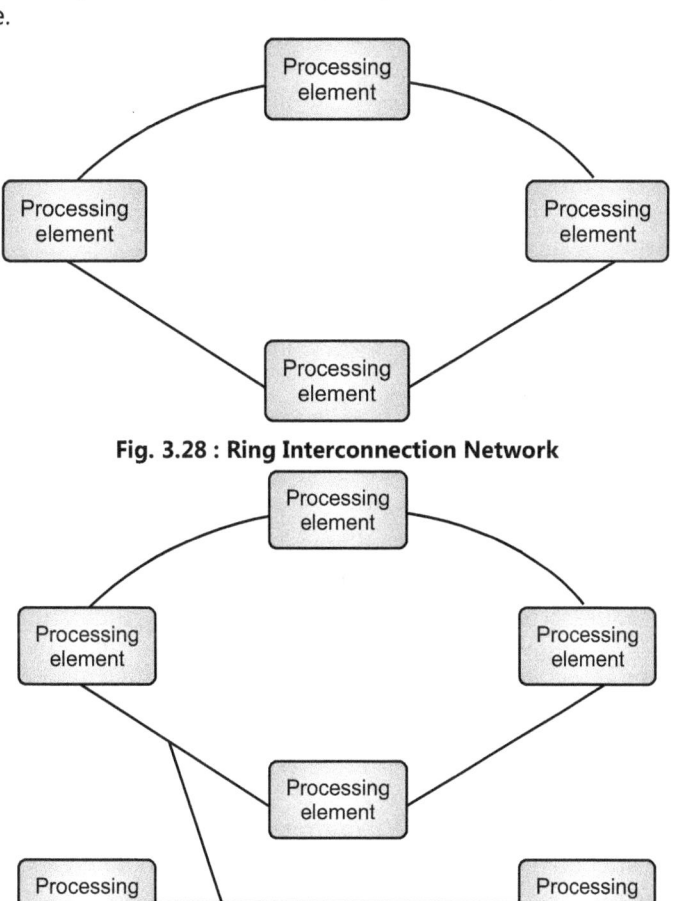

Fig. 3.28 : Ring Interconnection Network

Fig. 3.29 : Ring Based Two Tree Structures

Tree Interconnection Network

Tree structure is another important and useful interconnection topology. There are number of levels in a tree structure. The general form of an n-level tree structure is shown in figure 3.30. In this case any intermediate node can be used as a medium to establish communication between its parents and children. Through this mechanism communication could also be established between any two nodes in the structure. A tree structure can be highly effective if a small portion of traffic goes through the root node. The possibility of bottleneck problems is less in a flat tree structure because in such structures large number of nodes are present at the higher levels.

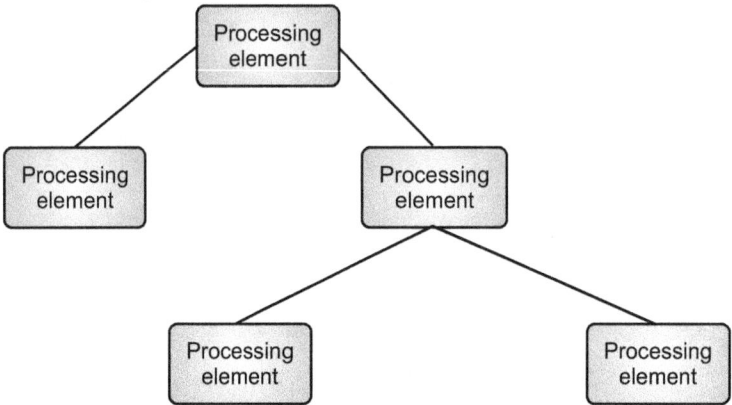

Fig. 3.30 : Tree interconnection Network

Hypercube Interconnection Network

Hypercube interconnection network falls under the category of static interconnection communication structure. It executes SPMD instructions. It is widely used interconnection network architecture, especially for NUMA multiprocessors. An n-dimensional hypercube can connect 2^n nodes. Each has a processor, a memory module and some I/O capability. A three dimensional hypercube is shown in figure 3.31. The edges of the cube represent bi-directional communication links between two neighbouring nodes. The nodes are normally labeled using binary addresses. Binary addresses of the two neighbouring nodes differ by one bit position. Messages are transferred from one node to another in a hypercube structure with the help of binary addresses assigned to each of the nodes. In this transferring scheme the binary address of the source node and the destination nodes are compared from least to most significant bits and transfer to the destination is performed through some intermediate nodes in between. For example, the transfer of message from node Pi to a node Pj takes place as follows. First the binary addressees of Pi and Pj are compared from least to most significant bits. Suppose they differ in bit position p. Node Pi then sends a message to the neighbouring node Pk whose address differs from Pi in bit position p. Node Pk then passes the message to its appropriate neighbours using the same scheme. The message gets closer to the destination node with each of these passes and finally reaches it after several passes. The hypercube structure is very reliable. If a faulty link is detected while passing a message from source to destination node through the shortest route; the message can be passed using another route. A hypercube is homogeneous in nature, as the system appears the same when viewed from any of its outside nodes. Thus, programming the hypercube is simple because all nodes can execute the same programs on different data when collaborating on a common task.

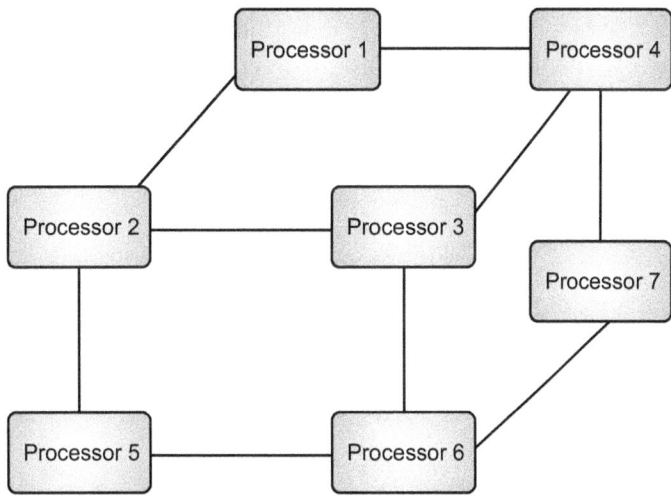

Fig. 3.31 : Hypercube Interconnection Structure

Complete Graph Interconnection Network

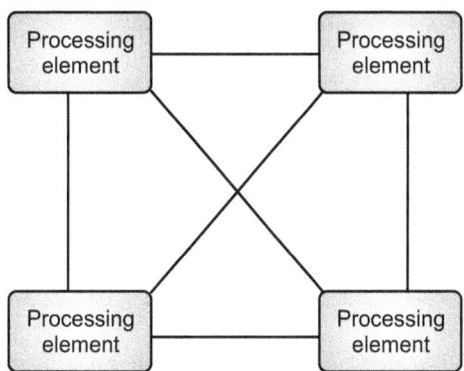

Fig. 3.32 : Complete Graph Interconnection Network

Complete graph interconnection network falls under the category of static interconnection communication structure. In a complete graph interconnection structure several processors are connected in the complete graph format as shown in figure 3.32. All the processors are connected to each other. Here, each node can directly communicate with any other node without going through or touching any intermediate node. However, it requires many buses. For a complete graph with *n* nodes the number of buses required is $n(n-1)/2$ and the maximum inter node distance is 1.

Switching or Dynamic Interconnection Structures

Dynamic parallel architectures are reconfigurable under system control and the control is generally achieved through different kinds of switching circuits. One such switch is shown in figure 3.33, which is an AND gate controlling the connection between two lines namely *m* and *n*. When line *n* is high (say, a binary 1) indicating that a connection is required to be made with the line *m*, the control line will go high and the connection will be established. Another two-state switching element is shown in figure 3.34. Each switch has a pair of input buses $x1$ and $x2$, and a pair of output buses $y1$ and $y2$, assisted by some form of control mechanism.

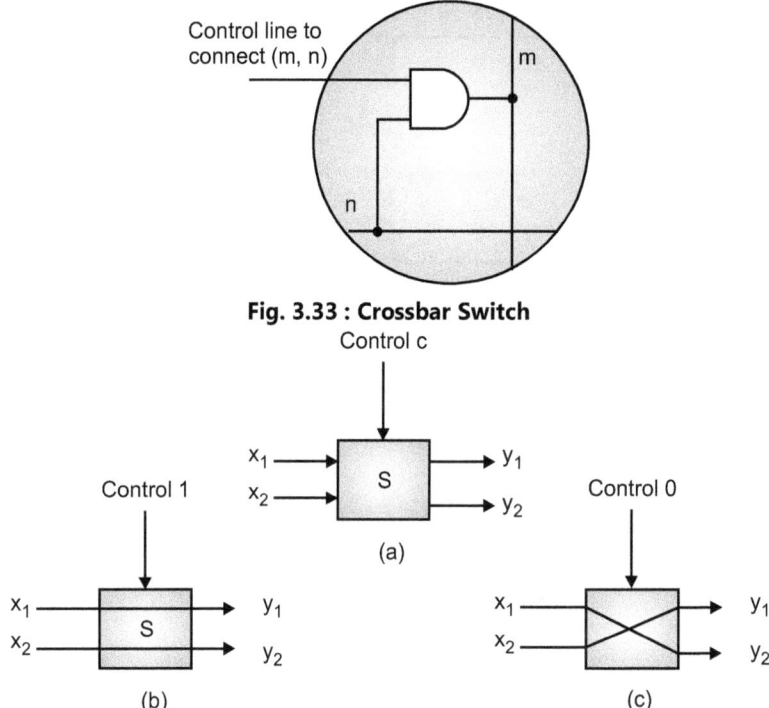

Fig. 3.33 : Crossbar Switch

Fig. 3.34 : Two States Switching Machine

The buses connected to the switch could be used to establish processor-to-processor or processor-to-memory links. The switch S has two states, determined by a control line, the through or direct state, as depicted in figure 3.34, where $y1=x1$ (i.e., $y1$ is connected to $x2$) and $y2=x2$ and a cross state where $y1=x2$ (i.e., $y1$ is connected to $x2$) and $y2=x1$. Using S as a building block, multistage switching networks of the type can be constructed for use as interconnection networks in parallel computers. A three-stage switching network of this type is shown in figure 3.35. The network contains 12 switching elements and is intended to provide dynamic connections between the processors. By setting the control signals of the switching elements in various ways, a large number of different interconnection patterns is possible. The number of stages, the fixed connections linking the stages, and the dynamic states of the switching elements, in general, determines the possibilities.

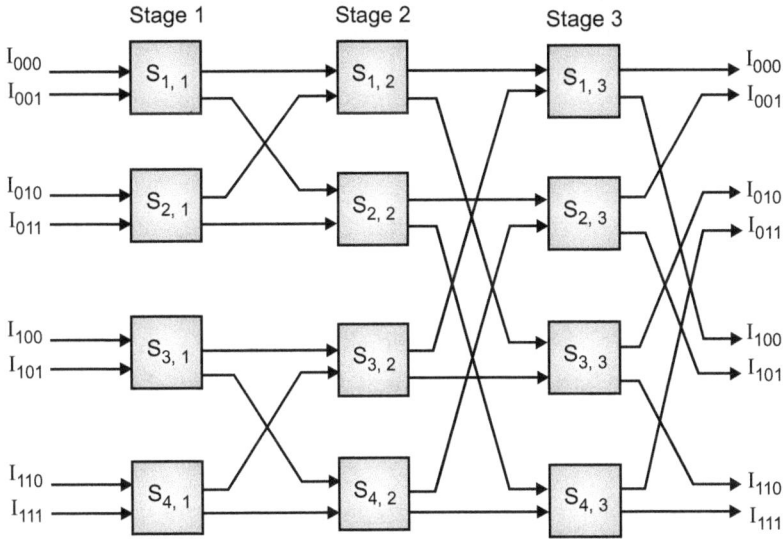

Fig. 3.35 : Three Stage Switching Network

3.10.4 Classification of Parallel Architectures Based on Characteristic Nature of Processing Elements

Parallel architectures can also be classified in terms of the nature of the processing elements comprising them. Architecture may consist of either only one type of processing elements or various types of processing elements.

When architecture consists of same type of processing elements, it is called as homogeneous parallel architecture. If the architecture consists of different types of processing elements, it is called as heterogeneous parallel architecture. The different types of processors that are commonly used to form parallel architectures are described below.

CISC Processors

Complex Instruction Set Computer (CISC) is a type of processor that uses a complex, powerful instruction set capable of performing many tasks including memory access, arithmetic calculations and address calculations.

Some important features of CISC processors are as follows :
- CISC instruction sets are large and powerful.
- CISC instructions are executed slowly as each instruction is normally capable of doing many tasks.
- CISC processors are difficult to program.
- CISC architectures have pipelines and more registers.
- CISC processors perform low number of operations.
- CISC processors are generally used in desktop machines.

RISC Processors

Reduced Instruction Set Computer (RISC) processors have a number of distinguishing characteristics, some of which are as follows:
- RISC processors handle more operations than CISC processors.
- Execution of instructions in a RISC processor is faster than execution of instructions in CISC processor.
- RISC processors support pipelined instruction execution.
- RISC processors contain large number of registers, most of which can be used as general-purpose registers.
- RISC processors are simple to program.

DSP and Vector Processors

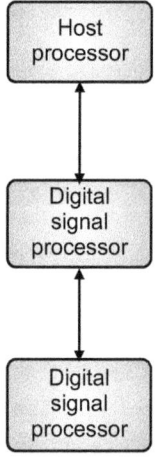

Fig. 3.36 : Homogeneous Architecture of DSP Processors

DSP chips are specially designed to execute signal processing algorithms and applications such as Fourier Transform, Fast Fourier Transform, correlation, convolution and digital filtering. Such algorithms are widely used in a variety of DSP applications such as radar, sonar, and weather forecasting, temperature sensing. As most digital signal processing operations require additions and multiplications together, DSP processors usually have number of adders and multipliers, which can be used in parallel within a single instruction. DSP chips are also capable of handling multiple memory access in a single instruction cycle.

One of the major differences between DSP chips and general-purpose processors is that DSP chips are required to deal with real-world problems frequently and they are designed to do so.

Vector processors are designed to execute vector-intensive algorithms faster than other types of general-purpose and specialized processors. In fact, many algorithms are of regular nature and contain numerous matrix operations. Vector processors are very efficient at executing these types of algorithms.

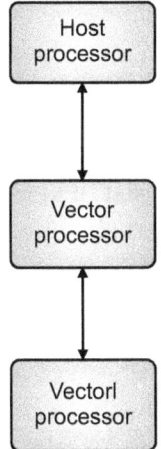

Fig. 3.37 : Homogeneous Architecture of Vector Processors

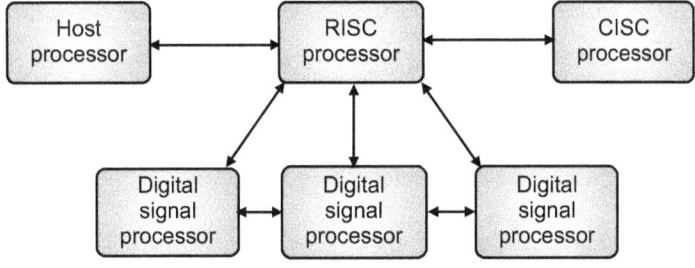

Fig. 3.38 : Heterogeneous Architecture

3.10.5 Specific Types of Parallel Architectures

Refer Article 3.9, Page 3.18.

3.10.6 Shore's Classification

Shore classified the computers on the basis of organization of the basic Computer elements. Shore classified the computers in six different categories.

Machine 1

These are conventional Von Neumann architectures with following units in single quantities

(a) Control Unit (CU)
(b) Processing Unit (PU)
(c) Instruction Memory (IM)
(d) Data Memory (DM)

- A single Data Memory (DM) read produces all the bits of any word for processing in parallel by the Processing Unit (PU).
- The PU may contain multiple functional units which may or may not be pipelined. Therefore,
- This group again includes both the scalar computers (e.g., IBM 360/91, CDC 7600, etc.) and the Pipelined vector computers (e.g., Cray YMX .Figure 3.39 (a) shows the organization of such a machine.
- The processing is characterized as horizontal (number of bits in parallel as a word).
- Machine 2 organization is similar to that of Machine 1, except that DM fetches a bit slice from all the words in the memory and PU are ordered to perform the operations in a bit serial manner on all the words (Fig.3.39 (b)).
- If the memory is regarded as a two dimensional array of bits with one word stored per row, then the Machine 2 reads vertical slice of bits and processes the same, whereas the machine 1 reads and processes a horizontal slice of bits.

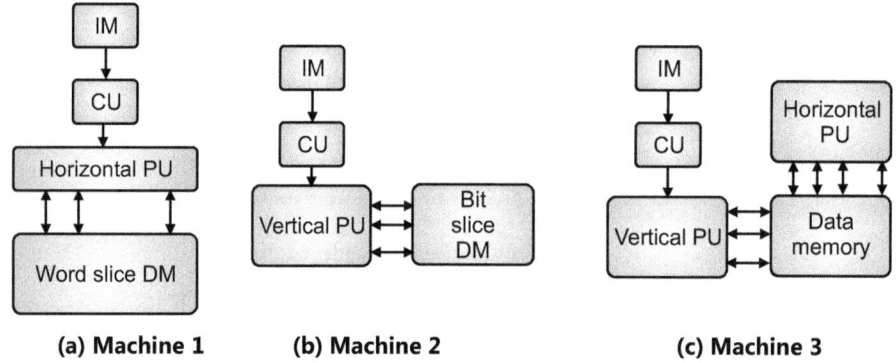

(a) Machine 1   (b) Machine 2   (c) Machine 3

Fig 3.39 : Shore's Classification : Machine 1,2 and 3

- Machine 3 is a combination of Machine 1 and Machine 2.
- It could be characterized with the memory as an array of bits with both horizontal and vertical reading and processing possible.
- The machine, thus, will have both the vertical and the horizontal processing units.
- Well known example is the machine OMENN 60. Figure 3.39(c) shows the architecture of Machine 3.

- Machine 4 architecture as shown in Fig. 3.40(a) is obtained by replicating the PU and DM of the Machine 1. An ensemble of PU and DM is called as Processing Element (PE). The instructions are issued to the PEs by a single control unit.
- There is no communication between PEs except through the CU. Absence of the connection between the PEs limits the applicability of the machine.
- Machine 5 is similar to Machine 4, with the addition of the communication between the PEs as shown in Fig. 3.40 (b). ILLIAC IV, CM2 and many SIMD processors fall in this category.
- Machines 1 to 5 maintain separation between data memory and processing units with some data bus or connection unit providing the communication between them.
- The machine 6 shown in Fig. 3.40 (c) includes the logic in the memory itself and is called an Associative processor. Machines based on this architecture have from simple associative memories to complex associative processors.

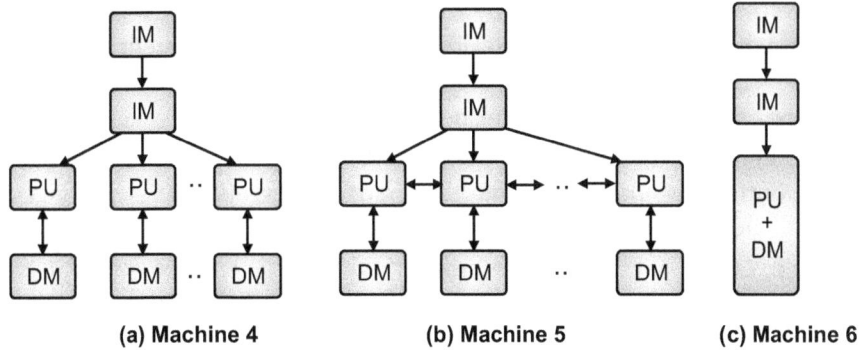

Fig. 3.40 : Shore's Classification : Machine 4, 5, 6

3.10.7 Feng's Classification

Feng also proposed a scheme on the basis of degree of parallelism to classify the computer architectures. Maximum number of bits that can be processed every unit of time by the system is called 'maximum degree of parallelism'.

Based on the Feng's scheme, we have sequential and parallel operations at the bit and the word levels to produce the following classification.

Classification	Examples
WSBS (Word Serial/Bit Serial)	It is not conceivable implementation
WPBS (Word Parallel/Bit Serial)	Staran
WSBP (Word Serial/Bit Parallel)	Conventional computers
WPBP (Word Parallel/Bit Parallel)	ILLIAC IV

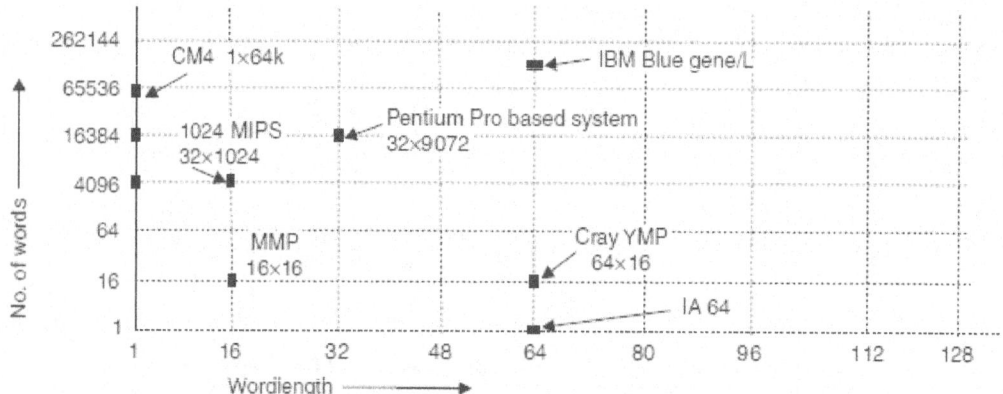

Fig. 3.41 : Feng's Classification

- The product of the number of bits and number of words processed gives the maximum degree of parallelism.
- Classification of some of the commercially available machines (current and past) is shown in the Fig. 3.41. One axis represents the word length and the other axis represents the number of words processed in parallel in the given diagram
- A machine is placed at a point in the space defined by these coordinates. The area of the rectangle formed by the origin and the point representing the machine gives the maximum degree of parallelism for the machine.
- For example, Cray 1 and IA-64 have areas of 64 each. The scheme fails to project the concurrency in pipeline processors.

3.10.8 Handler's Classification

Wolfgang Handler proposed a detailed document for articulating the pipelining and parallelism of computers. Handler's classification addresses the computer at three distinct levels :

- Processor control unit (PCU),
- Arithmetic logic unit (ALU),
- Bit-level circuit (BLC).

The PCU corresponds to a processor or CPU, the ALU corresponds to a functional unit or a processing element and the BLC corresponds to the logic circuit needed to perform one-bit operations in the ALU.

Handler's classification uses the following three pairs of integers to describe a computer :

Computer = (p * p', a * a', b * b')

Where p = number of PCUs

Where p'= number of PCUs that can be pipelined

Where a = number of ALUs controlled by each PCU
Where a' = number of ALUs that can be pipelined
Where b = number of bits in ALU or processing element (PE) word
Where b' = number of pipeline segments on all ALUs or in a single PE

The following rules and operators are used to show the relationship between various elements of the computer :

- The '*' operator is used to indicate that the units are pipelined or macro-pipelined with a stream of data running through all the units.
- The '+' operator is used to indicate that the units are not pipelined but work on independent streams of data.
- The 'v' operator is used to indicate that the computer hardware can work in one of several modes.
- The '~' symbol is used to indicate a range of values for any one of the parameters.
- Peripheral processors are shown before the main processor using another three pairs of integers. If the value of the second element of any pair is 1, it may omit for brevity.

Handler's classification is best explained by showing how the rules and operators are used to classify several machines.

- The CDC 6600 has a single main processor supported by 10 I/O processors.
- One control unit coordinates one ALU with a 60-bit word length.
- The ALU has 10 functional units which can be formed into a pipeline.
- The 10 peripheral I/O processors may work in parallel with each other and with the CPU.
- Each I/O processor contains one 12-bit ALU.
- The description for the 10 I/O processors is : 33.
- Elements of Parallel Computing and Architecture CDC 6600I/O = (10, 1, 12).

The description for the main processor is :
    CDC 6600main = (1, 1 * 10, 60).

The main processor and the I/O processors can be regarded as forming a macro-pipeline so the '*' operator is used to combine the two structures:

CDC 6600 = (I/O processors) * (central processor = (10, 1, 12) * (1, 1 * 10, 60)

Texas Instrument's Advanced Scientific Computer (ASC) has one controller coordinating four arithmetic units. Each arithmetic unit is an eight stage pipeline with 64-bit words. Thus we have :
    ASC = (1, 4, 64 * 8)

The Cray-1 is a 64-bit single processor computer whose ALU has twelve functional units, eight of which can be chained together to form a pipeline. Different functional units have from 1 to 14 segments, which can also be pipelined. Handler's description of the Cray-1 is :

Cray-1 = (1, 12 * 8, 64 * (1 ~ 14))
- Carnegie-Mellon University's C.mmp multiprocessor is another example
- This system was designed to facilitate research into parallel computer architectures and therefore can be broadly reconfigured.
- The system consists of 16 PDP-11 'minicomputers' (which have a 16-bit word length), interconnected by a crossbar switching network.
- Normally, the C.mmp operates in MIMD mode for which the description is (16, 1, 16).
- It can also operate in SIMD mode, where all the processors are coordinated by a single master controller. The SIMD mode description is (1, 16, 16).
- Finally, the system can be reorganized to operate in MISD mode.
- The processors are arranged in a chain with a single stream of data passing through all of them.
- The MISD modes description is (1 * 16, 1, and 16).
- The 'v' operator is used to combine descriptions of the same piece of hardware operating in differing modes.
- Hence, Handler's description for the complete C.mmp is :
C.mmp = (16, 1, 16) v (1, 16, 16) v (1 * 16, 1, 16)
- The '*' and '+' operators are used to combine several separate pieces of hardware.
- The 'v' operator is of a different form to the other two in that it is used to combine the different operating modes of a single piece of hardware.
- While Flynn's classification is easy to use, Handler's classification is cumbersome.
- The direct use of numbers in the taxonomy of Handler's classifications makes it much more abstract and hence difficult.
- Handler's classification is highly geared towards the description of pipelines and chains.
- While it is well able to describe the parallelism in a single processor, the variety of parallelism in multiprocessor computers is not addressed well.
- Flynn's classification discussed the behavioral concept and does not take into consideration the computer's structure.
- Parallel computers can be classified based on their structure.
- As we have seen, a parallel computer (MIMD) can be described as a set of multiple processors and shared memory or memory modules communicating via an interconnection network.
- When multiprocessors communicate through the global shared memory modules then this organization is called Shared memory computer or tightly coupled systems as shown in figure 3.42 (a).
- Similarly when every processor in a multiprocessor system has its own local memory and the processors communicate via messages transmitted between their local memories,

then this organization is called Distributed memory computer or loosely coupled system as shown in figure 3.42

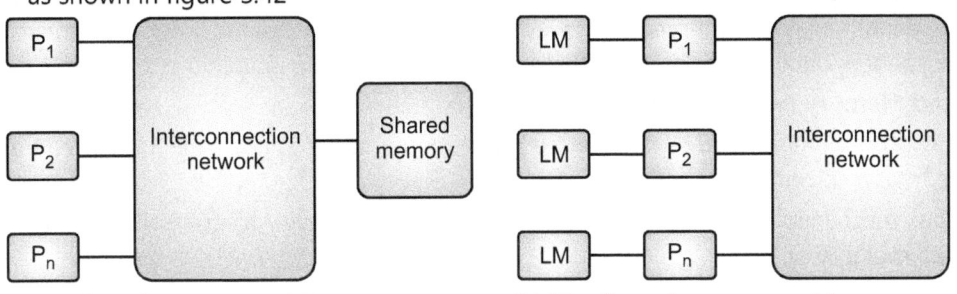

(a) **Shared memory multiprocessor**   (b) **Distributed memory multiprocessor**

Fig. 3.42 : Handler's Classification

The processors and memory in both organizations are interconnected via an interconnection network. This interconnection network may be in different forms like crossbar switch, multistage network, etc.

3.11 Parallel Programming Models

There are several parallel programming models in common use :
1. Shared Memory
2. Message Passing
3. Threads
4. Data Parallel
5. Hybrid
6. Single Program Multiple Data (SPMD)
7. Multiple Program Multiple Data (MPMD)

- Parallel programming models exist as an abstraction above the hardware and the memory architectures. These models are not specific to a particular type of machine or memory architecture, but are abstractions that could be built over any hardware. If the abstraction and the hardware have a wide gap, the program will suffer from exceedingly large access time. For example, a shared memory abstraction could be built over the message passing hardware, but it will have large access time for the shared global memory access. However, it could appear to the user as a single shared memory (global address space). Generically, this approach is referred to as "virtual shared memory". Message passing interface (MPI) model employs the Closely Coupled Non-Uniform Memory Access (CNUMA) type of shared memory architecture, where every task has direct access to global memory.

- The decision regarding which model to use is often a combination of personal choice and the availability. There is no "best" model, although there certainly are better implementations of some models over others. However one must look at the cost (time spent in data access) of using the model on the underlying architecture.

(1) Shared Memory (without Threads)
- In this programming model, tasks share a common address space, which they read and write to asynchronously.
- Various mechanisms such as locks / semaphores may be used to control access to the shared memory.
- An advantage of this model from the programmer's point of view is that the notion of data "ownership" is lacking, so there is no need to specify explicitly the communication of data between tasks. Program development can often be simplified.
- An important disadvantage in terms of performance is that it becomes more difficult to understand and manage data locality. Keeping data local to the processor that works on it conserves memory accesses, cache refreshes and bus traffic that occur when multiple processors use the same data. Unfortunately, controlling data locality is hard to understand and may be beyond the control of the average user.

Implementations
- On stand-alone shared memory machines, native operating systems, compilers and/or hardware provide support for shared memory programming. For example, the POSIX standard provides an API for using shared memory.
- On distributed shared memory machines, memory is physically distributed across a network of machines, but made global through specialized hardware and software.

Shared Memory Model
In the shared-memory programming model, tasks share a common address space, which they read and write asynchronously. Various mechanisms like locks/ semaphores are used to control the access to the shared memory. An advantage of this model from the programming point of view is that the notion of data "ownership" is not present, so there is no need to explicitly specify the communication of data between the tasks. This leads to simplified program development. Major disadvantage is due to the poor locality understanding and managing data locally. On shared memory platforms, the native compilers translate user program variables into actual memory addresses, which are global.

(2) Message Passing Model
Multiple tasks can reside on the same physical machine as well across an arbitrary number of machines. Tasks exchange data through communications by sending and receiving messages. Refer Fig. 3.43. Data transfer usually requires cooperative operations to be performed by each process. For example, a send operation must have a matching receive

operation. From a programming point of view, message passing implementations commonly comprise a library of subroutines that are embedded in the source code. The programmer determines all the parallelism required.

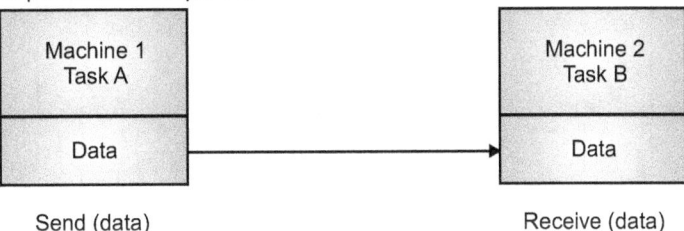

Fig. 3.43 : Message Passing Model

A variety of message passing libraries are available but their implementations differed from each other making it difficult for programmers to develop portable applications. The MPI (Message Passing Interface) Forum was established to suggest a standard interface for message passing implementations.

Message Passing Interface, MPI part-1 was released in 1994 while MPI-2 was released in 1996. MPI is now the industry standard for message passing, replacing most of the other message passing implementations.

MPI implementations usually don't use a network for task communications. Instead, they use shared memory (memory copies) for performance reasons since MPI was designed for high performance on both, the massively parallel machines and also on the workstation clusters.

(3) Threads Model

The thread model is shown in Fig. 3.44. Main program P is scheduled to run by the OS. P loads and gets all the system and the user resources so as to run. P runs its code and may create number of threads as entities that run in parallel. Threads can be scheduled and run by OS concurrently. Each thread may have a local data. A thread also shares the entire resources of P including global memory of P.

A thread's work may best be described as a subprogram within the main program. Any thread can execute any subroutine at the same time as the other threads. Threads communicate with each other through global memory (updating addressed locations). This requires synchronization constructs to ensure that more than one thread is not updating the same global address at any time.

Threads can come and go, but P remains present to provide the necessary shared resources until the application run has completed. Threads are commonly associated with shared memory architectures and also the operating systems and today Sun Micro system's Java programming language has excellent thread support.

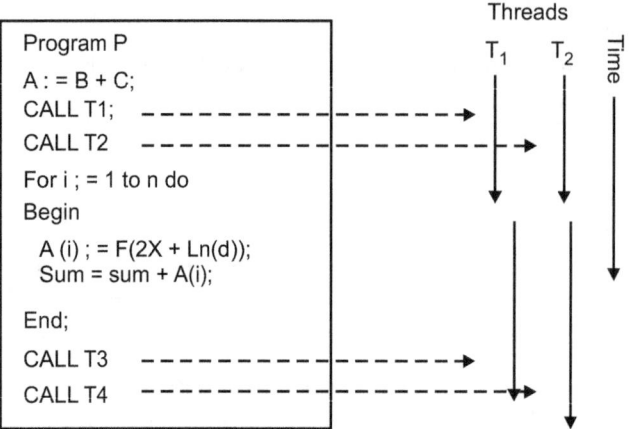

Fig. 3.44 : Threads Programming Model

Implementations

Usually hardware vendors implement their own proprietary versions of threads. These implementations differed substantially from each other making it difficult for programmers to develop portable threaded applications. Independent standardization efforts have resulted in two very different implementations of threads, Posix Threads and OpenMP.

POSIX Threads

It is a set of library functions to be used in C programs. It has support to create threads that run concurrently. The threads created by a process share all the resources of the process, other support includes joining and destroying the threads, synchronize the threads if required along with the other support required for parallel programming.

OpenMP

OpenMP is an Application Program Interface (API), jointly defined by a group of major computer hardware and software vendors. OpenMP provides a portable, scalable model for developers of shared memory parallel applications. The API supports C/C++ and FORTRAN on most of the architectures, including UNIX and Windows NT. The major features of OpenMP are its various constructs and directives for specifying parallel regions, work sharing, synchronization and data environment.

(4) Data Parallel Model

Parallel computing work in this model focuses on performing operations on a data set. The data set is organized into a common structure, such as an array. A set of tasks works collectively on the same data structure with each task working on part of it. Tasks perform the same operation on their part of work. For example, create an array X by multiplying Y elements by value of PI as shown in Fig. 3.45, where each processing element works on 20 distinct elements of the arrays. In shared memory architectures, all the tasks have access to the data structure through global memory. On the other hand, in the distributed memory architectures, the data structure is split up in pieces; each piece resides in the local memory of a task. Programming the data parallel model is accomplished by writing a program with data parallel constructs. The constructs can be calls to a data parallel subroutine library or, compiler directives recognized by a data parallel compiler. High Performance FORTRAN (HPF) support data parallel programming.

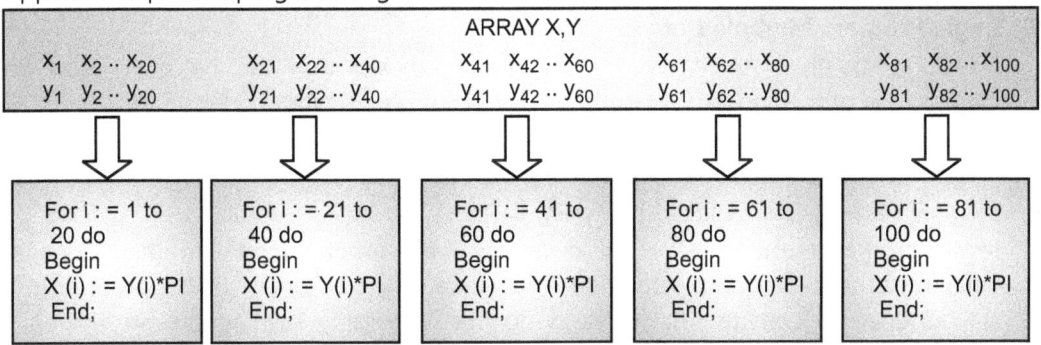

Fig. 3.45 : Data Parallel Model

(5) Hybrid Model

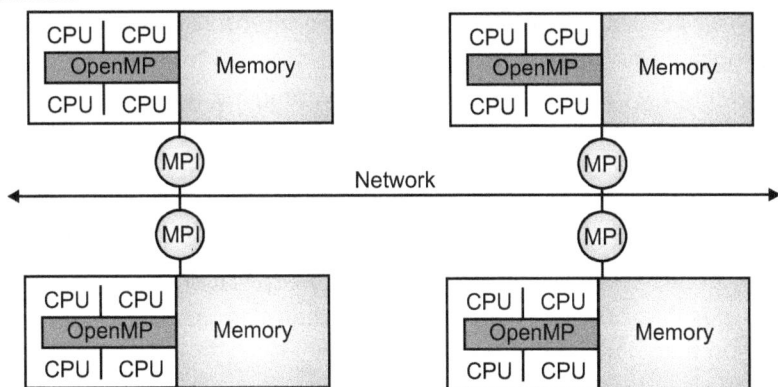

Fig. 3.46 : Hybrid Model

- A hybrid model combines more than one of the previously described programming models.
- Currently, a common example of a hybrid model is the combination of the message passing model (MPI) with the threads model (OpenMP).
- Threads perform computationally intensive kernels using local, on-node data.
- Communications between processes on different nodes occurs over the network using MPI.
- This hybrid model lends itself well to the increasingly common hardware environment of clustered multi/many-core machines.

- Another similar and increasingly popular example of a hybrid model is using MPI with GPU (Graphics Processing Unit) programming. GPUs perform computationally intensive kernels using local, on-node data.
- Communications between processes on different nodes occurs over the network using MPI.

(6) Single Program Multiple Data (SPMD)
- SPMD is actually a "high level" programming model that can be built upon any combination of the previously mentioned parallel programming models.
- Single Program : All tasks execute their copy of the same program simultaneously. This program can be threads, message passing, data parallel or hybrid.
- Multiple Data : All tasks may use different data.
- SPMD programs usually have the necessary logic programmed into them to allow different tasks to branch or conditionally execute only those parts of the program they are designed to execute. That is, tasks do not necessarily have to execute the entire program - perhaps only a portion of it.
- The SPMD model, using message passing or hybrid programming, is probably the most commonly used parallel programming model for multi-node clusters.

(7) Multiple Program Multiple Data (MPMD)
- Like SPMD, MPMD is actually a "high level" programming model that can be built upon any combination of the previously mentioned parallel programming models.
- Multiple Programs : Tasks may execute different programs simultaneously. The programs can be threads, message passing, data parallel or hybrid.
- Multiple Data : All tasks may use different data.
- MPMD applications are not as common as SPMD applications, but may be better suited for certain types of problems, particularly those that lend themselves better to functional decomposition than domain decomposition.

3.12 Parallel Algorithms

- Studies in the design of parallel algorithms are interesting. Any algorithm development and analysis studies involve how best algorithm out of many can do the given job. Sequential algorithms have been thoroughly studied for several important problems. One important measure of the performance of any algorithm is the time complexity. It is the time required to execute the algorithm specified as some function of the problem size. Another important performance measure is the space complexity defined as memory required by the algorithm. This performance measure is called as space complexity. It is also specified as some function of the problem size. Many times, the time and space complexities depend on the data structure used. Another important measure therefore, is the preprocessing time complexity to generate the desired data structure. Algorithms giving the best figures for the above measures naturally shall be preferred. To determine the theoretical lower bound on the time and space complexities is an important research activity.

- Parallel algorithms are the algorithms to be run on parallel machines. The most important measure of performance of a parallel algorithm is how fast one can solve a given problem using as many processors as required. Since the parallel algorithm uses several processors, the complexity of communication among the processors is also an important measure.

- The communication complexity in turn depends on the communication hardware supported by the machine. Therefore, an algorithm may fare badly on one machine and do much better on another. Due to this reason, the mapping of the algorithms on architectures is an important activity in the study of parallel algorithms. Speedup and efficiency are also important performance measures for a parallel algorithm when mapped on to a given architecture. A parallel algorithm for a given problem may be developed using one or more of the following:

  1. Detect and exploit the inherent parallelism available in the existing sequential algorithm.
  2. Independently invent a new parallel algorithm.
  3. Adapt an existing parallel algorithm that solves a similar problem.

Following are some problems that are broadly studied for understanding parallel algorithms.

Matrix Multiplication

Here we will study matrix multiplication in parallel. We present an algorithm for multiplying two n x n matrices. For clarity, we assume that n is a power of 2. We use the CREW (Concurrent Read Exclusive Write) PRAM model to allow multiple read operations from the same memory locations. In CREW PRAM, multiple read operations can be conducted concurrently, but multiple write operations are performed exclusively. We start by presenting the algorithm on a CREW PRAM with n*n*n processors. We assume that the two input matrices are stored in the shared memory in the arrays A[1 .. n, 1 .. n], B[1 .. n, 1 .. n].

Using n*n*n Processors.

We consider the n*n*n processors as being arranged into a three-dimensional array. Processor Pi, j, k is the one with index (i, j, k). A three-dimensional array C[i, j, k], where 1<= i, j, k <= n, in the shared memory will be used as working space. The resulting matrix will be stored in locations C[i, j, n], where 1 <=i, j <= n.

The algorithm consists of two steps. In the first step, all n*n*n processors operate in parallel to compute n*n*n multiplications. For each of the n*n cells in the output matrix, n products are computed. In the second step, the n products computed for each cell in the output matrix are summed to produce the final value of this cell. The two steps of the algorithm are given as:

1. Each processor Pi, j, k computes the product of A[i, k] * B[k, j] and stores it in C[i, j, k].
2. The idea of Algorithm Sum_EREW is applied along the k dimension n*n times in parallel to compute C[i, j, n], where $1 <= i, j <= n$.

The details are described in Algorithm Sum_EREW given below.

Algorithm Sum_EREW
for i=1 to log n do
for all Pj, where $1 <= j <= n/2$ do in parallel
if $(2^j \bmod 2^i) = 0$ then
A[2j] <- A[2j] + A[2j – $2^{(i-1)}$]
endif
endfor
endfor

The details of these two steps are presented in Algorithm MatMult_CREW :

Algorithm MatMult_CREW
/* Step 1 */
For all Pi, j, k, where $1 <= i, j, k <= n$ do in parallel
C[i,j,k] = A[i,k]*B[k,j]
endfor
/* Step 2 */
for l=1 to log n do
for all Pi, j, k, where $1 <= i, j <= n$ & $1 <= k <= n/2$ do in parallel
if $(2k \bmod 2^l) = 0$ then
C[i,j,2k] = C[i,j,2k] + C[i,j, 2k – $2^{(l-1)}$]
endif
endfor
/* The output matrix is stored in locations
C[i,j,n], where $1 <= i, j <= n$ */
Endfor

Sorting

Given an unsorted list of n elements a_1, a_2, . . . , a_i, . . . , a_n, an enumeration sort determines the position of each element a_i in the sorted list by computing the number of elements smaller than it. If c_i elements are smaller than a_i, then it is the $(c_i + 1)$th element in the sorted list. If two or more elements have the same value, the element with the largest index in the unsorted list will be considered as the largest in the sorted list. For example, suppose that $a_i = a_j$, then a_i will be considered the larger of the two if $i > j$, otherwise a_j is the larger. We present this simple algorithm on a CRCW PRAM with n*n processors. In a CRCW PRAM multiple read operations can be conducted concurrently; so are multiple write operations. However, write conflicts must be resolved according to a certain policy. In this algorithm, we assume that when multiple processors try to write different values into the same address, the sum of these values will be stored in that address. Consider the n2 processors as being arranged into n rows of n elements each. The processors are numbered as follows : Pi, j is the processor located in row i and column j in the grid of processors. We assume that the sorted list is stored in the global memory in an array A[1 .. n]. Another array C[1 .. n] will be used to store the number of elements smaller than every element in A.

The algorithm consists of two steps :

1. Each row of processors i computes C[i], the number of elements smaller than A[i]. Each processor Pi, j compares A[i] and A[j], then updates C[i] appropriately.

2. The first processor in each row Pi,1 places A[i] in its proper position in the sorted list (C[i] + 1).

The details of these two steps are presented in Algorithm Sort_CRCW :

Algorithm Sort_CRCW

```
/* Step 1 */
For all Pi, j, where 1 <= i, j <=n do in parallel
if A[i] > A[j] or (A[i]=A[j] and i > j) then
C[i] <-1
else
C[i]<- 0
endif
endfor
/* Step 2 */
For all Pi,1, where 1 <= i <= n do in parallel
A[C[i] + 1] <- A[i]
Endfor
```

Complexity Analysis : The complexity measures of the enumerating sort on CRCW PRAM are summarized as :

1. Run time, $T(n) = O(1)$.
2. Number of processors, $P(n) = n*n$.
3. Cost, $C(n) = O(n*n)$.

Linear programming problems, four color problems, are the few problems that are being widely studied. Few important problems that are broadly studied for parallel algorithms include Fast Fourier Transform (FFT), search and graph problems.

3.13 PERFORMANCE ANALYSIS OF PARALLEL ALGORITHMS

- Amdahl and Gustafson put forward laws that defined theories and suitable metrics for measuring performance of parallel algorithms.
- Gene Myron Amdahl's law specially discovers the limits of parallel computing while Gustafson's law rectified limitation due to fixed workload computation.
- Amdahl's law states that the performance improvement to be gained from using high performance parallel computing mode of execution is limited by the fraction of the time the faster mode can be used.
- Amdahl's model assumes the problem size does not change with the number of CPUs and wants to solve a fixed size problem as fast as possible.
- The model is also known as speedup, which can be defined as the maximum likely improvement to an overall system when only part of the system, is enhanced.
- Woo and Lee have understood and evaluated Amdahl and Gustafson's laws on measuring parallel computing performance in terms of various computing platforms.
- Hill and Marty analyzed performance of parallel system on multicore technology and evaluated how scalable a parallel system could be with pessimistic view.
- Xian He and Chen (2010) re-evaluated how scalable a parallel algorithm is by the analysis and application of Amdahl's theorem.

3.13.1 Performance Metrics

- The metrics used for evaluating the performance of the parallel architecture and the parallel algorithm are parallel runtime, speedup, efficiency, cost and parallel slowdown factor as follows :

Speedup is given as :

$$S_p = T_s/T_p \text{ or } T_s/T_1 \qquad \ldots (3.1)$$

Where,

T_s = Runtime of the Sq serial program

T_p = Runtime of the Sq parallel algorithm using p processors

T_1 = Runtime using one CPU

T_s = Runtime of the fastest sequential program.

- Speed of sequential algorithm individually depends largely on the methodology of array or matrices manipulation and programming structure.
- Thus, serial runtime, T_s, must be developed to be the fastest algorithm for a particular problem, on this premise Amdahl's law could be proven right and validated.
- Hence, it is rarely assumed that T_1 equals T_s.
- The interpretation of Amdahl's Law is that speedup is limited by the fact that not all parts of a code can run completely in parallel. Refer equation 1.

- According to Amdahl's laws, equation (3.2) defines speedup (Sp) as a function of sequential and parallel segments of a program with respect to number processors (p) used,

$$Sp = 1/f + 1-f/p \qquad ...(3.2)$$

- Where the term f denotes the fraction of program operations executed sequentially on a single processor.
- The term (1 - f) refers to the fraction of operations done in optimal parallelism with p processors.
- Normally, algorithm or program code is composed of parallel and serial code sections. Clearly, it is impossible to speed up parallel section completely due to bottleneck caused by sequential section.
- In equation (3.2), when the number of processors goes to infinity, the code speedup is still limited by 1 / f. Amdahl's law indicates that the sequential fraction of code has much effect on speedup and overall efficiency of the processors allocation.
- Hence, there is need for large and complex problem sizes when employing multiple parallel processors so that better performance can be achieved on a parallel computer. Amdahl proved that as the problem size increases the probability of having parallelism grows and the sequential fraction reduces.
- In addition to Amdahl's law, John L. Gustafson found out that complex problems show much better speedup than Amdahl predicted.
- Gustafson concentrated on computation time instead of the problem size. He explained that increasing number of CPUs to solve bigger problem would provide better results in the same time.
- Amdahl's law was simplified to re-define speedup with respect to computation time as follows :
- Computation time on the parallel system, Tp, can be expressed as :

$$Tp = ts + tp \qquad ...(3.3)$$

Where,
ts = computation time spent by the sequential section
tp = computation spent by the parallel section.

- While computation time on the sequential system, Ts, can be expressed as :

$$Ts = ts + p * tp \qquad ...(3.4)$$

Applying equation (3.1)

$$Sp = ts + p*tp / ts+tp \qquad ...(3.5)$$

- Applying equation (3.1) Therefore,

$$f = ts/ts+tp \qquad ...(3.6)$$

$$Sp = f + p(1-f) \qquad ...(3.7)$$

- The Gustafson's law clearly states that the variation of problem is indirectly proportional to sequential part available with respect to execution runtimes.
- These laws were previously applicable in mainframe, minicomputer and personal computer periods.
- Experimentally, these laws are still valid for evaluating parallel computing performance in the cluster and multi core technology eras.
- Amdahl's equations assume that the computation problem size would not change when running on enhanced machines.
- This means that the fraction of a program that is parallelizable remains fixed.
- Gustafson argued that Amdahl's law doesn't do justice to massively parallel machines because they allow computations previously intractable in the given time constraints.
- A machine with greater parallel computation ability lets computations operate on larger data sets in the same amount of time.

Questions

1. What is GPU? Write short note on GPU hardware.
2. Explain various alternatives of CUDA.
3. How parallelism can be achieved with the help of GPUs?
4. Differentiate between serial computing and parallel computing?
5. Explain the hardware overview and physical architecture of CUDA with neat diagram.
6. Explain why there is need of parallel computing?
7. Write short note on parallel architectures and explain.
8. General purpose computer architecture.
9. Special purpose computer architecture.
10. Draw neat diagrams to explain the parallel architectures.
11. Explain the following classification of parallel architecture.
12. Flynn Classification.
13. Classification based on memory arrangement and communication among processing elements.
14. Classification based on inter connections among processing elements and memory modules.
15. Classification based on characteristics nature of processing elements.
16. Explain various parallel programming models.
17. How matrix multiplication can be implemented in parallel?
18. How sorting of 'n' elements can be done in parallel?
19. Explain various metrics used for evaluating the performance of parallel algorithms.

UNIT - IV

DISTRIBUTED COMPUTING SYSTEMS

4.1 INTRODUCTION

- A computer system is a one that is able to take a set of inputs, process them and create a set of outputs.
- This is done by combination of hardware and software.
- Over the past two decades, advancements in electronics have resulted in the availability of fast, inexpensive processors, and advancements in communication technology have resulted in the availability of cost effective and highly efficient computer networks.
- The net result of the advancements in these two technologies is that the price performance ratio has now changed to favor the use of inter connected, multiple processors in place of a single, high-speed processor.
- A distributed system is a system in which components located on network of computers communicate and co-ordinate their actions by passing messages.
- These components interact with each other to accomplish a common goal.
- Distributed computing refers to the use of distributed system to solve computational problem.
- In distributed computing, a problem is divided into many tasks and each of these tasks is solved by one or more computer.
- Computers usually communicate with each other by message passing.

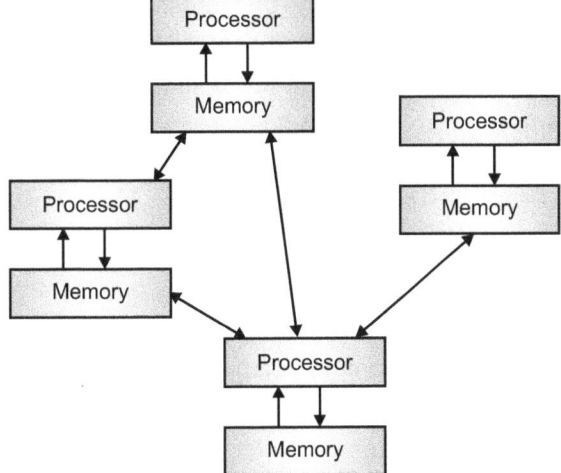

Fig. 4.1 : Distributed Systems

- The term distributed computing has got much wider sense now. Although there is no single definition of a distributed system, following properties are commonly used to refer distributed computing systems :
  1. There are several independent computational entities, usually computers, each of which has its own local memory.
  2. These computational entities communicate each other by message passing.
- Distributed computing systems may have a common goal of solving large computational problem.
- However, this is not the case always. Each computer may have its own user with unique needs.
- The purpose of distributed system is to co-ordinate the use of shared resources or provides communication services to the users.

4.2 Distributed Computing Systems

- Distributed computing is a method of computer processing in which different parts of a program are run simultaneously on two or more computers that are communicating with each other over a network.
- Distributed computing is a type of segmented or parallel computing, but the latter term is most commonly used to refer to process in which different parts of a program run simultaneously on two or more processors those are part of the same computer.
- While both types of processing require that a program be segmented or divided into sections that can run simultaneously, distributed computing also requires that the division of the program take into account the different environments on which the different sections of the program will be running. For example, two computers are likely to have different file systems and different hardware components.
- Distributed computing is a natural result of using networks to enable computers to communicate efficiently. But distributed computing is distinct from computer networking or fragmented computing.
- Fragmented computing refers to two or more computers interacting with each other, but not, typically, sharing the processing of a single program.
- The World Wide Web is an example of a network, but not an example of distributed computing.
- There are numerous technologies and standards used to construct distributed computations, including some which are specially designed and optimized for that purpose, such as Remote Procedure Calls (RPC) or Remote Method Invocation (RMI).

4.3 ARCHITECTURE

- Various hardware and software architectures are used for distributed computing.
- At a lower level, it is necessary to interconnect multiple CPUs with some sort of network, regardless of whether that network is printed onto a circuit board or made up of loosely coupled devices and cables.
- At a higher level, it is necessary to interconnect processes running on those CPUs with some sort of communication system.
- Distributed programming typically falls into one of several basic architectures or categories : Client-server, 3-tier architecture, N-tier architecture, Distributed objects, Loose coupling, or Tight coupling.
- **Client-server :** Smart client code contacts the server for data, then formats and displays it to the user. Input at the client is committed back to the server when it represents a permanent change. The Client-server architecture is a way to provide a service from a central source. There is a single server that provides a service, and many clients that communicate with the server to consume its services. In this architecture, clients and servers have different jobs. The server's job is to respond to service requests from clients, while a client's job is to use the data provided in response in order to perform some tasks.

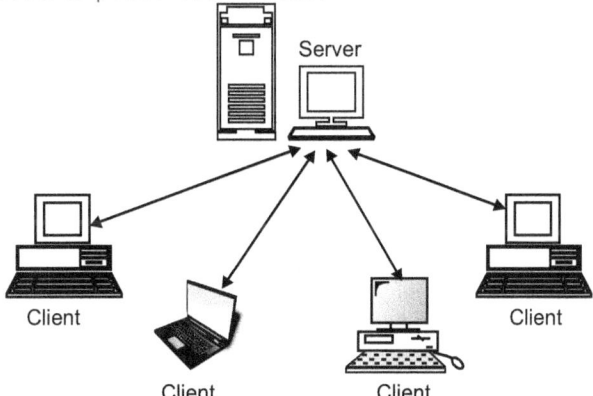

Fig. 4.2 : Client Server Architecture

- **3-tier Architecture :** Three tier systems move the client intelligence to a middle tier so that stateless clients can be used. This simplifies application deployment. Most web applications are 3-tier.

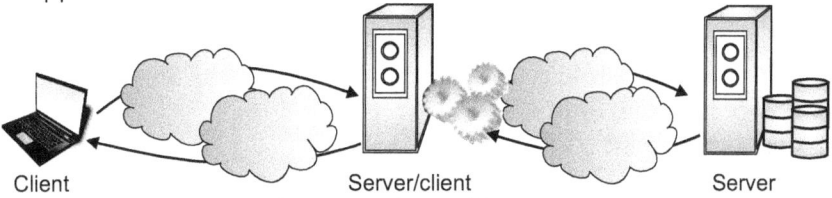

Fig. 4.3 : 3-tier Architecture

- **N-tier Architecture :** N-Tier refers typically to web applications which further forward their requests to other enterprise services. This type of application is the one most responsible for the success of application servers.

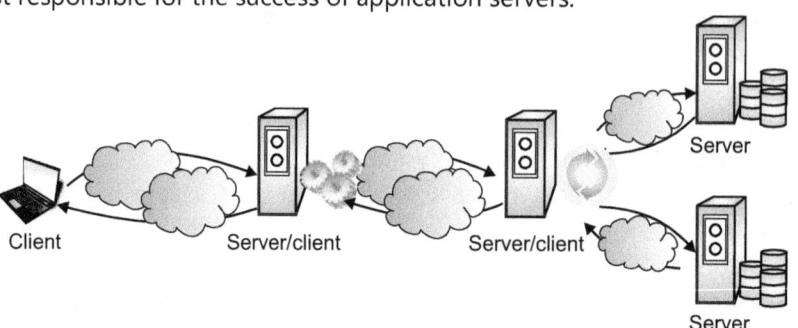

Fig. 4.4 : N-tier Architecture

- **Peer-to-peer Architecture :** An architecture where there is no special machine or machines that provide a service or manage the network resources. Instead all responsibilities are uniformly divided among all machines, known as peers. Peers can serve both as clients and servers. The term peer-to-peer is used to describe distributed systems in which labour is divided among all the components of the system. All the computers send and receive data, and they all contribute some processing power and memory. As a distributed system increases in size, its capacity of computational resources increases. In a peer-to-peer system, all components of the system contribute some processing power and memory to a distributed computation.

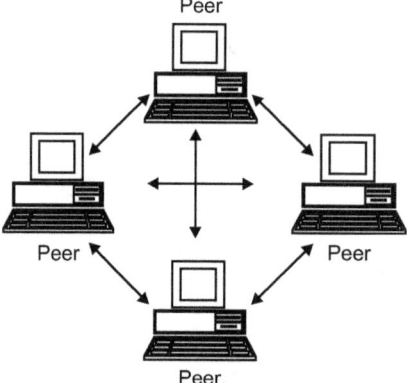

Fig. 4.5 : Peer to Peer Architecture

- Computer architectures consisting of interconnected, multiple processors are basically of two types :

(1) Tightly Coupled Systems

Tightly coupled computer architecture systems are also called as shared memory multiprocessor systems. In tightly coupled system one or more processors are attached by some interconnection mechanism. A memory module is also attached by same interconnection mechanism. All the attached processors share the memory module. In tightly coupled system communication between processors is usually take place through shared memory module using read-write operations. That means if any processor writes a value to some memory location, other processors can subsequently read that value from corresponding memory location. Refer figure 4.6

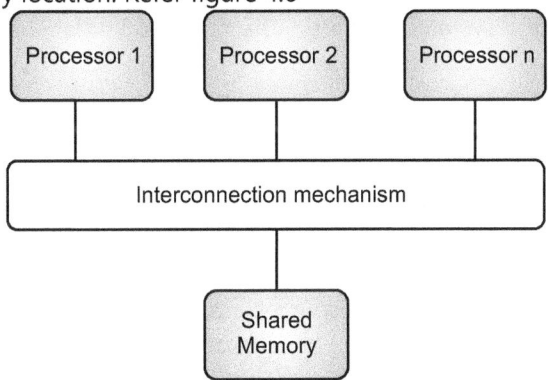

Fig. 4.6 : Tightly Coupled System

(2) Loosely Coupled System :

Unlike tightly coupled system loosely couples system processors do not share memory. Each processor has its own memory which is known as local memory. All the processors are attached by interconnection mechanism. Refer fig 4.7.

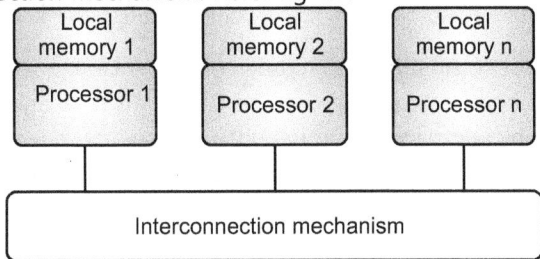

Fig. 4.7 : Loosely Coupled System

When a processor writes some value to some memory location, this write operation will only change the contents of its corresponding local memory and will not affect the contents of the local memories of remaining processors.

Since no shared memory is available in loosely coupled system, communication between processors cannot be done through read-write operations. In these systems, all physical communication between the processors is done by passing messages across the interconnection mechanism that interconnects the processors.

- Tightly coupled systems are referred to as parallel processing systems, and loosely coupled systems are referred to as distributed computing systems, or simply distributed systems.

- Processors in tightly coupled systems are at very close to each other, however the processoros of distributed computing systems can be located far from each other so that they can cover a wider geographical area. Furthermore, in tightly coupled systems, the numbers of processors that can be attached by some interconnection mechanism are usually small. Tightly couple system is having a limited scalability. This is because of limited availability of the bandwidth of the shared memory. This is not the case with distributed computing systems that are more freely expandable and can have an almost unlimited number of processors. So loosely coupled systems are highly scalable as compared to tightly coupled system
- In short, a distributed computing system is basically a collection of number of processors interconnected by a communication network. Each processor in distributed computing system has its own local memory and other peripherals, and the communication between any two processors of the system takes place by message passing over the communication network.
- For a particular processor, its own resources are local, whereas the other processors and their resources are global. Together, a processor and its resources are usually referred to as a node of the distributed computing system.

4.4 Guidelines for Organizing the Distributed Computing System

- Establishing and maintaining the communication between each computer is very important. For maintaining the proper communication between various types of computers, the communication protocol or interconnection mechanisms should use any information that is not compatible with some computers.
- The communication system must also ensure that right messages are delivered to right computers. Communication system must also ignore or reject the invalid messages because this may bring down the system and perhaps the rest of the network.

4.5 Distributed Computing System Models

Distributed computing system models can be broadly classified into five categories – minicomputer, workstation, workstation-server, processor pool, and hybrid. They are briefly described below.

4.5.1 Minicomputer Model

- In minicomputer model of distributed computing system number of minicomputers are interconnected by some interconnection or communication networking mechanism. Refer fig. 4.8
- Each minicomputer may have multiple users simultaneously logged on to it. Simultaneous logging of multiple users is possible in this model because number of terminal computers can be attached to each minicomputer.

- Each user that is logged on to one specific minicomputer, can interact with other minicomputers through remote access mechanism.

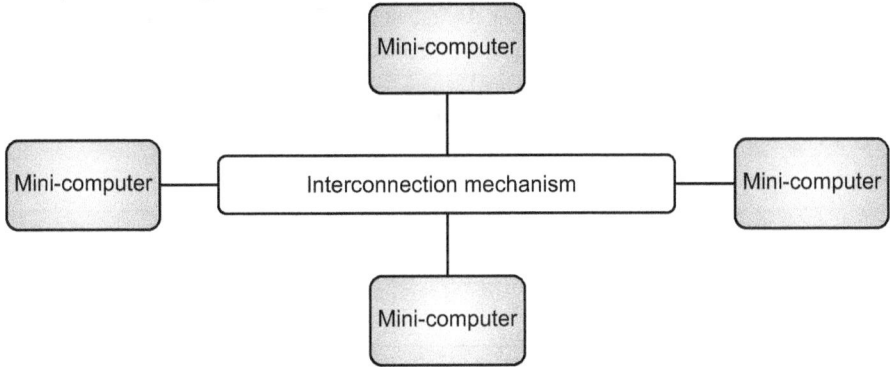

Fig. 4.8 : Distributed Computing System Based on Minicomputer Model

- User to access remote resources (resources available on machine other than the machine to which user is currently logged in).
- The minicomputer model may be used when resource sharing (Such as sharing of information databases of different types, with each type of database located on a different machine) with remote users is desired.
- Minicomputer model is well suited for small scale distributed computing systems.

4.5.2 Workstation Model

- In workstation model of distributed computing system several workstations are interconnected by some interconnection mechanism. Refer fig. 4.9.
- An organization may have number of workstations distributed throughout a organization's building or local area.
- Each workstation has with its own resources and it can be considered as single-user computer.
- In workstation style distributed computing systems it is usually observed that at some particular time instance (usually at night and vacation period of organization), a considerable number of the workstations are idle (in no utilized mode), resulting in the waste of large amounts of CPU time.
- So this situation can be overcome by interconnecting all these workstations by some interconnection mechanism such as high speed LAN. With this type interconnection it is possible to utilize idle workstations and users who are logged onto other workstations and do not have sufficient processing power at their own workstations to get their jobs processed efficiently.
- In workstation model, "home" workstation is a machine from which user logs on and submits jobs for execution. Assuming that workstations within the organization are interconnected when the system finds that the user's workstation does not have

sufficient processing power for executing the processes of the submitted jobs efficiently, it transfers one or more of the process from the user's workstation to some other workstation that is currently idle and gets the process executed there, and finally the result of execution is returned to the user's workstation.

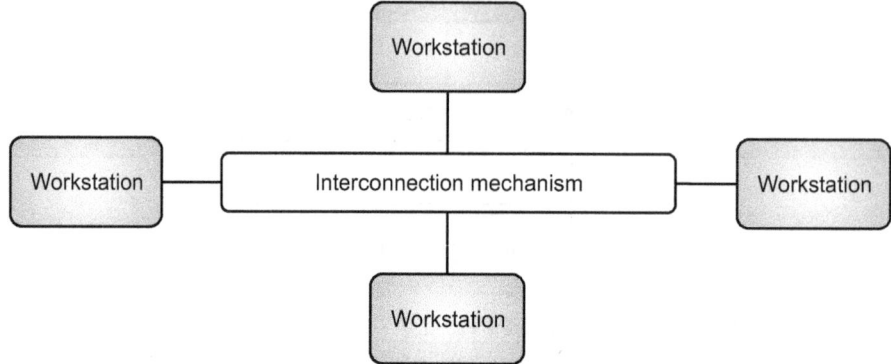

Fig. 4.9 : Distributed Computing System Based On Workstation Model

While implementing the workstation distributed computing system model following issues need to be addressed :

1. Finding an idle workstation
2. Migrating/Transferring the process from one workstation to another
3. Decision about remote process if a user's home workstation that was idle until now and was being used to execute a process of another workstation?

- For handling the above mentioned issues following approaches are usually considered

1. Allow the remote process share the resources of the workstation along with resources of user's home workstation. Although this method is easy to implement, it is impractical if home workstations are personal computers. This is because if remote processes are allowed to execute simultaneously with the user's own processes on his home workstation, the logged-on user will not get the desired response.
2. The second approach is to kill the remote process. The main drawbacks of this method are that all processing done for the remote process gets lost and the file system may be left in an inconsistent state, making this method unappealing.
3. The third approach is to migrate the remote process back to its home workstation, so that its execution can be continued there. This method is difficult to implement because it requires the system to support preemptive process migration facility.

- For a number of reasons, such as higher reliability, improved response time and better scalability, multiple servers are often used for managing the resources in a distributed computing system.
- For example, there may be multiple file servers, each running on a separate minicomputer and interacting via the network, for managing the files of all the users in the system.

- Deciding the priorities of processes and managing their execution accordingly is one of the better approaches. Normal processes required by user can be performed at the user's home workstation, but requests for services provided by special servers (such as a file server or a database server) are sent to a server providing that type of service that performs the user's requested activity and returns the result of request processing to the user's workstation.
- Therefore, in this model, the user's processes need not be migrated to the server machines for getting the work done by those machines.
- For improving the system performance, the local disk storage of a workstation is normally used for storing of temporary files, storage of unshared files, storage of shared files that are rarely changed.

4.5.3 Workstation-Server Model

- Workstation – server model has several advantages over traditional workstation model:
- In general, it is much cheaper to use a few minicomputers equipped with large, fast disks that are accessed over the network than a large number of diskful workstations, with each workstation having a small, slow disk.
- Diskless workstations are given more preference over diskful workstations from a system maintenance point of view. Backup and hardware maintenance are easier to perform with a few large disks than with many small disks distributed all over organization's area. Furthermore, installing new releases and versions of software is easier when the software is to be installed on a few file server machines than on every workstation.
1. In workstation model each workstation has its local file system and different mechanisms are needed to access local and remote files. In the workstation server model, since all files are managed by the file servers, user have the flexibility to use any workstation and access the files in the same manner irrespective of which workstation the user is currently logged on.

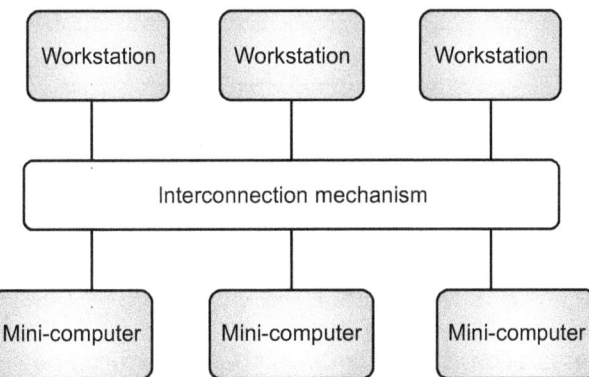

Fig. 4.10 : Distributed Computing System Based on Workstation-Server Model

2. In the workstation server model, accessing the services provided by server machines is done by request-response protocol. The entity which needs service request the server and server accordingly responds. Therefore, unlike the workstation model, this model does not need a process migration facility, which is difficult to implement.
- The request response protocol is known as the client-server model of communication. In this model, a client process sends a request to a server for providing the required service. The server executes the request and sends back a reply to the client that contains the result of request processing.
- The client-server model provides an effective general – purpose approach to the sharing of information and resources in distributed computing systems.
- The computers used to run the client and server processes need not necessarily be workstations and minicomputers. They can be of many types and there is no need to distinguish between them. It is even possible for both the client and server processes to be run on the same computer. That is, a server process may use the services of another server, appearing as a client to the latter.
3. A user has guaranteed response time because workstations are not used for executing remote processes. However, the model does not utilize the processing capability of idle workstations.

4.5.4 Processor Pool Model

- Most of the time a user does not need any computing power but user may need a very large amount of computing power for a short time depending on the type of process user want to execute.

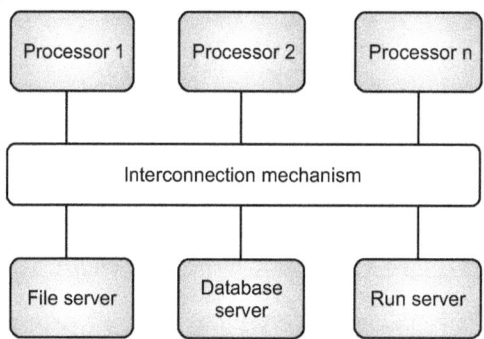

Fig. 4.11 : Distributed Computing System Model Based Processor Pool Model

- Processor pool model has been developed by keeping this issue in mind.
- Therefore, unlike the workstation – server model in which a processor is allocated to each user, in the processor-pool model the processors are pooled together to be shared by the users as needed.
- The pool of processors consists of a large number of microcomputers and minicomputers are attached to the network. Each processor in the pool has its own memory to load and run a system program or an application program of the distributed computing system.

- Even special servers can also be attached by some interconnection mechanism.
- In processor-pool model, the processors in the pool have no terminals attached directly to them, and users access the system from terminals that are attached to the network via special devices. Refer fig. 4.11.
- In processor pool model a special server (Called a run server) manages and allocates the processors in the pool to different users on a demand basis.
- When a user submits a job for computation, an appropriate number of processors are temporarily assigned for execution of job by the run server.
- In the processor-pool model there is no concept of a home machine. That is, a user does not log onto a particular machine but to the system as a whole.

4.5.5 Hybrid Model

- Till now we have seen four models minicomputer model, workstation model, workstation server model and processor pool model.
- Since a large number of computer users only perform simple and straight forward interactive tasks such as editing jobs, sending electronic mails, and executing small programs, the workstation server model, is the most widely used model for building distributed computing systems.
- The workstation-server model is ideal for simple and straight forward usage. However, in a working environment that has groups of users who often perform jobs needing massive computation, the processor-pool model is more attractive and suitable.
- By considering and analyzing the all the needs and advantages hybrid model is designed may be used to build a distributed computing system.
- The hybrid model is based on the workstation-server model but with the addition of a pool of processors. The processors in the pool can be allocated dynamically for computations that are too large for workstations or that requires several computers concurrently for efficient execution. So this provides the combined advantages of workstation server model and processor pool model.
- In addition to efficient execution of computation-intensive jobs, the hybrid model gives guaranteed response to interactive jobs by allowing them to be processed on local workstations of the users. However, the hybrid model is more expensive to implement than the workstation – server model or the processor-pool model.

4.6 Distributed Operating System

- As we call Central Processing Unit as a brain of computer, we can call an operating system as a heart of computer. It is basically a program that manages the resources of a computer system and provides an interface for the users of the machine so that they can utilize these resources.
- From the above definition we can easily conclude that operating system is an entity which is able

1. To provide the interface for users that is easier to program than the underlying hardware and users can easily interact with software and hardware resources.
2. To manage the various resources of the system. This involves performing such tasks as keeping track of who is using which resource, granting resource requests, accounting for resource usage, and mediating conflicting requests from different programs and users

- The operating systems commonly used for distributed computing systems can be broadly classified into two types-network operating systems and distributed operating systems.
- The three most important features commonly used to differentiate between these two types of operating systems are system image, autonomy, and fault tolerance capability.

(1) System image

Image of the distributed computing system from the user's point of view is the most important feature used to differentiate between the two types of operating systems. That is how user sees the operating system is very important perspective for distinguishing the operating systems

In case of a network operating system, the users view the distributed computing system as a collection of distinct machines connected by a communication subsystem.

A distributed operating system keeps the users unaware of the existence of multiple computers and provides a single-system image to its users. That is, it makes a collection of networked machines act as a virtual single processor. User is not aware of the presence of the multiple processors. Physically they will be interacting only with their own processors and utilizing the computing power of other processors.

(2) Autonomy

Each computer of the distributed computing system has its own local operating system in case of network operating system. Distributed computing system may be influenced by heterogeneous operating system i.e. the operating systems of different computers may be different, and there is essentially no coordination at all among the computers except for the rule that when two processes of different computers communicate with each other, they must use a mutually agreed on communication protocol.

With a distributed operating system, there is a single system wide operating system and each computer of the distributed computing system runs a part of this global operating system. The distributed operating system strongly associated with all the computers of the distributed computing system in the sense that they work in close cooperation with each other for the efficient and effective utilization of the various resources of the system. This system provides the additional computing power for executing user's processes. These will obviously accelerate the execution performance of user's processes.

(3) Fault tolerance capability

A network operating system provides very little fault tolerance capability. If particular number of computers in network operating system fail or crash down then that many number of users are unable to continue with their work.

This simply means that failure of number of computers is proportional the number of users who are unable to use their corresponding machines.

With a distributed operating system, most of the users are normally unaffected by the failed machines and can continue to perform their work normally, with loss in performance which is proportional to only the number of machines which are failed. Distributed computing system provides quite good fault tolerance capability.

4.7 Issues in Designing A Distributed Operating System

- A group of linked computers working co-operatively on tasks, referred to as a distributed system, often requires a distributed operating system to manage the distributed resources.
- Distributed operating systems must handle all the usual problems of operating systems.
- There are many different types of distributed computing systems and many challenges to overcome in successfully designing one. The main goal of a distributed computing system is to connect users and resources in a transparent, open, and scalable way. Ideally, this arrangement is drastically more fault tolerant and more powerful than many combinations of stand-alone computer systems.
- In general, designing a distributed operating system is more difficult than designing a centralized operating system for several reasons.
- In the design of a centralized operating system, it is assumed that the operating system has access to complete and accurate information about the environment in which it is functioning.
- However, a distributed operating system must be designed with the assumption that complete information about the system environment will never be available.
- In a distributed system, the resources are physically separated, there is no common clock among the multiple processors, delivery of messages is delayed, and messages could even be lost.
- Due to all these reasons, a distributed operating system does not have up-to-date, consistent knowledge about the state of the various components of the underlying distributed system.
- Thus, lack of up-to-date and consistent information makes many things (Such as management of resources and synchronization of co-operating activities) much harder in the design of a distributed operating system.
- Despite these complexities and difficulties, a distributed operating system must be designed to provide all the advantages of a distributed system to its users. That is, the users should be able to view a distributed system as a virtual centralized system that is flexible, efficient, reliable, secure and easy to use.
- To meet this challenge, the designers of a distributed operating system must deal with several design issues.

4.7.1 Transparency

- A distributed system that is able to present itself to user and application as if it were only a single computer system is said to be transparent.
- There are eight types of transparencies in a distributed system :

4.7.1.1 Access Transparency

- It hides differences in data representation and how a resource is accessed by a user.
- Example, a distributed system may have a computer system that runs different operating systems, each having their own file naming conventions.
- Differences in naming conventions as well as how files can be manipulated should be hidden from the users and applications.

4.7.1.2 Location Transparency

- It hides where exactly the resource is located physically.
- Example, by assigning logical names to resources like yahoo.com, one cannot get an idea of the location of the web page's main server.

4.7.1.3 Migration Transparency

- Distributed system in which resources can be moved without affecting how the resource can be accessed are said to provide migration transparency.
- It hides that the resource may move from one location to another.

4.7.1.4 Relocation Transparency

- This transparency deals with the fact that resources can be relocated while it is being accessed without the user who is using the application to know anything.
- Example: using a network service on mobile phones while moving from place to place without getting disconnected.

4.7.1.5 Replication Transparency

- It hides the fact that multiple copies of a resource could exist simultaneously.
- To hide replication, it is essential that the replicas have the same name.
- Consequently, as system that supports replication should also support location transparency.

4.7.1.6 Concurrency Transparency

- It hides the fact that the resource may be shared by several competitive users.
- Example, two independent users may each have stored their file on the same server and may be accessing the same table in a shared database.
- In such cases, it is important that each user does not notice that the others are making use of the same resource.

4.7.1.7 Failure Transparency
- It hides failure and recovery of the resources.
- It is the most difficult task of a distributed system and is even impossible when certain apparently realistic assumptions are made.
- Example: A user cannot distinguish between a very slow or dead resource. Same error message come when a server is down or when the network is overloaded of when the connection from the client side is lost.
- So here, the user is unable to understand what has to be done, either the user should wait for the network to clear up, or try again later when the server is working again.

4.7.1.8 Persistence Transparency
- It hides if the resource is in memory or disk.
- Example : Object oriented database provides facilities for directly invoking methods on storage objects.
- First the database server copies the object states from the disk i.e. main memory performs the operation and writes the state back to the disk.
- The user does not know that the server is moving between primary and secondary memory.

4.7.2 Performance Transparency
- The performance of the system must not be degraded in any case. The aim of performance transparency is to allow the system to be automatically reconfigured to improve performance, as loads vary dynamically in the system. This simply means that system should be capable of balancing the load even it varies dynamically.
- A situation in which one processor of the system is overloaded with jobs while another processor is idle should not be allowed to occur.
- That is, the processing capability of the system should be uniformly distributed among the currently available jobs in the system.
- This requirement creates the need for intelligent resource allocation and process migration facilities in distributed operating systems.

4.7.3 Scaling Transparency
- The aim of scaling transparency is to allow the system to expand in scale without disrupting the activities of the users.
- During the process of system expansion user should get the same execution performance. In fact user must not be aware of the situation that the scaling of system is going on.

4.7.4 Reliability
- In general, distributed systems are expected to be more reliable than centralized systems due to the existence of multiple instances of resources.

- However, the existence of multiple instances of the resources alone cannot increase the system's reliability. Rather, the distributed operating system, which manages these resources must be designed properly to increase the system's reliability.
- A fault in a system can cause system failure.
- Depending on the manner in which a failed system behaves, system failures are of two types – fail stop and Byzantine.
- In the case of fail-step failure, the system stops functioning after changing to a state in which its failure can be detected.
- On the other hand, in the case of Byzantine failure, the system continues to function but produces wrong results.
- Byzantine failures are much more difficult to deal with than fail-stop failures.
- For higher reliability, the fault-handling mechanisms of a distributed operating system must be designed properly to avoid faults, to tolerate faults, and to detect and recover from faults.

4.7.5 Fault Handling Mechanisms

4.7.5.1 Fault Avoidance

- Fault avoidance deals with designing the components of the system in such a way that the occurrence of faults in minimized.
- High reliability components are often used for improving the reliability of the system based on the idea of fault avoidance.
- Although Distributed operating system often has little or no role to play in improving the fault avoidance capability of a hardware component, the designers of the various software components of the distributed operating system must test them thoroughly to make these components highly reliable.

4.7.5.2 Fault Tolerance

- Fault tolerance is the ability of a system to continue functioning in the event of partial system failure.
- The performance of the system might be degraded due to partial failure, but otherwise the system functions properly.
- Some of the important concepts that may be used to improve the fault tolerance ability of a distributed operating system are as follows :

(1) Redundancy Techniques

- The basic idea behind redundancy techniques is to avoid single points of failure by replicating critical hardware and software components, so that if one of them fails, the others can be used to continue.
- Obviously, having two or more copies of a critical component makes it possible to continue operations in case of occasional partial failures.

- For example, a critical process can be simultaneously executed on two nodes so that if one of the two nodes fails, the execution of the process can be completed at the other node.
- Similarly, a critical file may be replicated on two or more storage devices for better reliability.
- Notice that with redundancy techniques additional system overhead is needed to maintain two or more copies of a replicated resource and to keep all the copies of a resource consistent.
- For example, if a file is replicated on two or more nodes of a distributed system, additional disk storage space is required and for corrects functioning, it is often necessary that all the copies of the file are mutually consistent.
- This raises an important question: How much replication is enough? A system is said to be k-fault tolerant if it can continue to function even in the event of the failure of k components.
- Therefore, if the system is to be designed to tolerance k fail – stop failures, $k + 1$ replicas are needed. If k replicas are lost due to failures, the remaining one replica can be used for continued functioning of the system.

4.7.5.3 Distributed Control

- For better reliability, many of the particular algorithms or protocols used in a distributed operating system employ a distributed control mechanism to avoid single points of failure.
- For example, a highly available distributed file system should have multiple and independent file servers controlling multiple and independent storage devices.
- In addition to file servers, a distributed control technique could also be used for name servers, scheduling algorithms, and other executive control functions.

4.7.5.4 Fault Detection and Recovery

- The faulty detection and recovery method of improving reliability deals with the use of hardware and software mechanisms to determine the occurrence of a failure and then to correct the system to a state acceptable for continued operation.
- Some of the commonly used techniques for implementing this method in a distributed operating system are as follows.

(1) Atomic Transactions
- A transaction is a computation consisting of a collection of operation that take place indivisibly in the presence of failures and concurrent computations.
- That is, all of the operations are performed successfully or none of their effects exists.
- Other processes executing concurrently cannot modify or observe intermediate states of the computation.
- Transactions help to preserve the consistency of a set of shared date objects (e.g. files) in the case of failures and concurrent access.

- They make crash recovery much easier, because transactions can only end in two states: Either all the operations of the transaction are performed or none of the operations of the transaction is performed.

(2) Stateless Servers
- The client-server model is frequently used in distributed systems to service user requests.
- In this model, a server may be implemented as either stateful or stateless.
- The stateful approach depends on the history of the serviced requests, that means history of the serviced requests between a client and a server affects the execution of the next service request.
- The stateless approach does not depend on it. Stateless servers have a distinct advantage over stateful servers in the event of a failure. That is, the stateless service paradigm makes crash recovery very easy because no client state information is maintained by the server. On the other hand, the stateful service paradigm requires complex crash recovery procedures.
- The server needs to detect client crashes so that it can discard any state it is holding for the client, and the client must detect server crashes so that it can perform necessary error – handling activities.

Acknowledgments and Timeout-Based Retransmission of Messages.
- In a distributed system, events such as a node crash or a communication link failure may interrupt a communication that was in progress between two processes which resulting in the loss of a message.
- Therefore, a reliable inter process communication mechanism must have ways to detect lost messages so that they can be retransmitted.
- Handling of lost messages usually involves return of acknowledgment messages and retransmissions on the basis of timeouts.
- That is, the receiver must return an acknowledgment message for every message received, and if the sender does not receive any acknowledgement for a message within a fixed timeout period, it assumes that the message was lost and retransmits the message.
- A problem associated with this approach is that of duplicate message. Duplicates messages may be sent in the event of failures or because of timeouts. Therefore, a reliable inter process communication mechanism should also be capable of detecting and handling duplicate messages. Handling of duplicate messages usually involves a mechanism for automatically generating and assigning appropriate sequence numbers to messages.

4.7.6 Flexibility
- Another important issue in the design of distributed operating systems is flexibility. Flexibility is the most important features for distributed systems.
- The design of a distributed operating system should be flexible due to the following reasons :

4.7.6.1. Ease of Modification
- From the experience of system designers, it has been found that some parts of the design often need to be replaced / modified either because some bug is detected in the design or because the design is no longer suitable for the changed system environment or new-user requirements.
- Therefore, it should be easy to incorporate changes in the system in a user-transparent manner or with minimum interruption caused to the users.

4.7.6.2. Ease of Enhancement
- In every system, new functionalities have to be added from time to time it more powerful and easy to use.
- Therefore, it should be easy to add new services to the system.
- Furthermore, if a group of users do not like the style in which a particular service is provided by the operating system, they should have the flexibility to add and use their own service that works in the style with which the users of that group are more familiar and feel more comfortable.
- The most important design factor that influences the flexibility of a distributed operating system is the model used for designing its kernel.
- The kernel of an operating system is its central controlling part that provides basic system facilities.
- It is the only part of an operating system that a user cannot replace or modify.
- The two commonly used models for kernel design in distributed operating systems are the monolithic kernel and the microkernel. In the monolithic kernel model, most operating system services such as process management, memory management, device management, file management, name management, and inter-process communication are provided by the kernel. As a result, the kernel has a large, monolithic structure.
- On the other hand, in the microkernel model, the main goal is to keep the kernel as small as possible.
- Therefore it provides only the minimal facilities necessary for implementing additional operating system services. The only services provided by the kernel in this model are inter-process communication low level device management, a limited amount of low-level process management and some memory management.
- All other operating system services, such as file management, name management, additional process, and memory management activities and much system call handling are implemented as user-level server processes.
- As compared to the monolithic kernel model, the microkernel model has several advantages.
- In the monolithic kernel model, the large size of the kernel reduces the overall flexibility and configurability of the resulting operating system. On the other hand, the resulting operating system of the microkernel model is highly modular in nature.

- Due to this characteristic feature, the operating system of the microkernel model is easy to design, implement, and install. Moreover, since most of the services are implemented as user-level server processes, it is also easy to modify the design or add new services. In spite of its potential performance cost, the microkernel model is being preferred for the design of modern distributed operating systems.

4.7.7 Performance

- Performance of distributed system must be at least as good as a centralized system.
- That is, when a particular application is run on a distributed system, its overall performance should be better than or at least equal to that of running the same application on a single processor system.
- However, to achieve his goal, it is important that the various components of the operating system of a distributed system be designed properly; otherwise, the overall performance of the distributed system may turn out to be worse than a centralized system.
- Some design principles considered useful for better performance are as follows :

1. **Batch if Ppossible**
   Batching often helps in improving performance greatly. For example, transfer of data across the network in large chunks rather than as individual pages is much more efficient.
2. **Cache Whenever Possible**
   Caching of data at clients' sites frequently improves overall system performance because it makes data available wherever it is being currently used, thus saving a large amount of computing time and network bandwidth. In addition, caching reduces contention on centralized resources.
3. **Minimize Copying of Data**
   Data copying overhead (e.g. moving data in and out of buffers) involves a substantial CPU cost of many operations.
4. **Minimize Network Traffic**
   System performance may also be improved by reducing inter node communication costs. For example, accesses to remote resources require communication, possibly through intermediate nodes. Therefore, migrating a process closer to the resources it is using most heavily may be helpful in reducing network traffic in the system.

4.7.8 Scalability

- Scalability refers to the strength of the system.
- It is basically a measure how much load your system can carry before degrading the performance of execution.
- A distributed system will grow with time since it is very common to add new machines or an entire sub network to the system to take care of increased workload or organizational changes in a company.

- Therefore, a distributed operating system should be designed to easily cope with the growth of nodes and users in the system.
- That is, such growth should not cause serious disruption of service or significant loss of performance to users.
- Guidelines for designing a scalable distributed system are given below

1. **Avoid Centralized Entities**
   In the design of a distributed operating system, use of centralized entities such as a single central file server or a single database for the entire system makes the distributed system non-scalable. These central entities may also become single point of failure.
2. **Avoid Centralized Algorithms**
   Use of centralized algorithms should be avoided to protect from central point of failure.
3. **Perform Most Operations on Client Workstations**
   By performing most operations at client side most of the processes can be executed faster as transmission is reduced to great extent.

4.7.9 Heterogeneity

- A heterogeneous distributed system consists of interconnected sets of dissimilar hardware or software systems.
- Because of the diversity, designing heterogeneous distributed systems is far more difficult than designing homogeneous distributed systems, in which each system is based on the same, or closely related, hardware and software.
- However heterogeneity is unavoidable part of distributed systems.
- Furthermore, often heterogeneity is preferred by many users because heterogeneous distributed systems provide the flexibility to their users of different computer platforms for different applications.

4.7.10 Security

- Users are the people who use the resources of a computer for executing their processes and tasks. These resources are either software or hardware. Resources of the computer system must be protected against destruction, unauthenticated and unauthorized access.
- Users will trust the computing system only if its resources are properly protected.
- Enforcing security in a distributed system is more difficult than in a centralized system because there is no as such single point of control and the use of insecure networks for data communication.
- Therefore, as compared to a centralized system, enforcement of security in a distributed system has the following additional requirements:

1. It should be possible for the receiver of a message to know that the message was by the intended receiver. Both the sender and receiver must be authorized entities.
2. It should be possible for the receiver of a message to know that the message was sent by the genuine sender.

3. It should be possible for both the sender and receiver of a message to be guaranteed that the contents of the message were not changed while it was in transfer.

- Cryptography is used to ensure contents of the message are not hampered during transmission process. It is very useful technique for imposing security on information during transmission. Distributed computing systems often require transmission of information from computer at one location to computer at another location. So it is very useful in distributed computing system. In this method private information is prevented by encrypting the information, which can then be decrypted only by authorized users.

4.8 Distributed Computing Environment

- With Distributed Computing Environment (DCE) it is possible to install an integrated set of services, applications and tools on existing operating systems.
- It acts as a platform for distributed applications.
- DCE acts as a middleware software layer between the services, applications, tools and the operating system and networking layer as shown in Fig. 4.12.
- Important functions handled by DCE are given below :
    1. Take collection of existing machines from different vendors.
    2. Interconnect them by a communication network.
    3. Add DCE software platform on the top of the existing operating system and transport services
    4. On this DCE platform, distributed applications, tools, services run.

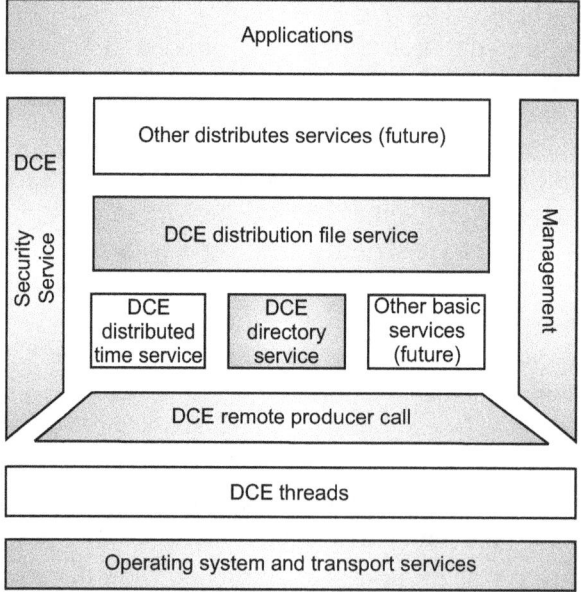

Fig. 4.12 : DCE Acts as a Middleware Between Application and Operating System

Following are the Main Components of DCE

1. **Thread Package :** This package is better used for concurrent applications. It creates and controls multiple threads in a single process.
2. **Remote Procedure Call (RPC) Facility :** This service is used to build client-server applications. RPC facility provides all communication platforms in DCE.
3. **Distributed Time Service :** This service is used to synchronize the clocks of all the computers in the distributed system.
4. **Name Service :** All the resources like files, devices, servers etc. must have unique name, so that they can be accessed irrespective of their location in distributed system.
5. **Security Service :** This service is needed for authentication and authorization. This prevents malicious and legitimate access into the system.
6. **Distributed File Service :** This service provides a file system that has high performance, high availability and location transparency
   - In DCE, it is difficult to manage the large system because of the high scalability of the system.
   - Hence the larger system is decomposed into number of smaller systems called as 'cells'.
   - These cells are easy to manage and called as unit of management in DCE.
   - These cells can be considered as a group of users, group of computers and different resources that have some common properties.
   - They may or may not have similar purpose and services.
   - While decomposing a larger system into cells, following four factors must be taken into account
     1. **Purpose :**
        The computers performing some common operations must be put together in the same cell.
     2. **Administration :**
        The highest privileges within a cell are assigned to a role called cell administrator. This cell administrator controls the access rights of the user community.
     3. **Security :**
        Cell administrator also decides the trust on user machines. User machines that have greater trust must be put into the same cell.
     4. **Overhead :**
        To avoid the overhead of name resolution and user authentication, machines of the user those use each other's resources frequently must be placed in the same cell.

Questions

1. In what respect are distributed computing systems better than parallel processing systems?
2. Discuss the main guiding principles that a distributed operating system designer must keep in mind for good performance of the system?
3. What are the major issues of designing a Distributed OS?
4. What is the major difference between Network OD and Distributed OS?
5. Why is scalability an important feature in the design of a distributed OS? Discuss the guiding principles for designing a scalable distributed system.
6. Explain the various transparencies of a distributed system.
7. How are location, relocation and migration transparencies different from each other? Explain with examples.
8. Explain the flexibility of a DS.
9. Discuss the security aspects of a DS.
10. Why Distributed Computing Environment (DCE) is important? What are the different DCE components?
11. Why DCE cells are created? What are the factors that must be taken into consideration while decomposing a large system into cells?

UNIT - V

VIRTUALIZATION AND PROGRAMMING FOR XEN

5.1 Introduction

- The IT industry's focus on virtualization technology has increased considerably in the past few years.
- The concept of virtualization has its origins in the mainframe days in the late 1960s and early 1970s, when IBM invested a lot of time and effort in developing robust time-sharing solutions.
- At that time main intention behind virtualization was to allow large expensive mainframes to be easily shared among different application environments.
- Time-sharing refers to the shared usage of computer resources among a large group of users, aiming to increase the efficiency of both the users and the expensive computer resources they share.
- This model represented a major breakthrough in computer technology : The cost of providing computing capability dropped considerably and it became possible for organizations, and even individuals, to use a computer without actually owning one.
- IT industry is constantly searching for a way to utilize the resources in most efficient way.
- The best way to improve resource utilization, and at the same time simplify data center management, is through virtualization.
- Data centers today use virtualization techniques to make abstraction of the physical hardware, create large pools of logical resources consisting of CPUs, memory, disks, file storage, applications, networking, and offer those resources to users or customers in the form of agile, scalable, consolidated virtual machines.
- The core meaning of virtualization is to enable a computing environment to run multiple independent systems at the same time.
- Virtualization is an industry-changing movement that will touch all aspects of IT infrastructure and drive new levels of flexibility and dynamism in IT.

5.2 Overview of Virtualization

- Virtualization is a technique for hiding the physical characteristics of computing resources from the way other systems, applications or end users interact with them.
- Virtualization is a framework or methodology of dividing the resources of a computer into multiple execution environments, by applying one or more concepts or technologies such as hardware and software partitioning, time-sharing, partial or complete machine simulation, emulation, quality of service, and many others.

- We all are aware of the simple mechanism that one physical machine runs one operating system at any given time.
- By virtualizing the machine, we are able to run several operating systems (and all of their applications) at the same time.
- Virtualization provides following two functionalities :
    1. Making multiple physical resources appear to function as a single logical resource. Refer Fig. 5.1

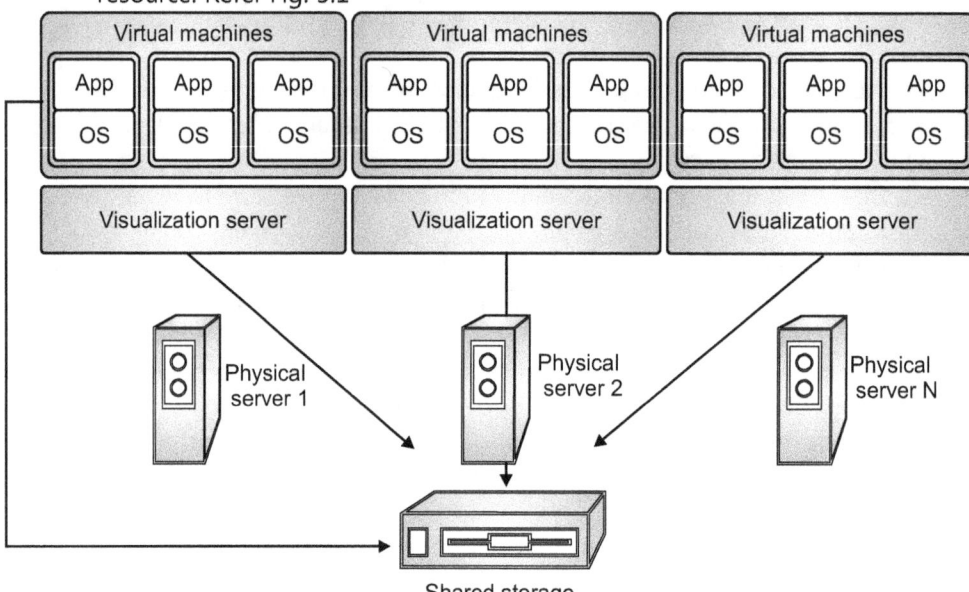

Fig. 5.1 : Multiple Physical Resources as A Single Logical Resource

2. Making a single physical resource appear to function as multiple logical resources. Refer Fig. 5.2.

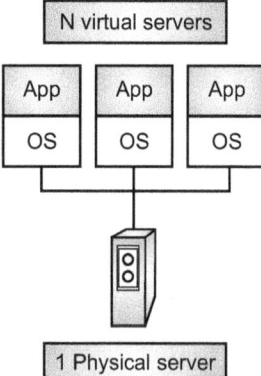

Fig. 5.2 : Single Physical Resource as A Multiple Logical Resources

- Now let's understand the difference between multitasking, multithreading and virtualization.

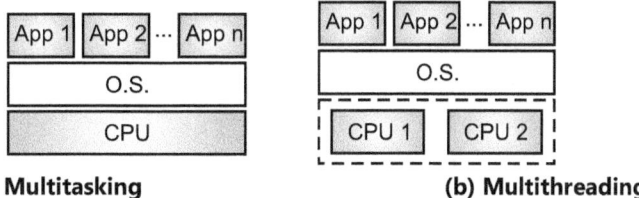

(a) Multitasking   (b) Multithreading

Fig. 5.3

- In case of multitasking, there is only one Central Processing Unit (CPU) and one operating system which can be used for running several applications. Refer Fig. 5.3 (a)
- Whereas in case of multithreading there can be two or more physical as well as logical instances of CPU, called as threads which can be used for running several applications. Refer Fig. 5.3 (b)
- Parallel processing is made possible by letting the number of applications to run on multiple cores.
- Virtualization describes a process which enables the sharing of resources of one or more computers, namely its CPU, memory or hard disk, through the creation of virtual hardware platforms, operating systems, storage devices or network resources.
- This improves the performance existing system, allowing users to run more software and applications without the need to install new hardware or appliances. Refer Fig. 5.4.
- With the virtualization it is possible to create several instances of CPUs, called as virtual CPU and operating systems.
- Each instance (CPU + Operating System) is treated as separate entity and it is responsible for running number of applications.

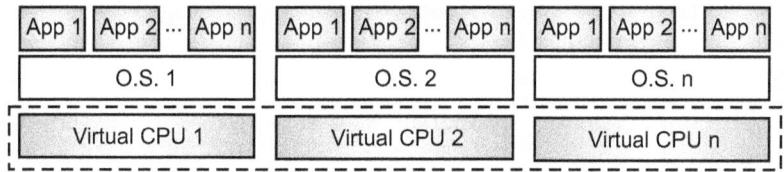

Fig. 5.4 : Virtualization

- Till now we have seen the virtualization and what can be done using virtualization. Now let's turn towards the basic entities which are used for creating virtual environment.

1. **Virtual Machines**
   - Virtual machines are presentation of a real machine using software that provides an operating environment which can run or host a guest operating system. Virtual machines are created and managed by virtual machine monitors.

- Virtual machines are simply implementation of a machine that executes programs as if it were a real machine.
- These virtual machines are basically categorized into two types.
  (a) Process virtual machines.
  (b) System virtual machines.

(a) Process Virtual Machines
- Process virtual machines run as a normal application inside an operating system to abstract away the details of the underlying hardware.
- These are designed to provide a platform-independent environment to a single process (i.e., program).
- The environment is created when its associated process is started and destroyed when that process exits.
- Process virtual machines allow program to execute in the same way regardless of the physical platform it is running on.
- They are implemented using an interpreter.
- The programmer's code is not compiled, but the interpreter requires compilation before providing the processing environment.

(b) System Virtual Machine
- System virtual machines allow multiplexing (time sharing) of the underlying hardware between different operating systems.
- These are designed to provide a complete platform which can support the execution on multiple, and different, operating systems.
- They allow time-sharing of underlying hardware between virtual machines.
- In system virtual operating systems remain isolated from one another.
- The Instruction Set Architecture (ISA) provided by the virtual machine can be different from that of the real machine.
- System virtual machines implemented through the use of a Virtual Machine Monitor (VMM) also-known-as a Hypervisor.

2. Guest Operating System
- Guest operating system is an operating system which is running inside the created virtual machine.

3. Hypervisor
- Hypervisor is a thin layer of software that generally provides virtual partitioning capabilities, which runs directly on hardware, but below the higher-level virtualization services.
- Hypervisors are classified into two categories.

(a) Native Hypervisor (Hardware-Level)
- Native hypervisor is a software which runs directly on top of a given hardware platform as a control program for operating systems. Refer Fig. 5.5

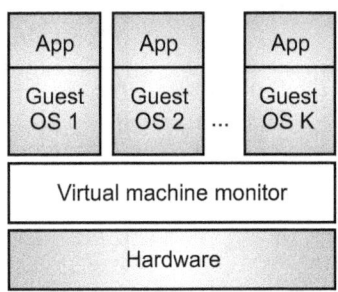

Fig. 5.5 : Native Hypervisor

- It is where actual virtualization begins.

(b) Hosted Hypervisor (OS-Level)
- Hosted hypervisor is software which runs within an operating system environment as a control program for other operating systems.
- Virtual Machine Monitor layer is moved one level higher as compared to Native VMs.
- Hosted hypervisor runs within a Host operating system environment.
- An operating system is installed first; as usual, on top of Hardware.
- A Virtual Machine Monitor is then installed within the Host OS.
- Guest operating systems can be installed on top of the VMM layer.
- Host OS sees the VMM as a process.
- VMM controls the allocation of time between Guest operating systems.
- Guest operating system is segregated from the rest of the environment. Refer Fig. 5.6.

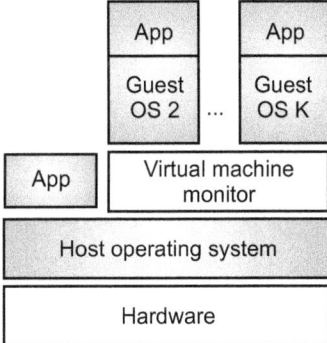

Fig. 5.6 : Hosted Hypervisor

4. **Virtual Machine Monitor**
   - Above entities use the terms like hypervisor and virtual machine monitor, but they are conceptually different.
   - Virtual Machine Monitor (VMM) is a software that runs in a layer between host operating system and one or more virtual machines that provides the virtual machine abstraction to the guest operating systems. Refer Fig. 5.7.

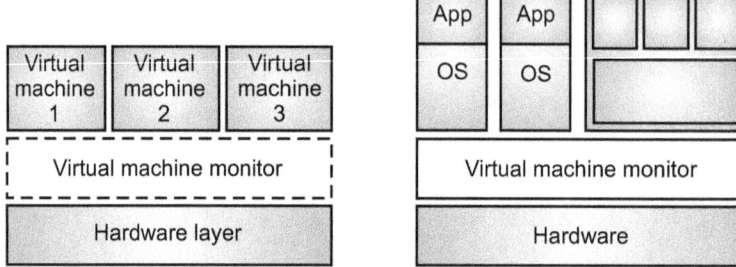

Fig. 5.7 : Role of Virtual Machine Monitor in Virtualization

- With full virtualization, the virtual machine monitor exports a virtual machine abstraction identical to a physical machine, so that standard operating systems can run just as they would on physical hardware.

5.3 THE VIRTUAL SERVER

- Before directly moving to the virtual server concept, first we must understand the traditional server concept.
- Servers can be considered as a whole unit that includes the hardware, the OS, the storage, and the applications.
- Servers are often referred to by their function i.e. the Web server, the SQL server, the File server, etc. Refer Fig. 5.8.

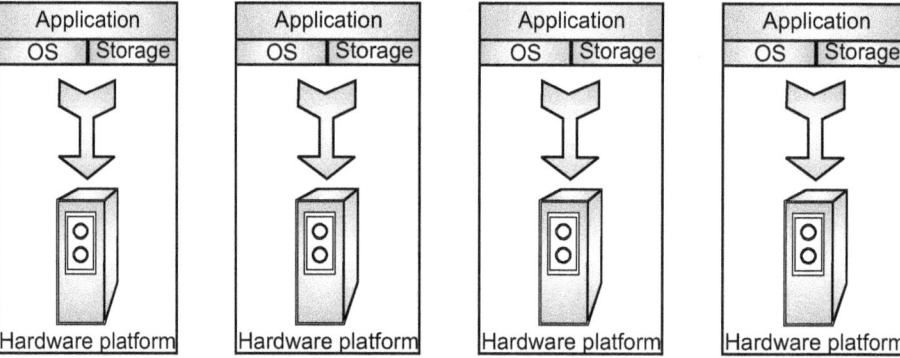

Fig. 5.8 : Traditional Servers

- If the any of the server is overloaded or that server fills up then the system administrators must add in a new server.
- If there are no multiple servers and if a service experiences a hardware failure, then the service is down completely. Refer Fig. 5.9.

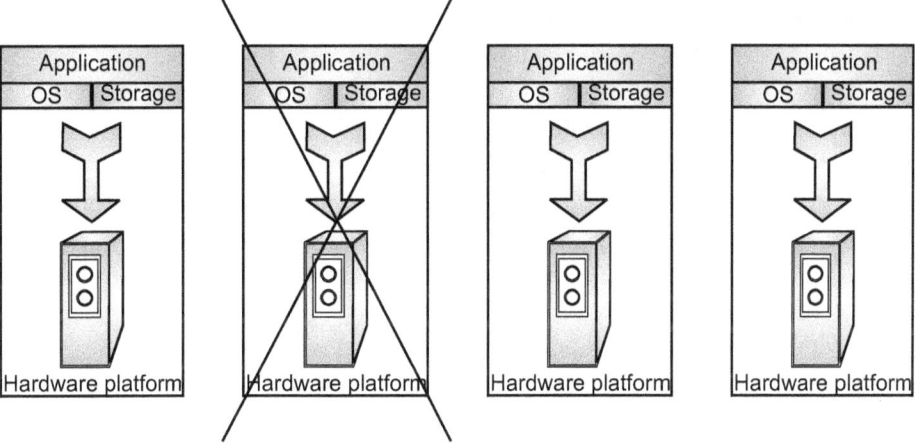

Fig. 5.9 : Service is Completely Down if Server Fails

- It is also possible to implement clusters of servers to make them more fault tolerant. However, even clusters have limits on their scalability, and not all applications work in a clustered environment.
- Although traditional servers mentioned above provide many advantages such as easy deployment, easy to backup, less complexity we must not ignore disadvantages such as expenses to maintain hardware, limited scaling, difficulty in replication, difficulty in maintaining redundancy, under utilization of processor etc.
- Virtual servers are implemented using virtualization to overcome the disadvantages of traditional servers mentioned above.

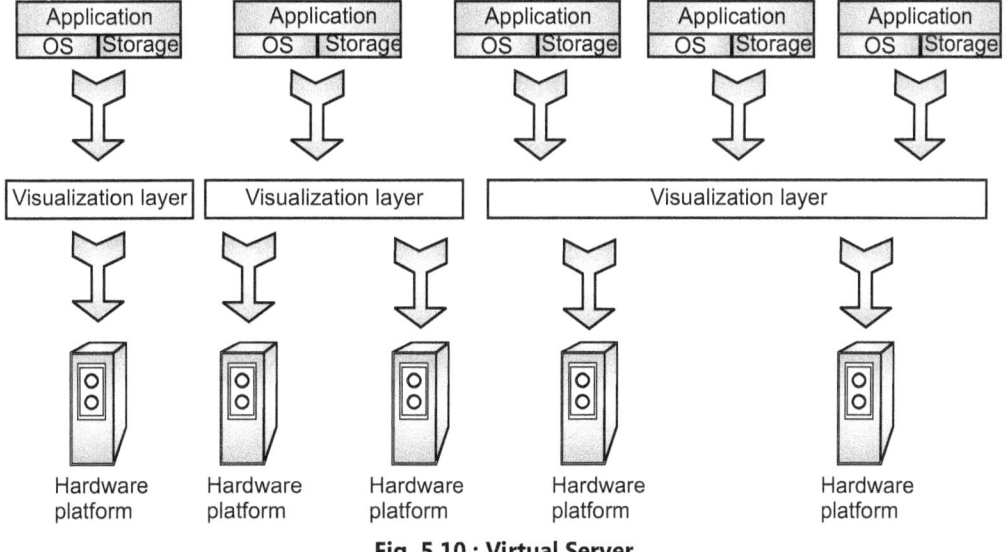

Fig. 5.10 : Virtual Server

- Virtual servers seek to encapsulate the server software away from the hardware.
- This includes the OS, the applications, and the storage for that server.
- Servers end up as mere files stored on a physical box, or in enterprise storage.
- A virtual server can be serviced by one or more hosts, and one host may contain more than one virtual server. Refer Fig. 5.10.
- Virtual servers can still be referred to by their function i.e. email server, database server, etc.
- If the environment is built correctly, virtual servers will not be affected by the loss of a host.
- Hosts may be removed or added at any time and as per requirement to fulfill the requirements.
- Virtual servers can be scaled out easily.
- If the administrators find that the resources supporting a virtual server are being taxed too much, they can adjust the amount of resources allocated to that virtual server.
- Server templates can be created in a virtual environment to be used to create multiple, identical virtual servers.
- Virtual servers themselves can be migrated from host to host almost at will.

Advantages of Virtual Servers
- Resource pooling.
- Highly redundant.
- Highly available.
- Rapidly deploy new servers.
- Easy to deploy.
- Reconfigurable while services are running.
- Optimizes physical resources by doing more with less.

Disadvantages of Virtual Servers
- Slightly harder to conceptualize.
- Slightly more costly (must buy hardware, OS, Apps and now the abstraction layer).

5.4 Types Of Virtualization

- Virtualization approaches are classified into following five types :

5.4.1 Emulation

- In this approach virtual machine simulates the entire hardware set needed to run unmodified guests for completely different hardware architectures.
- It is used to create new operating systems for the hardware which is in design phase and not in physical form.

- Virtual Machine provides a "guest" operating system the (simulated) hardware environment it expects.
- Software is unaware that it is really talking to a virtualized device. Refer Fig. 5.11.

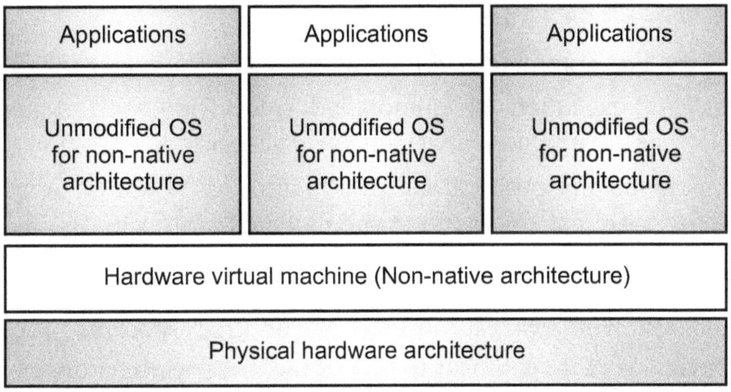

Fig. 5.11 : Emulation

- Each interaction between Guest device driver with the emulated device hardware requires transaction with VMM.
- The real hardware does its job as usual, but the VMM must now translate the result for the guest.
- **Advantage :** Guest Software need not be modified
- **Disadvantage :** Must pay Performance Penalty.

5.4.2 Full Virtualization

- Full virtualization is a native kind of virtualization in which hypervisor runs directly on top of a given hardware platform as a control program for operating systems.
- It is similar to emulation except it is designed to simulate the underlying hardware which is physically available.

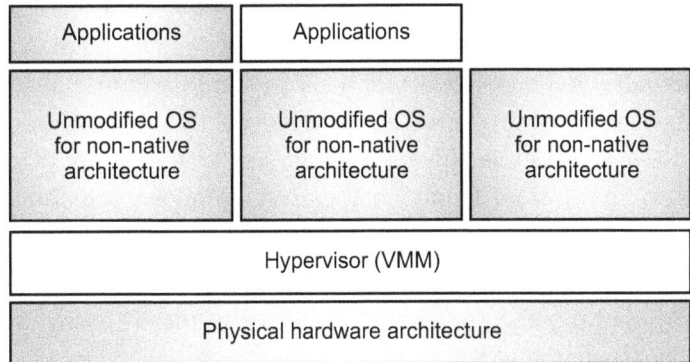

Fig. 5.12 : Full Virtualization

- It runs unmodified guests on a physical machine.

- It gives the flexibility to move entire virtual machines from one host to another host very easily, but for the cost of performance due to the overhead added by the emulator Layer. Refer Fig. 5.12.
- Examples : Virtual PC and VMware Workstation.
- VMware is the first commercial virtualization product provider for x86 architecture.
- It enables the execution of unmodified guest operating systems through the translation of x86 instructions that cannot be virtualized.
- Hyper-V, a standalone product and as a feature for Windows Server 2008, windows edition translates guest kernel mode and real mode into x86 user mode.

5.4.3 Para Virtualization

- Para virtualization is a virtualization technique that presents a software interface to virtual machines that is similar to that of the underlying hardware.
- Application Programming Interface (API) is provided to the Guest OS by the VMM so the guest may utilize the hardware.
- The hypervisor exports a modified version of the underlying physical hardware.
- The intent of the modified interface is to reduce the portion of the guest's execution time spent performing operations which are substantially more difficult to run in a virtual environment compared to a non-virtualized environment.
- A successful para virtualized platform may allow the virtual machine monitor (VMM) to be simpler (by relocating execution of critical tasks from the virtual domain to the host domain), and/or reduce the overall performance degradation of machine-execution inside the virtual-guest.
- Para virtualization requires the guest operating system to be explicitly ported for the para-API. This is because a conventional OS distribution that is not para virtualization-aware cannot be run on top of a para virtualizing VMM.
- However, even in cases where the operating system cannot be modified, components may be available that enable many of the significant performance advantages of para virtualization. For example, the Xen Windows GPLPV project provides a kit of para virtualization-aware device drivers, licensed under the terms of the GPL, that are intended to be installed into a Microsoft Windows virtual-guest running on the Xen hypervisor.
- Thus with para virtualization guest interacts with VMM at a higher level of abstraction
- Instead of supplying the specifics of how to use the hardware, software provides general requests to the VMM.
- Para virtualization decreases the number of interactions between Guest and VMM for a specific operation. Refer Fig. 5.13.

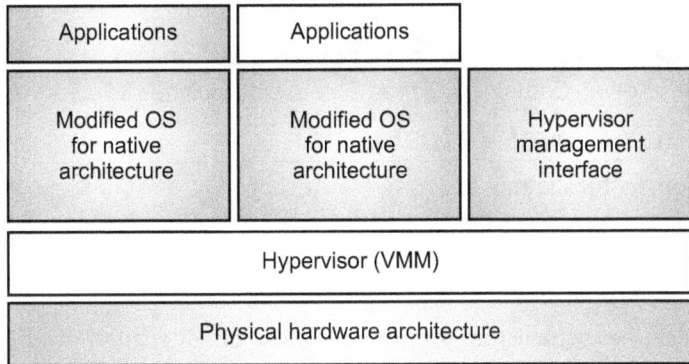

Fig. 5.13 : Para Virtualization

- **Advantage :** Better Performance.
- **Disadvantage :** Guest OS must be modified to use API.

5.4.4 Operating System Level Virtualization

- With operating system level virtualization virtual machine monitor software is not required.
- With this technique of virtualization single OS image handles all the guest images in different isolated containers.
- There is host OS that handles all other guest OS images present in respective containers.
- OS level virtualization does not support running different operating systems (Specifically, different kernel) at a time.
- With OS level virtualization instead of virtualizing the hardware, it is possible to run multiple virtual instances of same OS on single hardware.
- Thus with OS level virtualization only single kernel runs at a time.
- Single kernel means very low overhead (1 to 3%) compared to standalone server.
- Containers are the entities which provide isolation between processes.
- Each process appears as separate OS. Refer Fig. 5.14.

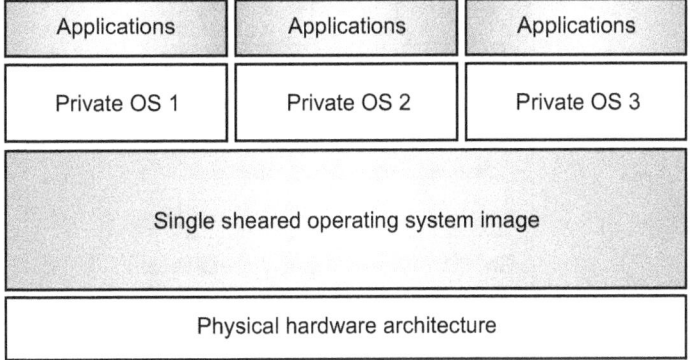

Fig. 5.14 : OS Level Virtualization

- **Advantage :** Best Performance / Scalability, Ease of Administration.
- **Disadvantage :** Only virtualizes copies of same OS.
- **Examples :** Solaris Containers/Zones, FreeBSD Jails, Linux VServers and OpenVZ.

5.4.5 Application Level Virtualization

- Application virtualization is software technology that encapsulates application software from the underlying operating system on which it is executed.
- A fully virtualized application is not installed in the traditional sense, although it is still executed as if it were.
- The application behaves at runtime like it is directly interfacing with the original operating system and all the resources managed by it, but can be isolated or sandboxed to varying degrees.
- In this context, the term "virtualization" refers to the object being encapsulated (application), which is quite different from its meaning in hardware virtualization, where it refers to the object being abstracted (physical hardware).
- Application level virtualization is also known as process virtualization.
- Application virtualization is the approach of running applications inside a virtual execution environment.
- The virtual execution environment provides a standard API for cross platform execution and manages the consumption of application's local resources such as threading model, environment variables, user interface libraries and objects.
- Modern operating systems such as Windows and Linux can include limited application virtualization.
- For example, Windows 7 provides Windows XP Mode that enables older Windows XP application to run unmodified on Windows 7.

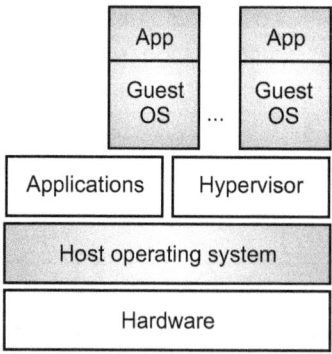

Fig. 5.15 : Application Virtualization

- Full application virtualization requires a virtualization layer.
- Application virtualization layers replace part of the runtime environment normally provided by the operating system.

- The layer intercepts all disk operations of virtualized applications and transparently redirects them to a virtualized location, often a single file.
- The application remains unaware that it accesses a virtual resource instead of a physical one.
- Since the application is now working with one file instead of many files spread throughout the system, it becomes easy to run the application on a different computer and previously incompatible applications can be run side-by-side.

5.5 NEED AND ADVANTAGES OF VIRTUALIZATION

5.5.1 Need of Virtualization

- We have already learnt about virtualization concepts, virtual machine and types of virtualization.
- Still we are not really sure of why there is need of virtualization.
- Most of the businesses often use a combination of a number of application servers, web servers, image servers, audio-video servers, document servers and database servers.
- Above mentioned hardware infrastructure is not being used well almost all the time.
- If the 75% of the hardware appears as being used at any point of time on the basis of average number of server requests recorded, the servers are still largely under-utilized.
- The servers typically take only about 1-10 ms to service each request. However it should be much faster.
- Given this extremely short amount of time taken to service the request, the amount of time the server machine is kept up and running relative to the actual time spent by it servicing the requests, is much higher.
- This clearly indicates that a significant amount of energy is wasted per server in the process of keeping the servers up and ever-ready to service requests upon their arrival.
- Cumulative energy wasted is actually high considering the fact that we use not one server for each purpose, but a number of them for different purposes.
- Maximizing the server utilization is limited by the number of incoming server requests.
- Even if we have done our best to ensure that server spends a good fraction of time servicing requests, this equivalent to the number of requests the server receives at any point of time.
- Virtualization is the technique for eliminating this wastage and maximizing the profit.
- We already know that virtualization essentially means to create multiple, logical instances of software or hardware on a single physical hardware resource.

- This technique simulates the available hardware and gives every application running top of it, the feeling that it is the unique holder of the resource.
- The details of the virtual, simulated environment are kept transparent from the application.
- Organizations use this technique to perform the tasks away from many of their physical servers and map these functions onto one robust, evergreen physical server.
- This is beneficial in terms of cost of maintenance and reduced energy wastage.
- Since we have fewer physical servers, we need only their maintenance and therefore maintenance becomes much easier and cheaper.
- Also the amount of energy wasted is a function of the number of physical servers which is clearly much lower in virtualized environment.

5.5.2 Advantages of Virtualization

- Allows applications to run in environments that do not suit the native application :
  1. Wine allows some Microsoft_Windows applications to run on Linux.
  2. CDE, a lightweight application virtualization, allows Linux applications to run on another platform.
- May protect the operating system and other applications from poorly written or buggy code and in some cases provide memory protection and IDE style debugging features.
- Uses fewer resources than a separate virtual_machine.
- Run applications that are not written correctly, for example applications that try to store user data in a read-only system-owned location.
- Run incompatible applications side-by-side, at the same time and with minimal regression testing against one another.
- Reduce system integration and administration costs by maintaining a common software baseline across multiple diverse computers in an organization.
- Implement the security principle of least privilege by removing the requirement for end-users to have Administrator privileges in order to run poorly written applications.
- Simplified operating system migrations.
- Improved security, by isolating applications from the operating system.
- Allows applications to be copied to portable media and then imported to client computers without need of installing them, so called Portable software.

5.5.3 Limitations of Virtualization

- Not all software can be virtualized. Some examples include applications that require a device driver and 16 bit applications that need to run in shared memory space.
- Some types of software such as anti-virus packages and applications that require heavy OS integration are difficult to virtualize.
- Only file and registry-level compatibility issues between legacy applications and newer operating systems can be addressed by application virtualization.

- For example, applications that don't manage the heap correctly will not execute on Windows Vista as they still allocate memory in the same way, regardless of whether they are virtualized or not.
- For this reason, specialist application compatibility fixes (shims) may still be needed, even if the application is virtualized.
- Moreover, in software licensing, application virtualization bears great licensing pitfalls mainly because both the application virtualization software and the virtualized applications must be correctly licensed.

5.6 XEN OVERVIEW

5.6.1 Introduction to XEN

- Virtualization of operating systems is used in many different computing areas. It finds its applications in server consolidation, energy saving efforts, or the ability to run older software on new hardware.
- Number of systems have been designed which use virtualization to subdivide the many resources of a modern computer.
- Some require specialized hardware, or cannot support commodity operating systems.
- Some target 100% binary compatibility at the expense of performance. Others sacrifice security or functionality for speed.
- Few offer resource isolation or performance guarantees; most provide only best effort provisioning, risking denial of service.
- Xen, an x86 virtual machine monitor which allows multiple commodity operating systems to share conventional hardware in a safe and resource managed fashion, but without sacrificing either performance or functionality.
- Xen is a virtualization system supporting both para-virtualization (PV) and hardware assistant full virtualization (HVM).
- The name XEN has evolved from ne**X**t g**EN**eration virtualization.
- This is achieved by providing an idealized virtual machine abstraction to which operating systems such as Linux, BSD and Windows, can be ported with minimal effort.

5.6.2 Basic Components of XEN Environment

- A Xen virtual environment consist of several items that work together to deliver the virtualization environment.
- The basic components of a Xen-based virtualization environment are the Xen hypervisor, the Domain0, any number of other VM Guests, and the tools, commands, and configuration files that let you manage virtualization.
- Collectively, the physical computer running all these components is referred to as a virtual machine host because together these components form a platform for hosting virtual machines.

- Xen virtualization environment consists of following components :
1. Xen Hypervisor.
2. Domain 0 Guest.
3. Domain Management and Control (Xen DM&C).
4. Domain U Guest (Dom U).
5. PV Guest.
6. HVM Guest.

The diagram below shows the basic organization of these components.

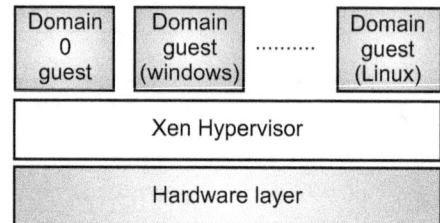

Fig. 5.16 : Block diagram of Xen virtualization Environment

1. The Xen Hypervisor

- The Xen hypervisor sometimes referred to generically as a virtual machine monitor, is an open-source software program that coordinates the low-level interaction between virtual machines and physical hardware.
- The Xen hypervisor is the basic abstraction layer of software that sits directly on the hardware below any operating systems. It is responsible for CPU scheduling and memory partitioning of the various virtual machines running on the hardware device.
- The hypervisor not only abstracts the hardware for the virtual machines but also controls the execution of virtual machines as they share the common processing environment.
- It has no knowledge of networking, external storage devices, video, or any other common I/O functions found on a computing system.

2. The Domain 0

- The virtual machine host environment, also referred to as domain0 or controlling Domain.
- The term "Domain 0" refers to a special domain that provides the management environment. This may be run either in graphical or in command line mode.
- Domain 0, a modified Linux kernel, is a unique virtual machine running on the Xen hypervisor that has special rights to access physical I/O resources as well as interact with the other virtual machines (Domain U : PV and HVM Guests) running on the system.
- All Xen virtualization environments require Domain 0 to be running before any other virtual machines can be started.

- Two drivers are included in Domain 0 to support network and local disk requests from Domain U PV and HVM Guests; the Network Backend Driver and the Block Backend Driver. Refer Fig. 5.17.

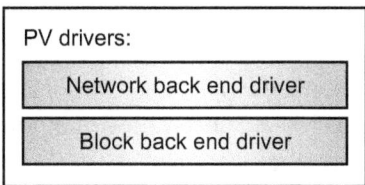

Fig. 5.17 : Drivers of Domain 0

- The Network Backend Driver communicates directly with the local networking hardware to process all virtual machines requests coming from the Domain U guests.
- The Block Backend Driver communicates with the local storage disk to read and write data from the drive based upon Domain U requests.

3. **Domain U**
- Domain U guests have no direct access to physical hardware on the machine as a Domain 0 Guest does and is often referred to as unprivileged.
- All para-virtualized virtual machines running on a Xen hypervisor are referred to as Domain U PV Guests and are modified Linux operating systems, Solaris, FreeBSD, and other UNIX operating systems.
- All fully virtualized machines running on a Xen hypervisor are referred to as Domain U **HVM Guests** and run standard Windows or any other unchanged operating system.

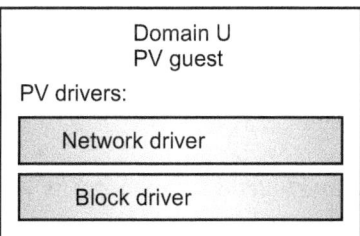

Fig. 5.18 : Divers of Domain U

- The Domain U PV Guest virtual machine is aware that it does not have direct access to the hardware and recognizes that other virtual machines are running on the same machine.
- The Domain U HVM Guest virtual machine is not aware that it is sharing processing time on the hardware and that other virtual machines are present.
- A Domain U PV Guest contains two drivers for network and disk access, PV Network Driver and PV Block Driver. Refer Fig. 5.18.

- A Domain U HVM Guest does not have the PV drivers located within the virtual machine; instead a special daemon is started for each HVM Guest in Domain 0.

4. **Qemu-DM**
   - Qemu-DM supports the Domain U HVM Guest for networking and disk access requests.
   - The Domain U HVM Guest must initialize as it would on a typical machine so software is added to the Domain U HVM Guest, Xen virtual firmware, to simulate the BIOS an operating system would expect on startup.
   - Every HVM Guest running on a Xen environment requires its own Qemu daemon.
   - This tool handles all networking and disk requests from the Domain U HVM Guest to allow for a fully virtualized machine in the Xen environment.
   - Qemu-DM must exist outside the Xen hypervisor due to its need for access to networking and I/O and is therefore found in Domain 0. Refer Fig. 5.19.
   - A new tool, Stub-dm, is in development for future versions of Xen that will remove the need for a Qemu-DM running for every Domain U HVM Guest and will instead provide a set of services available to every Domain U HVM Guest.

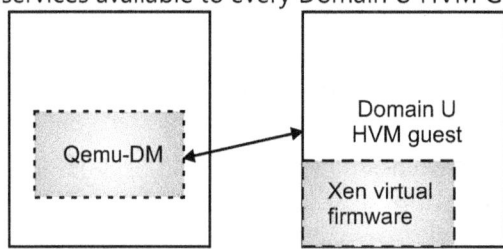

Fig. 5.19 : Qemu-DM

5. **Domain Management and Control**
   - A series of Linux daemons are classified as Domain Management and Control by the open source community.
   - These services support the overall management and control of the virtualization environment and exist within the Domain 0 virtual machine.

6. **Xend**
   - The Xend daemon is a python application that is considered the system manager for the Xen environment.
   - It leverages the libXenctrl library to make requests of the Xen hypervisor.
   - All requests processed by the Xend are delivered to it via an XML RPC interface by the Xm tool. Refer Fig. 5.20.
   - The Xend daemon (Xend) stores configuration information about each virtual machine and controls how virtual machines are created and managed.

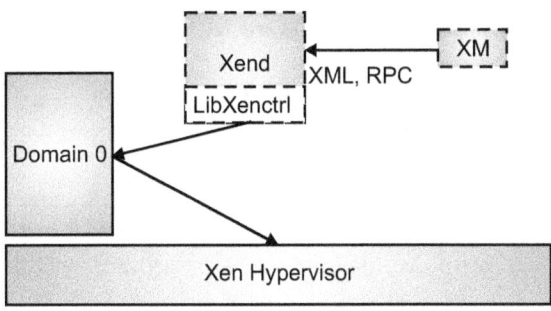

Fig. 5.20 : Xend Daemon

7. **Xm**
   - Xm is the command line tool that takes user input and passes to Xend via XML RPC.
8. **Xenstored**
   - The Xenstored daemon maintains a registry of information including memory and event channel links between Domain 0 and all other Domain U Guests.
   - The Domain 0 virtual machine leverages this registry to setup device channels with other virtual machines on the system.
9. **LibXenctrl**
   - LibXenctrl is a C library that provides Xend the ability to talk with the Xen hypervisor via Domain 0.
   - A special driver within Domain 0, privcmd delivers the request to the hypervisor. Refer Fig. 5.21.

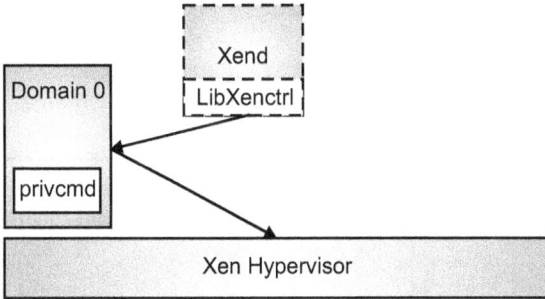

Fig. 5.21 : LibXenctrl

10. **Xen Virtual Firmware**
    - The Xen Virtual Firmware is a virtual BIOS that is inserted into every Domain U HVM Guest to ensure that the operating system receives all the standard start-up instructions it expects during normal boot-up providing a standard PC-compatible software environment.
11. **Xen PCI Passthru**
    - A new feature in Xen designed to improve overall performance and reduce the load on the Domain 0 Guest is PCI Passthru which allows the Domain U Guest to

have direct access to local hardware without using the Domain 0 for hardware access.
- The Domain U Guest is given rights to talk directly to a specific hardware device instead of the previous method of using Fronted and Backend drivers.

5.6.3 Xen Operation

- This subsection demonstrates how a para-virtualized Domain U is able to communicate with external networks or storage via the Xen hypervisor and Domain 0.

5.6.3.1 Domain 0 to Domain U Communication

- As stated earlier, the Xen hypervisor is not written to support network or disk requests thus a Domain U PV Guest must communicate via the Xen hypervisor with the Domain 0 to accomplish a network or disk request.
- The example shown below shows a Domain U PV Guest writing data to the local hard disk.
- The Domain U PV Guest PV block driver receives a request to write to the local disk and writes the data via the Xen hypervisor to the appropriate local memory which is shared with Domain 0.
- An event channel exists between Domain 0 and the Domain U PV Guest that allows them to communicate via asynchronous inter-domain interrupts in the Xen hypervisor.
- Domain 0 will receive an interrupt from the Xen hypervisor causing the PV Block Backend Driver to access the local system memory reading the appropriate blocks from the Domain U PV Guest shared memory.
- The data from shared memory is then written to the local hard disk at a specific location.

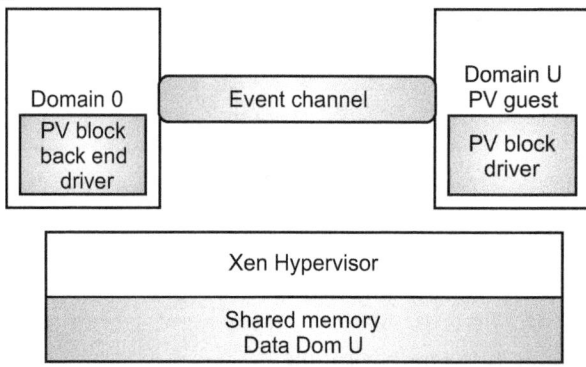

Fig. 5.22 : Domain 0 to Domain U Communication

- The event channel is shown in Fig. 5.22 as a direct link between Domain 0 and Domain U PV Guest which is a simplified view of the way the system works.

- In fact, the event channel runs through the Xen hypervisor with specific interrupts registered in Xenstored allowing both the Domain 0 and Domain U PV Guest to quickly share information across local memory.

5.6.4 Understanding Virtualization Modes

- Guest operating systems are hosted on virtual machines in either full virtualization mode or para-virtual mode.(Refer 5.4)
- There are several ways to implement virtualization.
- Two leading approaches are full virtualization and para-virtualization. Each virtualization mode has advantages and disadvantages.
- Full virtualization is designed to provide total abstraction of the underlying physical system and creates a complete virtual system in which the guest operating systems can execute.
- No modification is required in the guest OS or application; the guest OS or application is not aware of the virtualized environment so they have the capability to execute on the VM just as they would on a physical system.
- This approach can be advantageous because it enables complete decoupling of the software from the hardware.
- As a result, full virtualization can streamline the migration of applications and workloads between different physical systems.
- Full virtualization also helps provide complete isolation of different applications, which helps make this approach highly secure.
- However, full virtualization may incur a performance penalty. The VM monitor must provide the VM with an image of an entire system, including virtual BIOS, virtual memory space, and virtual devices.
- The VM monitor also must create and maintain data structures for the virtual components, such as a shadow memory page table.
- These data structures must be updated for every corresponding access by the VMs.
- In contrast, para-virtualization presents each VM with an abstraction of the hardware that is similar but not identical to the underlying physical hardware.
- Para-virtualization techniques require modifications to the guest operating systems that are running on the VMs.
- As a result, the guest operating systems are aware that they are executing on a VM allowing for near-native performance.
- Para-virtualization methods are still being developed and thus have limitations; including several insecurities such as the guest OS cache data, unauthenticated connections, and so forth.

5.6.5 The Virtual Machine Interface

- Table 5.1 presents an overview of the para-virtualized x86 interface, classified into three broad aspects of the system : memory management, the CPU, and device I/O.

Table 5.1 : Virtual Machine Interfaces

Memory Management	
Segmentation	Cannot install fully-privileged segment descriptors and cannot overlap with the top end of the linear address space.
Paging	Guest OS has direct read access to hardware page tables, but updates are batched and validated by the hypervisor. A domain may be allocated discontinuous machine pages.
CPU	
Protection	Guest OS must run at a lower privilege level than Xen.
Exceptions	Guest OS must register a descriptor table for exception handlers with Xen. A side from page faults, the handlers remain the same.
System Calls	Guest OS may install a 'fast' handler for system calls, allowing direct calls from an application into its guest OS and avoiding in directing through Xen on every call.
Interrupts	Hardware interrupts are replaced with a lightweight event system.
Time	Each guest OS has a timer interface and is aware of both `real' and `virtual' time.
Device I/O	
Network, Disk, etc.	Virtual devices are elegant and simple to access. Data is transferred using asynchronous I/O rings.
	An event mechanism replaces hardware interrupts for notifications.

5.6.5.1 Memory Management

- Virtualizing memory is the most difficult part of para-virtualizing an architecture in terms of the mechanisms required in the hypervisor and modifications required to port each guest OS.
- The task is easier if the architecture provides a software managed TLB as these can be efficiently virtualized in a simple manner.
- Associating an address-space identifier tag with each TLB entry allows the hypervisor and each guest OS to efficiently coexist in separate address spaces because there is no need to flush the entire TLB when transferring execution.
- Unfortunately, x86 does not have a software managed TLB; instead TLB misses are serviced automatically by the processor by walking the page table structure in hardware.

- Thus to achieve the best possible performance, all valid page translations for the current address space should be present in the hardware-accessible page table.
- Moreover, because the TLB is not tagged, address space switches typically require a complete TLB flush.
- Given these limitations, two decisions are made :
  (a) Guest OSes are responsible for allocating and managing the hardware page tables, with minimal involvement from Xen to ensure safety and isolation; and
  (b) Xen exists in a 64MB section at the top of every address space, thus avoiding a TLB flush when entering and leaving the hypervisor.
- Each time a guest OS requires a new page table, for example a new process is being created, it allocates and initializes a page from its own memory reservation and registers it with Xen.
- At this point the OS must give up direct write privileges to the page-table memory : All subsequent updates must be validated by Xen.
- This restricts updates in a number of ways, including only allowing an OS to map pages that it owns, and disallowing writable mappings of page tables.
- Guest OSes may batch update requests to pay back the overhead of entering the hypervisor.
- The top 64MB region of each address space, which is reserved for Xen, is not accessible or remappable by guest OSes.
- This address region is not used by any of the common x86 architectures.
- So this restriction does not break application compatibility.
- Segmentation is virtualized in a similar way, by validating updates to hardware segment descriptor tables. The only restrictions on x86 segment descriptors are :
  (a) They must have lower privilege than Xen.
  (b) They may not allow any access to the Xen reserved portion of the address space.

5.6.5.2 CPU

- Virtualizing the CPU has several implications for guest OSes.
- Principally, the insertion of a hypervisor below the operating system violates the usual assumption that the OS is the most privileged entity in the system.
- In order to protect the hypervisor from OS misbehavior (and domains from one another) guest OSes must be modified to run at a lower privilege level.
- Many processor architectures only provide two privilege levels.
- In these cases the guest OS would share the lower privilege level with applications.
- The guest OS would then protect itself by running in a separate address space from its applications, and indirectly pass control to and from applications via the hypervisor to set the virtual privilege level and change the current address space.
- Again, if the processor's TLB supports address-space tags then expensive TLB flushes can be avoided.

- Efficient virtualizing of privilege levels is possible on x86 because it supports four distinct privilege levels in hardware.
- The x86 privilege levels are generally described as rings, and are numbered from zero (most privileged) to three (least privileged). Refer Fig. 5.23.

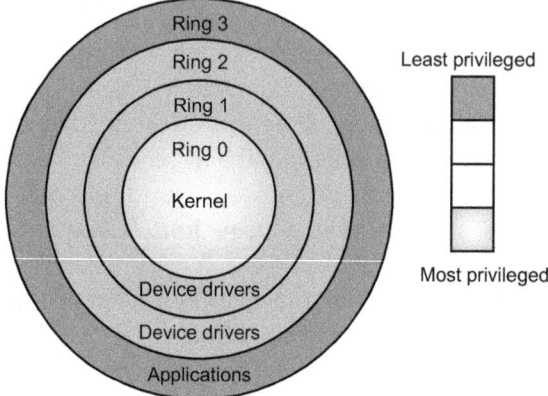

Fig. 5.23 : x86 Privilege Rings

- OS code typically executes in ring 0 because no other ring can execute privileged instructions, while ring 3 is generally used for application code. To our knowledge, rings 1 and 2 have not been used by any well-known x86 OS.
- Any OS which follows this common arrangement can be ported to Xen by modifying it to execute in ring 1. This prevents the guest OS from directly executing privileged instructions, yet it remains safely isolated from applications running in ring 3.
- Privileged instructions are para-virtualized by requiring them to be validated and executed within Xen. This applies to operations such as installing a new page table, or yielding the processor when idle.
- Any guest OS attempt to directly execute a privileged instruction is failed by the processor, either silently or by taking a fault, since only Xen executes at a sufficiently privileged level.
- Exceptions, including memory faults and software traps, are virtualized on x86 very straightforwardly.
- A table describing the handler for each type of exception is registered with Xen for validation.
- The handlers specified in this table are generally identical to those of real x86 hardware. This is possible because the exception stack frames are unmodified in our para-virtualized architecture. The sole modification is to the page fault handler, which would normally read the faulting address from a privileged processor register (CR2); since this is not possible, we write it into an extended stack frame2.
- When an exception occurs while executing outside ring 0, Xen's handler creates a copy of the exception stack frame on the guest OS stack and returns control to the appropriate registered handler.

- Typically only two types of exception occur frequently enough to affect system performance : System calls (which are usually implemented via a software exception), and page faults.
- Performance of system calls can be improved by allowing each guest OS to register a 'fast' exception handler which is accessed directly by the processor without indirecting via ring 0; this handler is validated before installing it in the hardware exception table.
- Unfortunately it is not possible to apply the same technique to the page fault handler because only code executing in ring 0 can read the faulting address from register CR2; page faults must therefore always be delivered via Xen so that this register value can be saved for access in ring 1.
- Safety is ensured by validating exception handlers when they are presented to Xen. The only required check is that the handler's code segment does not specify execution in ring 0.
- Since no guest OS can create such a segment, it suffices to compare the specified segment selector to a small number of static values which are reserved by Xen.

5.6.5.3 Device I/O

- Rather than emulating existing hardware devices, as is typically done in fully-virtualized environments, Xen exposes a set of clean and simple device abstractions.
- This allows us to design an interface that is both efficient and satisfies requirements for protection and isolation. To this end, I/O data is transferred to and from each domain via Xen, using shared-memory, asynchronous buffer descriptor rings.
- These provide a high-performance communication mechanism for passing buffer information vertically through the system, while allowing Xen to efficiently perform validation checks (for example, checking that buffers are contained within a domain's memory reservation).
- Similar to hardware interrupts, Xen supports a lightweight event delivery mechanism which is used for sending asynchronous notifications to a domain. These notifications are made by updating a bitmap of pending event types and, optionally, by calling an event handler specified by the guest OS.

5.6.6 Xen Architecture

- Xen is open source virtualization software based on para-virtualization technology. This subsection provides an overview of the Xen architecture.
- Fig. 5.24 shows the architecture of Xen hosting four VMs (Domain 0, VM 1, VM 2, and VM 3). This architecture includes the Xen Virtual Machine Monitor (VMM), which abstracts the underlying physical hardware and provides hardware access for the different virtual machines.

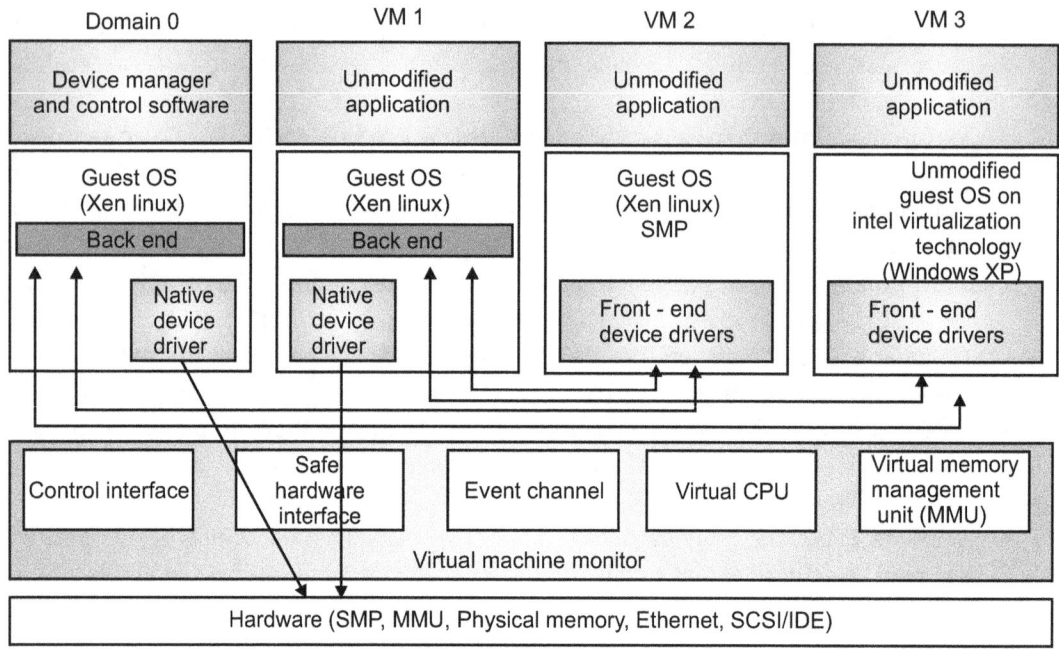

Fig. 5.24 : Xen Architecture

- Fig. 5.24 also shows the special role of the VM called Domain 0. Only Domain 0 can access the control interface of the VMM, through which other VMs can be created, destroyed, and managed.
- Management and control software runs in Domain 0.
- Administrators can create virtual machines with special privileges such as VM 1 that can directly access the hardware through secure interfaces provided by Xen.
- Administrators can create other virtual machines that can access the physical resources provided by Domain 0's control and management interface in Xen.

5.6.6.1 CPU Operations

- The Intel x86 architecture provides four levels of privilege modes. These modes, or rings, are numbered 0 to 3, with 0 being the most privileged.
- In a non-virtualized system, the OS executes at ring 0 and the applications at ring 3. Rings 1 and 2 are typically not used.
- In Xen para-virtualization, the VMM executes at ring 0, the guest OS at ring 1, and the applications at ring 3. This approach helps to ensure that the VMM processes the highest privilege, while the guest OS executes in a higher privileged mode than the applications and is isolated from the applications.
- Privileged instructions issued by the guest OS are verified and executed by the VMM.

5.6.6.2 Memory Operations

- In a non-virtualized environment, the OS expects contiguous memory.

- Guest operating systems in Xen para-virtualization are modified to access memory in a non-contigious manner.
- Guest operating systems are responsible for allocating and managing page tables. However, direct writes are intercepted and validated by the Xen VMM.

5.6.6.3 I/O Operations
- In a fully virtualized environment, hardware devices are emulated.
- Xen para-virtualization exposes a set of clean and simple device abstractions. For example, I/O data to and from guest operating systems is transferred using shared memory ring architecture (memory is shared between Domain 0 and the guest domain) through which incoming and outgoing messages are sent.
- Modifying the guest OS is not feasible for non–open source platforms Windows operating systems.
- As a result, such operating systems are not supported in a para-virtualization environment.

5.7 x86 Virtualization

5.7.1 Introduction to x86 Virtualization
- x86 virtualization refers to hardware virtualization for the x86 architecture.
- It allows multiple operating systems to simultaneously share x86 processor resources in a safe and efficient manner.
- In the early days of x86 virtualization, all CPUs were implemented essentially the same 32-bit architecture and the virtual machine monitor (VMM) always used software techniques to run guest operating systems.
- Later uniformity no longer exists. CPUs today come in 32 and 64 bit variants. Some CPUs have hardware support for virtualization; others do not. Moreover, this hardware support comes in multiple forms for virtualizing different aspects of the x86 architecture.
- This subsection provides description of x86 architecture from virtualization point of view along with the understanding of :
   (a) Which CPU features are required.
   (b) Which CPU features can be utilized (but are not required).
   (c) Which CPU features can be virtualized that is, made available to software running in the virtual machine.
- With a better understanding of how CPU features are required, used, and virtualized we can more precisely talk about what can be virtualized, what performance levels may result for a given combination of CPU, guest operating system, and how workloads may respond to adjusting configuration parameters both for software running in the virtual machine and at the underlying hardware level.

5.7.2 x86 Architecture- History

- The x86 architecture has roots that link back to 8 bit processors built by Intel in the late 1970s.
- As manufacturing capabilities improved and software demands increased, Intel extended the 8-bit architecture to 16 bits with the 8086 processor.
- With the arrival of the 80386 CPU in 1985, Intel extended the architecture to 32 bits known as IA-32, but the vendor use the generalized term as x86.
- From the last two decades, the basic 32-bit architecture remained the same, although successive generations of CPUs added many new features such as chip floating point unit, support for large physical memories and vector instructions.
- In 2003, AMD introduced a 64-bit extension to the x86 architecture, after that Intel announced its own 64-bit architectural extension of IA-32 known as IA-32e. The AMD and Intel 64-bit extensions are extremely similar, with some minor differences which is crucial for virtualization.

5.7.3 VMware ESX

- VMware released the first version of VMware Workstation in 1999. It ran on, and virtualized, 32 bit x86 CPUs.
- Later VMware switched to the ESX Server product. This ESX server used a custom built kernel instead of workstation which relies on either Linux or Windows.
- The custom built kernel also known as VMkernel is designed to be scalable and efficiently run a workload that consists primarily of virtual machines while providing strong information and performance isolation among the virtual machines.
- The VMkernel row in Table 5.2 shows the architectural requirements for running the VMkernel itself in different versions of ESX.

Table 5.2 Physical and Virtual CPU Options

	ESX 1.0-2.5	ESX 3.0	ESX 3.5	ESX 4.0
VMkernel	32 bit	32 bit	32 bit	64 bit
Virtual CPU	32 bit	32-64 bit	32-64 bit	32-64 bit

- All versions of ESX before 4.0 can run on the 32-bit x86 architecture. They also can run on x64 CPUs but do not take advantage of the 64-bit architectural extensions.
- With VMware ESX 4.0, a 64-bit CPU is required to run the VMkernel. However this requirement causes a slight loss of hardware compatibility.
- After 2009 the majority of server CPUs implements the x64 architecture, making it desirable to use the large 64 bit address space and other architectural advances to improve performance and scalability.

5.7.4 Virtualizing 32- and 64-bit CPUs

- The VMkernel does not run virtual machines directly. Instead, it runs a VMM that in turn is responsible for execution of the virtual machine.
- Each VMM is dedicated to one virtual machine. To run multiple virtual machines, the VMkernel starts multiple VMM instances.
- Because the VMM decouples the virtual machine from the VMkernel, it is possible to run 64 bit guest operating systems on a 32 bit VMkernel (and vice versa) as long as the underlying physical CPUs have all the required features.
- VMM can also be designed which can take advantage of a 64-bit physical CPU to run a 64-bit guest operating system efficiently, even if the underlying VMkernel runs in 32-bit mode.
- The Virtual CPU row in Table 5.2 shows which versions of ESX can run just 32-bit virtual machines and which can run both 32- and 64-bit virtual machines.

5.7.5 Execution Modes

- The VMM implements the virtual hardware on which the virtual machine runs. This hardware includes a virtual CPU, virtual I/O devices, timers, and other devices.
- The virtual CPU has three important features :
  a. The virtual instruction set.
  b. The virtual memory management unit (MMU).
  c. The virtual interrupt controller (PIC or APIC).
- The VMM can implement each of these aspects using either software techniques or hardware techniques. The combination of techniques used to virtualize the instruction set and memory determines an execution mode.

5.7.5.1 Instruction Set Virtualization

- In order to run one or more virtual machines safely on a single host, ESX must isolate the virtual machines so that they can not interfere with each other or with the VMkernel.
- In particular, it must prevent the virtual machines from directly executing privileged instructions that could affect the state of the physical machine as a whole. Instead, it must intercept such instructions and emulate them so their effect is applied to the virtual machine's hardware, not the physical machine's hardware. For example, issuing the reboot command in a virtual machine should reboot just that virtual machine, not the entire host.
- Now we will see some software and hardware techniques for x86 virtualization.

Software Technique : Binary Translation

- The original approach to virtualizing the 32 bit x86 instruction set is just-in-time binary translation (BT).

- This approach is implemented in all versions of VMware ESX, and it is the only approach used in VMware ESX 1.x and 2.x. This approach is actually called as BT32 as this technique virtualizes the 32-bit architecture.
- When running a virtual machine's instruction stream using binary translation, the virtual machine instructions must be translated before they can be executed. Refer Fig. 5.25.
- When a virtual machine is about to execute a block of code for the first time, ESX sends this code through a just-in-time binary translator, much like a Java virtual machine (JVM) which translates Java byte code on the fly into native instructions.

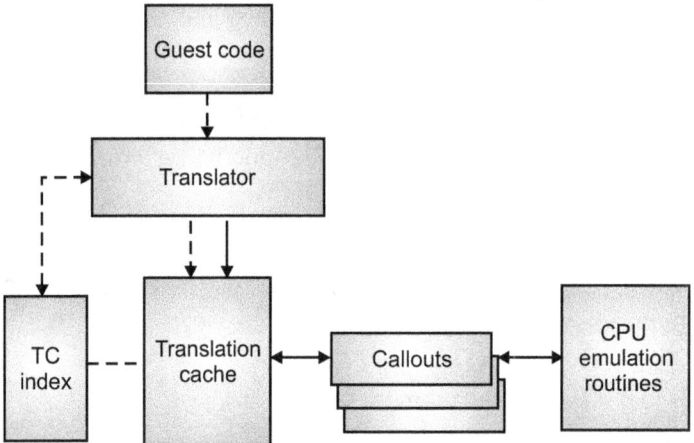

Fig. 5.25 : Binary Translation

- The translator in the VMM does not perform a mapping from one architecture to another, but instead translates from the full unrestricted x86 instruction set to a subset that is safe to execute. In particular, the binary translator replaces privileged instructions with sequences of instructions that perform the privileged operations in the virtual machine rather than on the physical machine.
- This translation enforces encapsulation of the virtual machine while preserving the x86 semantics as seen from the perspective of the virtual machine.
- To keep translation overheads low, the VMM translates virtual machine instructions the first time they are about to execute, placing the resulting translated code in a translation cache.
- If the same virtual machine code executes again in the future, the VMM can reuse the translated code from the translation cache, thereby amortizing the translation costs over all future executions.
- To reduce translation cost further and to minimize memory usage by the translation cache, the VMM combines binary translation of kernel code running in the virtual machine with direct execution of user mode code running in the virtual machine. This is safe because user mode code cannot execute privileged instructions.

- A Binary Translation-based VMM must enforce a strict boundary between the part of the address space that is used by the virtual machine and the part that is used by the VMM. The VMware VMM enforces this boundary using segmentation.
- Segmentation is a hardware feature of the x86 CPU that links back to its 16 bit ancestors. A segment is a consecutive range of memory, identified by a base (the starting address) and a limit (the length of the segment).
- Whenever an x86 instruction accesses memory, it does so with respect to a particular segment.
- The segmentation hardware checks the memory address against the segment limit. If it is within the limit, the base address is added and the access is permitted to proceed. If the address exceeds the limit, the memory access is aborted and the processor raises a protection fault.
- Since most of the modern operating systems, including Windows, Linux make limited use of segmentation, it is possible for the VMM to use segmentation to enforce the boundary between virtual machine and VMM.
- In rare cases when the uses of segmentation by the virtual machine and the VMM conflict, the VMM can perform software segmentation checks again, causing a slight loss of performance.
- In 2003, when AMD extended the x86 architecture from 32 to 64 bits, it eliminated segment limit checks for 64-bit code although 32 bit code still retained segment limit checks for backwards compatibility. This change meant that a BT-based VMM could not use segmentation to protect the VMM from a 64-bit virtual machine. In other words, BT32 could virtualize the 32-bit x86 architecture efficiently, but BT64 could not virtualize the 64-bit architecture efficiently.
- To overcome this AMD added segment limits back into 64-bit code. Thus, all 64-bit AMD CPUs can run virtual machines with BT64.
- The Intel 64-bit extensions to the x86 architecture also omitted support for segment limit checks for 64-bit code. Unlike AMD, however, Intel has not added support for segment limit checks in subsequent processors. This limitation makes it inefficient to run 64-bit virtual machines using BT64 on Intel CPUs.

Table 5.3 : Support for Binary Translation (BT)

	ESX 1.0-2.5	ESX 3.0	ESX 3.5	ESX 4.0
AMD	BT32	BT32, BT64	BT32, BT64	BT32, BT64
Intel	BT32	BT32	BT32	BT32

Hardware Technique : VT-x and AMD-V

- During the transition from 32-bit to 64-bit hardware, both Intel and AMD recognized the importance of virtualization. Both companies began designing hardware that made it easier for a VMM to run virtual machines.

- The first hardware designs by both of them focused on how to virtualize the 32- and 64-bit x86 instruction set.
- The Intel design, called VT-x got the importance because it provided a way to virtualize 64-bit virtual machines efficiently. (BT64 is not efficient because of the lack of segment limit checks in 64 bit mode on Intel CPUs.)
- AMD subsequently introduced AMD-V to provide hardware support for instruction set virtualization (virtualization of 64 bit virtual machines using BT64 was possible already for AMD CPUs).
- VT-x and AMD-V are similar in aim. Both designs allow a VMM to do away with binary translation while still being able to fully control the execution of a virtual machine by restricting which kinds of (privileged) instructions the virtual machine can execute without intervention by the VMM.
- VT-x and AMD-V both allow a VMM to give the CPU to a virtual machine for direct execution (an action called a VM entry) up until the point when the virtual machine tries to execute a privileged instruction.
- At that point, the virtual machine execution is suspended and the CPU is given back to the VMM (an action called a VM exit). The VMM then follows the inspection of the virtual machine instruction that caused the exit as well as other information provided by the hardware in response to the exit.
- With the relevant information collected, the VMM emulates the virtual machine instruction against the virtual machine state and then resumes execution of the virtual machine with another VM entry.

Table 5.4 : Support for Hardware Instruction Set Virtualization

	ESX 1.0-2.5	ESX 3.0	ESX 3.5	ESX 4.0
AMD	-	AMD-V32, AMD-V64	AMD-V32, AMD-V64	AMD-V32, AMD-V64
Intel	-	VT-x64	VT-x64	VT-x64

5.7.5.2 Memory and MMU Virtualization

- All modern x86 CPUs implement virtual memory, which is a technique for flexibly mapping multiple virtual address spaces (typically one per process) into a possibly smaller amount of physical memory.
- However, for the x86 architecture, the mapping is specified using a set of memory-resident hierarchical 4KB page tables. A tree of such page tables, identified by a root page table, specifies the entire mapping of a virtual address space into physical memory.
- The x86 MMU contains two main structures : a page table walker and a content-addressable memory called a translation lookaside buffer (TLB) to accelerate address translation lookups.

- When an instruction accesses a virtual address, segmentation hardware converts the virtual address to a linear address by adding the segment base. Then the page table walker receives the logical address and traverses the page table tree to produce the corresponding physical address. Refer Fig. 5.26.

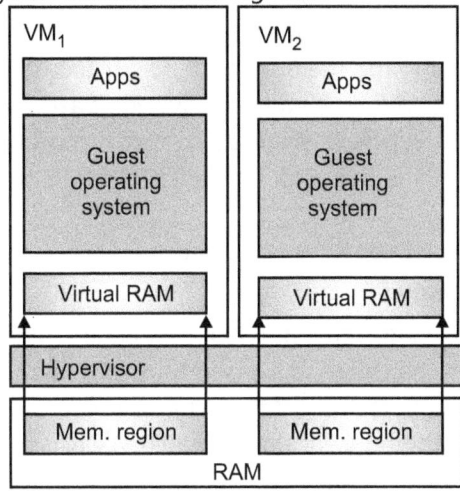

Fig. 5.26 : Memory Virtualization

- When the page table walk completes, the pair is inserted into the TLB to accelerate future accesses to the same address.
- Accordingly, the task of the VMM is not only to virtualize memory but to virtualize virtual memory so that the guest operating system can use virtual memory.
- To accomplish this task, the VMM must virtualize the x86 MMU. It does so by having the VMM remap addresses a second time, below the virtual machine, from physical address to machine address, to confine the virtual machine to the machine memory that the VMM and VMkernel have allowed it to use.

Software Technique : Shadow Page Tables

- To virtualize memory without special hardware support, the VMM creates a shadow page table for each primary page table that the virtual machine is using.
- The VMM populates the shadow page table with the composition of two mappings :
  a. **The Logical address :** Physical Address mapping specified by the guest operating system, obtained from the primary page tables.
  b. **The Physical address :** Logical Address mapping defined by the VMM and VMkernel.
- By building shadow page tables that capture this composite mapping, the VMM can point the hardware MMU directly at the shadows, allowing the virtual machine's memory accesses to run at native speed while being assured that the virtual machine cannot access machine memory that does not belong to it.
- However, shadow page tables incur overheads in following situations.

a. When the virtual machine updates a primary page table, the VMM must trap the update and propagate the change into the corresponding shadow page table or tables. This slows down memory mapping operations as well as creation of new processes in virtual machines.
b. When the virtual machine touches memory for the first time, the shadow page table entry mapping this memory must be created on demand, slowing down the first access to memory. (The native equivalent is a TLB miss.)
c. When the virtual machine switches context from one process to another, the VMM must intervene to switch the physical MMU to the new process' shadow page table root.
d. Shadow page tables consume additional memory.

Hardware Technique : RVI and EPT

- To address the overheads inherent in shadow page tables, both AMD and Intel now build special purpose hardware to support MMU virtualization.
- AMD introduced support for MMU virtualization, called RVI, in the quad-core Opteron CPU. Intel introduced similar functionality, called EPT, in its "Nehalem" generation of CPUs.
- Just as AMD-V and VT-x are similar in their aim, so are RVI and EPT. Both designs permit the two levels of address mapping to be performed in hardware by pointing the physical MMU at two distinct sets of page tables.
- The first is defined by the virtual machine and the second, invisible to the virtual machine, is controlled by the VMM.
- Given these two mappings, the physical CPU's page walker can walk the two sets of page tables to produce pairs that are cached in the TLB.
- This arrangement does away with shadow page tables at the cost of a single set of nested or extended page tables that map from physical address to machine address.
- Because the nested or extended page tables are largely static and need no update whenever the virtual machine creates or modifies page tables, the VMM need not interfere when virtual machine page tables are updated. Moreover, the VMM does not need to be involved in virtual machine context switches. The virtual machine can change the page table root on its own.
- Although RVI and EPT have compelling advantages, there is one potential downside : A TLB miss is now more expensive because it must be serviced by a two-level page walker.
- For most workloads, RVI or EPT provides an overall performance win over shadow page tables.
- For workloads that suffer frequent TLB misses or perform few context switches or page table updates RVI or EPT does not perform well.

Table 5.5 : Support RVI and EPT

	ESX 1.0-2.5	ESX 3.0	ESX 3.5	ESX 4.0
AMD	-	-	yes	yes
Intel	-	-	-	yes

5.7.5.3 Monitor Modes

- This subsection describes a two way choice between software and hardware techniques for instruction set virtualization (BT on one hand and AMD-V or VT-x on the other hand) and for memory virtualization (shadow page tables on one hand and RVI or EPT on the other hand).
- However the two forms of hardware support are not orthogonal. RVI is inseparable from AMD-V and EPT is inseparable from VT-x. This leaves only three valid combinations :
  a. BT(software) and MMU - binary translation and shadow page tables.
  b. HV(software) MMU –AMD-V or VT-x and shadow page tables.
  c. HV(hardware) MMU –AMD-V with RVI or VT-x with EPT.
  (HV stands for hardware support for instruction virtualization)
- Above three options are called as monitor modes because they describe the way the VMM runs a particular virtual machine on a given physical CPU.

Choice of Monitor Mode

- When a virtual machine is powering on, the VMM inspects the physical CPUs features and the guest operating system type to determine the set of possible execution modes.
- On ESX 3.0 and earlier only one monitor mode can be executed. Refer tables 5.2, 5.3, 5.4, 5.5.
- However from ESX 3.5, and especially with ESX 4.0, there are cases in which more than one execution mode is possible.
- In such a case VMM first finds the set of modes allowed. Then it restricts the allowed modes by configuration file settings. Finally, among the remaining sets, it chooses the "preferred" mode. The following examples illustrate the process :
  a. ESX 3.5 on an AMD CPU and a 64 bit virtual machine - The allowed modes are BT-(software) + MMU and HV-(hardware) + MMU (AMD-V with RVI). The preferred option for a 64 bit virtual machine is HV(hardware) + MMU, so the VMM chooses this mode at power on time.
  b. ESX 3.5 on an Intel Nehalem CPU and a 64 bit virtual machine - Run with HV(software) + MMU (because ESX 3.5 does not support EPT).
  c. ESX 4.0 on an AMD CPU and a 64-bit virtual machine - The choice is among BT-(software) + MMU, HV-(software) + MMU, and HV-(hardware) MMU. HV-(hardware) + MMU wins.

d. ESX 4.0 on an older Opteron CPU and a 64-bit virtual machine - Only one option is available : BT-(software) + MMU (because ESX cannot use AMD-V on this CPU).
   e. ESX 4.0 on an Intel Nehalem CPU and a 64-bit virtual machine - The allowed modes are HV-(software) + MMU and HV-(hardware) + MMU (BT is not allowed for 64-bit virtual machines on Intel CPUs because segment limit checks are missing). The VMM chooses HV-(hardware) + MMU.
- Certain features may restrict the available modes. For example, VMware Fault Tolerance cannot use RVI or EPT because of their lack of determinism, and it avoids BT, thus only choice left is HV-(software) + MMU.
- When multiple choices remain, a prioritization algorithm runs to choose the best mode :
   a. For ESX 3.5, the only case in which there is a choice is on AMD CPUs on which BT-(software) + MMU and HV-(hardware) + MMU might both be available. The default choice for 32-bit virtual machines is BT-(software) + MMU. For 64-bit virtual machines, it is HW-(hardware) + MMU.
   b. For ESX 4.0, many more situations can result in multiple allowable execution modes.
   c. The general priority for CPUs that have hardware support for APIC virtualization is : HV-(hardware) + MMU, followed by HV-(software) + MMU, followed by BT-(software) + MMU.
   d. For CPUs without hardware support for APIC virtualization, the order for 32-bit Windows guest operating systems is : HV-(hardware) + MMU, followed by BT-(software) + MMU, followed by HV-(software) + MMU.

Specifying the Preferred Monitor Mode
- In some cases, an explicit specification of monitor mode preference may be needed.
- Although this situation is rare, the complexity of workloads and virtual machine configurations makes a manual approach more desirable in cases in which the default choice leads to less than optimal performance.
- In virtual machine configuration files, we can restrict the set of modes by setting one or both of the following options :
monitor.virtual_mmu = software | hardware | automatic
monitor.virtual_exec = software | hardware | automatic
- Choose from software, hardware, or automatic can be made for each variable. Both ESX 3.5 and ESX 4.0 recognize the monitor.virtual_mmu setting. Only ESX 4.0 recognizes monitor.virtual_exec.
- We can express all possible ESX 3.5 mode choices with the monitor.virtual_mmu option alone.
- If a setting is not specified, the effect is the same as automatic. If it is set to hardware, it forces the use of the given form of hardware support if the feature is available and

supported. Likewise, if the setting is software, the VMM attempts to run the virtual machine without the given form of hardware support, if allowed.
- Although the configuration file settings are flexible enough to express all of the 2×2 possible combinations, only three of the four combinations are valid. Valid combinations are used to select one of the three execution modes.
- If the CPU does not support the requested execution mode, the settings are ignored. In addition, the settings are ignored if the CPU implements the execution mode but the version of ESX does not support it.

5.8 Installation and Configuration

- Xen is an open-source para-virtualizing virtual machine monitor (VMM), or "hypervisor", for a variety of processor architectures including x86. Xen can securely execute multiple virtual machines on a single physical system with near native performance.
- Xen can be used for
a. **Server Consolidation**
   Move multiple servers onto a single physical host with performance and fault isolation provided at the virtual machine boundaries.
b. **Hardware Independence**
   Allow legacy applications and operating systems to exploit new hardware.
c. **Multiple OS Configurations**
   Run multiple operating systems simultaneously, for development or testing purposes.
d. **Cluster Computing**
e. Management at VM granularity provides more flexibility than separately managing each physical host, but better control and isolation than single-system image solutions, particularly by using live migration for load balancing.
f. **Hardware Support for Custom OSes.**
   Allow development of new OSes while benefiting from the wide-ranging hardware support of existing OSes such as Linux.

5.8.1 Installation

- The Xen distribution includes three main components : Xen itself, ports of Linux and NetBSD to run on Xen, and the user-space tools required to manage a Xen-based system.
- The following is a full list of basic items. Items marked '†' are required by the xend control tools, and hence required if you want to run more than one virtual machine; items marked '*' are only required if you wish to build from source.
1. A working Linux distribution using the GRUB boot loader and running on a P6- class or newer CPU.

2. The iproute2 package.
3. The Linux bridge-utils1 (e.g., /sbin/brctl).
4. The Linux hotplug system2 (e.g., /sbin/hotplug and related scripts). On newer distributions, this is included alongside the Linux udev system3.
- All above mentioned tools are required by the xend control tools.
1. Build tools (gcc v3.2.x or v3.3.x, binutils, GNU make).
2. Development installation of zlib (e.g., zlib-dev).
3. Development installation of Python v2.2 or later (e.g., python-dev).
4. LaTex and transFig. are required to build the documentation.
- Above mentioned tools are required only if user wish to build virtual machine from source.
- Once these prerequisites are satisfied, it is possible to install either a binary or source distribution of Xen.

5.8.2 Installing from Binary Tarball

- Pre-built tarballs are available for download from the XenSource downloads page : http://www.xensource.com/downloads/
- Once user has downloaded the tarball, simply unpack and install :
  # tar zxvf xen-3.0-install.tgz
  # cd xen-3.0-install
  # sh ./install.sh
- Once the binaries are installed user need to configure your system.

5.8.3 Installing from RPMs

- Pre-built RPMs are available for download from the XenSource downloads page : http://www.xensource.com/downloads/
- Once user has downloaded the RPMs, he typically install them via the RPM commands :
  rpm -iv rpmname

5.8.4 Installing from Source

This part describes how to obtain, build and install Xen from source.

5.8.4.1 Obtaining the Source

- The Xen source tree is available as either a compressed source tarball or as a clone of master Mercurial repository.
- **Obtaining the Source Tarball**
  Stable versions and daily snapshots of the Xen source tree are available from the Xen download page :
  http://www.xensource.com/downloads/

- **Obtaining the Source via Mercurial**

    The source tree may also be obtained via the public Mercurial repository at : http://xenbits.xensource.com

5.8.4.2 Building from Source

The top-level Xen Makefile includes a target "world" that will perform following functionalities :

- Build Xen.
- Build the control tools, including xend.
- Download (if necessary) and unpack the Linux 2.6 source code, and patch it for use with Xen.
- Build a Linux kernel to use in domain 0 and a smaller unprivileged kernel, which can be used for unprivileged virtual machines.
- After the build has completed top-level directory is created called dist/ in which all resulting targets will be placed. Two XenLinux kernel images are very important one with a "-xen0" extension which contains hardware device drivers and drivers for Xen's virtual devices, and one with a "-xenU" extension that just contains the virtual ones.
- These are found in dist/install/boot/ along with the image for Xen itself and the configuration files used during the build.
- To customize the set of kernels built user needs to edit the top-level Makefile.

    KERNELS ?= linux-2.6-xen0 linux-2.6-xenU. This can be changed to include any set of operating system kernels which have configurations in the top-level buildconFig.s/ directory.

5.8.4.3 Custom Kernels

- If you wish to build a customized XenLinux kernel (e.g. to support additional devices or enable distribution-required features), you can use the standard Linux configuration mechanisms, specifying that the architecture being built for is xen, e.g :

    ```
    # cd linux-2.6.12-xen0
    # make ARCH=xen xconFig.
    # cd..
    # make
    ```

- It is also possible to copy an existing Linux configuration (.conFig.) into e.g. linux-2.6.12-xen0 and execute :

    ```
    # make ARCH=xen oldconFig.
    ```

- Only difference between the two types of Linux kernels that are built is the configuration file used for each. The "U" suffixed (unprivileged) versions don't contain any of the physical hardware device drivers, leading to a 30% reduction in size; hence you may prefer these for your non-privileged domains. The "0" suffixed privileged versions can be used to boot the system, as well as in driver domains and unprivileged domains.

5.8.4.4 Installing Generated Binaries

- The files produced by the build process are stored under the dist/install/ directory.
- To install them in their default locations, use the coomand :
  # make install
- Alternatively, users with special installation requirements may wish to install them manually by copying the files to their appropriate destinations.
- The dist/install/boot directory will also contain the conFig. files used for building the XenLinux kernels, and also versions of Xen and XenLinux kernels that contain debug symbols such as (xen-syms-3.0.0 and vmlinux-syms-2.6.12.6-xen0) which are essential for interpreting crash dumps.

5.8.5 Configuration

- Once you have built and installed the Xen distribution, it is simple to prepare the machine for booting and running Xen.

5.8.5.1 GRUB Configuration

- An entry should be added to grub.conf (often found under /boot/ or /boot/grub/) to allow Xen / XenLinux to boot. This file is sometimes called menu.lst, depending on your distribution. The entry should look something like the following :

  title Xen 3.0 / XenLinux 2.6

  kernel /boot/xen-3.0.gz dom0_mem=262144

  module /boot/vmlinuz-2.6-xen0 root=/dev/sda4 ro console=tty0

- The kernel line tells GRUB where to find Xen itself and what boot parameters should be passed to it (setting the domain 0 memory allocation in kilobytes and the settings for the serial port).
- The module line of the configuration describes the location of the XenLinux kernel that Xen should start and the parameters that should be passed to it. These are standard Linux parameters, identifying the root device and specifying it be initially mounted read only and instructing that console output be sent to the screen.
- When installing a new kernel, it is recommended that you do not delete existing menu options from menu.lst, as you may wish to boot your old Linux kernel in future, particularly if you have problems.

5.8.5.2 Serial Console

- Serial console access allows you to manage, monitor, and interact with your system.
- This can allow access from another nearby system via a null modem ("LapLink") cable or remotely via a serial concentrator.

- System's BIOS, bootloader (GRUB), Xen, Linux, and login access must each be individually conFig.ured for serial console access. It is not strictly necessary to have each component fully functional, but it can be quite useful.

a. Serial Console BIOS Configuration

- Enabling system serial console output neither enables nor disables serial capabilities in GRUB, Xen, or Linux, but may make remote management of your system more convenient by displaying POST and other boot messages over serial port and allowing remote BIOS configuration.
- It is advised to refer your hardware vendor's documentation for capabilities and procedures to enable BIOS serial redirection.

b. Serial Console GRUB Configuration

- Enabling GRUB serial console output neither enables nor disables Xen or Linux serial capabilities, but may made remote management of your system more convenient by displaying GRUB prompts, menus, and actions over serial port and allowing remote GRUB management.
- Adding the following two lines to your GRUB configuration file, typically either /boot/grub/menu.lst or /boot/grub/grub.conf will enable GRUB serial output.

  serial --unit=0 --speed=115200 --word=8 --parity=no --stop=1

  terminal --timeout=10 serial console
- Note that when both the serial port and the local monitor and keyboard are enabled, the text "Press any key to continue" will appear at both. Pressing a key on one device will cause GRUB to display to that device. The other device will see no output. If no key is pressed before the timeout period expires, the system will boot to the default GRUB boot entry.

5.8.5.3 Serial Console Xen Configuration

- Enabling Xen serial console output neither enables nor disables Linux kernel output or logging in to Linux over serial port. It does however allow you to monitor and log the Xen boot process via serial console and can be very useful in debugging.
- In order to conFig.ure Xen serial console output, it is necessary to add a boot option to your GRUB conFig.; e.g. kernel / boot / xen.gz dom0_mem = 131072 com1 = 115200, 8n1 console=com1,vga This conFig.ures Xen to output on COM1 at 115,200 baud, 8 data bits, no parity and 1 stop bit.
- It is also possible to conFig.ure XenLinux to share the serial console; to achieve this append "console=ttyS0" to your module line.

5.8.5.4 Serial Console Linux Configuration

- Enabling Linux serial console output at boot neither enables nor disables logging in to Linux over serial port. It does however allow you to monitor and log the Linux boot process via serial console and can be very useful in debugging.

- To enable Linux output at boot time, add the parameter console=ttyS0 (or ttyS1, ttyS2, etc.) to your kernel GRUB line. Under Xen, this might be :
  module /vmlinuz-2.6-xen0 ro root=/dev/VolGroup00/LogVol00 \
  console=ttyS0, 115200to enable output over ttyS0 at 115200 baud.

5.8.5.5 Serial Console Login Configuration

- Logging in to Linux via serial console, under Xen or otherwise, requires specifying a login prompt be started on the serial port. To permit root logins over serial console, the serial port must be added to /etc/securetty.
- To automatically start a login prompt over the serial port, add the line :
  c:2345:respawn:/sbin/mingetty ttyS0 to /etc/inittab. Run init q to force a reload of your inttab and start getty.
- To enable root logins, add ttyS0 to /etc/securetty if not already present.

5.8.5.6 TLS Libraries

- Users of the XenLinux kernel should disable Thread Local Storage (TLS) (e.g. by doing a mv /lib/tls /lib/tls.disabled) before attempting to boot a Xen- Linux kernel4.
- It is always possible to run TLS by restoring the directory to its original location (i.e. mv /lib/tls.disabled /lib/tls). The reason for this is that the current TLS implementation uses segmentation in a way that is not permissible under Xen. If TLS is not disabled, an emulation mode is used within Xen which reduces performance substantially. To ensure full performance you should install a 'Xen-friendly' (nosegneg) version of the library.

5.8.6 Booting Xen

- It should now be possible to restart the system and use Xen. Reboot and choose the new Xen option when the Grub screen appears.
- It should look much like a conventional Linux boot. The first portion of the output comes from Xen itself, supplying low level information about itself and the underlying hardware. The last portion of the output comes from XenLinux.
- You may see some error messages during the XenLinux boot. These are not necessarily anything to worry about—they may result from kernel configuration differences between your XenLinux kernel and the one you usually use.
- When the boot completes, you should be able to log into your system as usual. If you are unable to log in, you should still be able to reboot with your normal Linux kernel by selecting it at the GRUB prompt.
- Booting the system into Xen will bring you up into the privileged management domain, Domain0. At that point you are ready to create guest domains and "boot" them using the xm create command.

- The first step in creating a new domain is to prepare a root filevsystem for it to boot. Typically, this might be stored in a normal partition, an LVM or other volume manager partition, a disk file or on an NFS server.
- A simple way to do this is simply to boot from your standard OS install CD and install the distribution into another partition on your hard drive.
- To start the xend control daemon, type

  # xend start
- Once the daemon is running, you can use the xm tool to monitor and maintain the domains running on your system.

5.8.7 Booting Guest Domains

5.8.7.1 Creating a Domain Configuration File

- Before you can start an additional domain, you must create a configuration file.
- Two example files are provided here which you can use as a starting point :

  /etc/xen/xmexample1 is a simple template configuration file for describing a single VM.

  /etc/xen/xmexample2 file is a template description that is intended to be reused for multiple virtual machines.

  Setting the value of the vmid variable on the xm command line fills in parts of this template.
- Copy one of these files and edit it as appropriate. Typical values you may wish to edit include :

  kernel

  Set this to the path of the kernel you compiled for use with Xen

  (e.g. kernel ="/boot/vmlinuz-2.6-xenU").

  memory

  Set this to the size of the domain's memory in megabytes (e.g. memory = 64).

  disk

  Set the first entry in this list to calculate the offset of the domain's root partition, based on the domain ID. Set the second to the location of /usr if you are sharing it between domains (e.g. disk = ['phy:your hard drive%d,sda1,w' % (base partition number + vmid), 'phy:your usr partition,sda6,r'].

  dhcp

  Uncomment the dhcp variable, so that the domain will receive its IP address from a DHCP server (e.g. dhcp="dhcp").
- You may also want to edit the **vif** variable in order to choose the MAC address of the virtual ethernet interface yourself. For example: vif = ['mac=00:16:3E:F6:BB:B3'] If you do not set this variable, xend will automatically generate a random MAC address

from the range 00:16:3E:xx:xx:xx, assigned by IEEE to XenSource as an OUI (organizationally unique identifier). XenSource Inc. gives permission for anyone to use addresses randomly allocated from this range for use by their Xen domains.

5.8.7.2 Booting the Guest Domain

- The xm tool provides a variety of commands for managing domains. Use the create command to start new domains. Assuming you've created a configuration file myvmconf based around /etc/xen/xmexample2, to start a domain with virtual machine ID 1 you should type :
  # xm create -c myvmconf vmid=1
- The -c switch causes xm to turn into the domain's console after creation. The vmid=1 sets the vmid variable used in the myvmconf file.
- Now you should be able to see the console boot messages from the new domain appearing in the terminal in which you typed the command, culminating in a login prompt.

5.8.7.3 Starting / Stopping Domains Automatically

- It is possible to have certain domains start automatically at boot time and to have dom0 wait for all running domains to shutdown before it shuts down the system.
- To specify a domain is to start at boot-time, place its configuration file under /etc/xen/auto/.
- You can then enable it in the appropriate way for your distribution.
- For instance, on Red Hat :
  # chkconFig. --add xendomains.
- By default, this will start the boot-time domains in runlevels 3, 4 and 5. You can also use the service command to run this script manually, e.g :
  # service xendomains start- Starts all the domains with conFig. files under / etc / xen / auto/.
- # service xendomains stop - Shuts down all running Xen domains.

5.8.8 Domain Management Tools

5.8.8.1 Xend

- The Xend node control daemon performs system management functions related to virtual machines. It forms a central point of control of virtualized resources, and must be running in order to start and manage virtual machines.
- Xend must be run as root because it needs access to privileged system management functions. An initialization script named /etc/init.d/xend is provided to start Xend at boot time.
- Use the tool appropriate (i.e. chkconFig.) for your Linux distribution to specify the run levels at which this script should be executed, or manually create symbolic links in the correct run level directories.

- Xend can be started on the command line as well, and supports the following set of parameters :
  # xend start start xend, if not already running
  # xend stop stop xend if already running
  # xend restart restart xend if running, otherwise start it
  # xend status indicates xend status by its return code

  A SysV init script called xend is provided to start xend at boot time make install installs this script in /etc/init.d. To enable it, you have to make symbolic links in the appropriate run level directories or use the chkconFig. tool, where available. Refer Fig. 5.27.

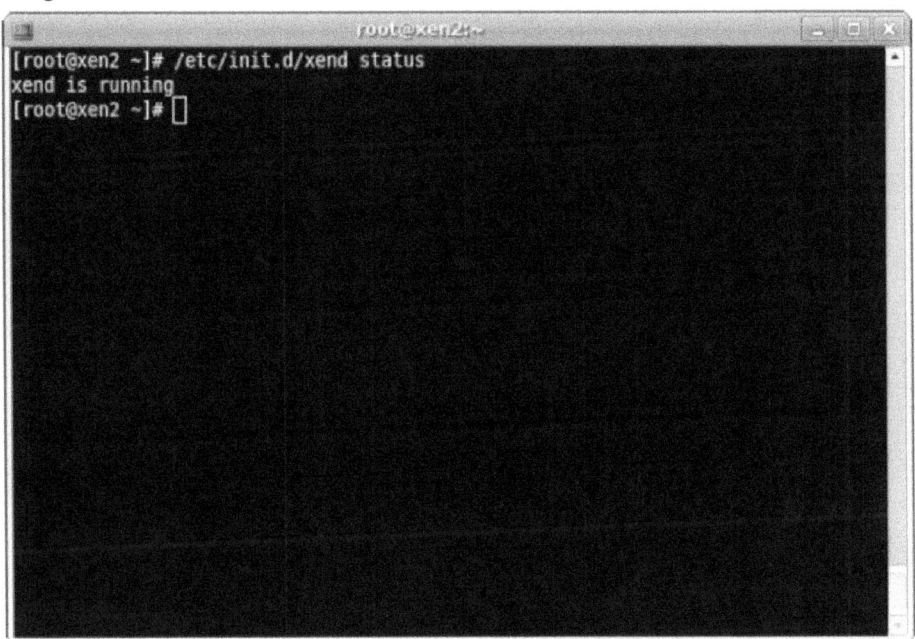

Fig. 5.27 : Status Message Showing Xend Is Running

- Once xend is running, administration can be done using the xm tool.
- As xend runs, events will be logged to /var/log/xen/xend.log and (less frequently) to /var/log/xen/xend-debug.log. These, along with the standard syslog files, are useful when troubleshooting problems.

5.8.8.2 ConFig.uring Xend

- Xend is written in Python. At startup, it reads its configuration information from the file /etc/xen/xend-conFig.sxp.
- The Xen installation places an example xend-conFig.sxp file in the /etc/xen subdirectory which should work for most installations.

- Some of the most important parameters are discussed below.
- An HTTP interface and a Unix domain socket API are available to communicate with Xend. This allows remote users to pass commands to the daemon. By default, Xend does not start an HTTP server. It does start a Unix domain socket management server, as the low level utility xm requires it.
- For support of cross-machine migration, Xend can start a relocation server. This support is not enabled by default for security reasons.
- Here important point to note that xend configuration file modifies the defaults and starts up Xend as an HTTP server as well as a relocation server.
- From the file :

  #(xend-http-server no)
  (xend-http-server yes)
  #(xend-unix-server yes)
  #(xend-relocation-server no)
  (xend-relocation-server yes)

  Comment or uncomment lines in that file to disable or enable features that you require.

  Connections from remote hosts are disabled by default :

- # Address xend should listen on for HTTP connections.
  # Specifying 'localhost' prevents remote connections.
  # Specifying the empty string " (the default) allows all connections.
  #(xend-address ")
  (xend-address localhost)
- It is recommended that if migration support is not needed, the xend-relocation-server parameter value be changed to "no".

5.8.8.3 Xm

- The xm tool is the primary tool for managing Xen from the console. The general format of an xm command line is :

  # xm command [switches] [arguments] [variables]

- The available switches and arguments are dependent on the command chosen. The variables may be set using declarations of the form variable=value and command line declarations override any of the values in the configuration file being used, including the standard variables described above and any custom variables (for instance, the xmdefconFig. file uses a vmid variable).

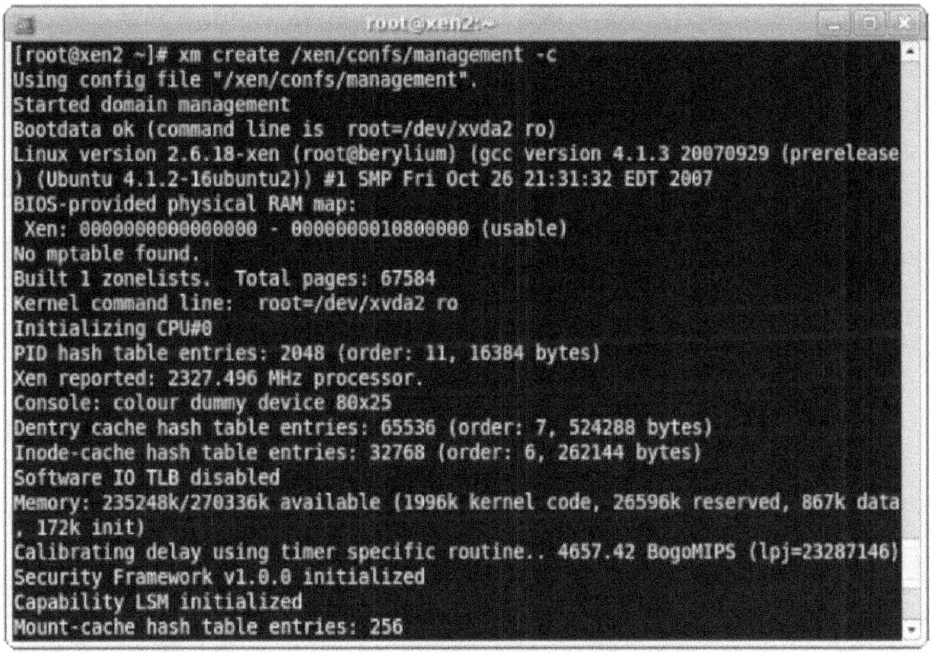

Fig. 5.28 : Xm Create Command

5.8.8.4 Basic Management Commands

- One useful command is # xm list which lists all domains running in rows of the following format :

    name domid memory vcpus state cputime

- The meaning of each field is as follows :

    name - The descriptive name of the virtual machine.

    domid - The number of the domain ID this virtual machine is running in.

    memory - Memory size in megabytes.

    vcpus - The number of virtual CPUs this domain has.

    state - Domain state consists of 5 fields :

    r - running

    b - blocked

    p - paused

    s - shutdown

    c - crashed

    cputime - How much CPU time (in seconds) the domain has used so far. Refer Fig. 5.29.

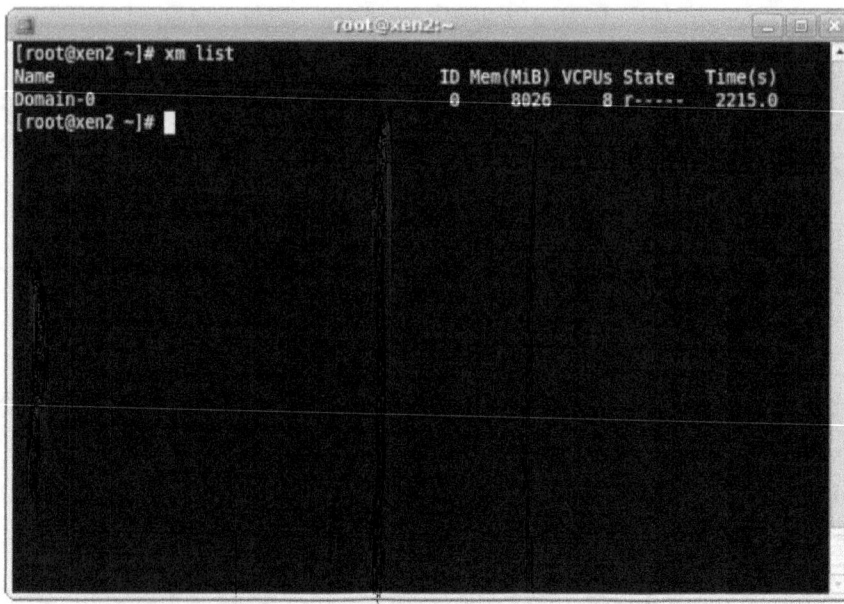

Fig. 5.29 : Xm List On A Machine With No Guest Running

- The xm list command also supports a long output format when the -1 switch is used. This outputs the full details of the running domains in xend's SXP configuration format. Refer Fig. 5.30.

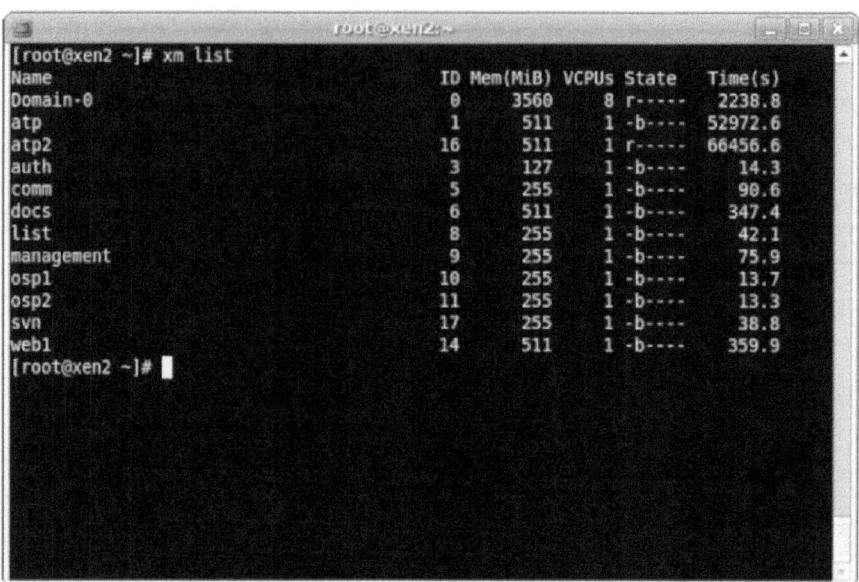

Fig. 5.30 : Xm List Showing Several Vms Running

- If you want to know how long your domains have been running for, then you can use the # xm uptime command.
- You can get access to the console of a particular domain using the # xm console command (e.g. # xm console myVM).

5.8.8.5 Domain Scheduling Management Commands

- The credit CPU scheduler automatically load balances guest VCPUs across all available physical CPUs on an SMP host. The user need not manually pin VCPUs to load balance the system. However, user can restrict which CPUs a particular VCPU may run on using the xm vcpu-pin command.
- Each guest domain is assigned a weight and a cap. A domain with a weight of 512 will get twice as much CPU as a domain with a weight of 256 on a contended host. Legal weights range from 1 to 65535 and the default is 256.
- The cap optionally fixes the maximum amount of CPU a guest will be able to consume, even if the host system has idle CPU cycles. The cap is expressed in percentage of one physical CPU : 100 is 1 physical CPU, 50 is half a CPU, 400 is 4 CPUs and so on. The default, 0, means there is no upper cap.
- When you are running with the credit scheduler, you can check and modify your domain's weights and caps using the xm sched-credit command :
  xm sched-credit -d <domain> lists weight and cap.
  xm sched-credit -d <domain> -w <weight> sets the weight.
  xm sched-credit -d <domain> -c <cap> sets the cap.

5.9 VIRTUAL MACHINE BOOTING AND CONFIGURATION

- Virtual machine configuration is the arrangement of resources assigned to a virtual machine. The resources allocated to a virtual machine (VM) typically include allocated processors, memory, disks, network adapters and the user interface.
- Before you can use virtualization, the virtualization packages must be installed on your computer. Virtualization packages can be installed either during the host installation sequence or after host installation using Subscription Manager.

- Many users install Virtualization Workstation on a dual-boot or multiple-boot computer so they can run one or more of the existing operating systems in a virtual machine. Sometimes you may want to use the existing installation of an operating system rather than reinstall it in a virtual machine.

- To support such installation virtual machine booting makes it possible for you to use a physical IDE disk or partition, also known as a raw disk, inside a virtual machine.

- You may sometimes want to run an operating system inside a virtual machine and at other times want to run that same installation of the operating system by booting the host computer directly into that operating system. If you want to use this approach, you must be aware of some special considerations.

- The issues arise because the virtual hardware that the operating system sees when it is running in a virtual machine is different from the physical hardware it sees when it is running directly on the host computer. It is as if you were removing the boot drive from one physical computer and running the operating system installed there in a second computer with a different motherboard, video card and other peripherals - then moving it back and forth between the two systems.

- The general approach for resolving these issues is to set up platforms for each of the two operating environments - the virtual machine and the physical computer. You can then choose the appropriate platform when you start the operating system. On some hardware, however, booting a previously installed operating system within a virtual machine may not work.

- Virtual machine uses description files to control access to each raw IDE device on the system. These description files contain access privilege information that controls a virtual machine's access to certain partitions on the disks. This mechanism prevents users from accidentally running the host operating system again as a guest or running a guest operating system that the virtual machine was not conFig.ured to use. The description file also prevents accidental corruption of raw disk partitions by badly behaved operating systems or applications.

- If a boot manager is installed on the computer system, the boot manager runs inside the virtual machine and presents you with the choice of guest operating systems to run. You must manually choose the guest operating system that this configuration was intended to run.

- If an operating system is installed directly into a virtual machine, the operating system properly detects all the virtual devices by scanning the hardware. However, if an operating system is already installed on the physical computer (for example, in a dual-boot configuration), the operating system already is conFig.ured to use the physical hardware devices. In order to boot such a preinstalled operating system in a virtual machine, you need to create separate hardware profiles in order to simplify the boot process.

5.9.1 Creating Up Hardware Profiles in Virtual Machines

- Certain operating systems use hardware profiles to load the appropriate drivers for a given set of hardware devices. If you have a dual-boot system and want to use a virtual machine to boot a previously installed operating system from an existing partition, you must set up "physical" and "virtual" hardware profiles.
- Each virtual machine provides a platform that consists of the following set of virtual devices :
- Virtual DVD/CD-ROM
- Virtual hard disk drives
- Standard PCI graphics adapter
- Standard floppy disk drive
- PCI Bus Master IDE controller
  (includes primary and secondary IDE controllers)
- BusLogic BT-958 compatible SCSI host adapter
- Standard 101/102-key keyboard
- Mouse
- Ethernet adapter
- Serial ports (COM1-COM4)
- Parallel ports (LPT1-LPT2)
- Two-port USB hub
- Sound card compatible with the Sound Blaster AudioPCI

- This set of virtual devices is different from the set of physical hardware devices on the host computer and is independent of the underlying hardware with a few exceptions (the processor itself is such an exception).
- This feature provides a stable platform and allows operating system images installed within a virtual machine to be migrated to other physical machines, regardless of the configuration of the physical machine.

Questions

1. Explain functionalities provided by Virtualization.
2. Explain difference between multitasking, multithreading and virtualization.
3. Explain XEN Architecture with suitable diagram.
4. Write short note on :
   (a) Virtual machines
   (b) Hypervisor
   (c) Virtual machine monitor
5. Why virtual servers are used ? State its advantages and disadvantages ?
6. State types of virtualization and explain any three of them.
7. Explain Need, Advantages and Limitations of virtualization.
8. What is XEN ? What are the components of XEN Environment ?
9. Explain software and hardware techniques for X86 virtualization.

UNIT - VI
CLOUD, MOBILE COMPUTING AND CUDA PRINCIPLES

6.1 Introduction to Cloud Computing

- Cloud computing is a computing area, where a large pool of systems (resources) are connected in private or public networks, to provide dynamically scalable infrastructure for application, data and file storage.
- With the advancements in this technology, the cost of computation, application hosting, content storage, sharing and delivery is reduced significantly.
- Cloud computing is a practical approach to experience direct cost benefits and data can be accessed from any part of the world.

  The idea of cloud computing is based on a very fundamental principal of "reusability of IT capabilities".
- Cloud Computing is built on top of several other technologies, for example : Distributed Computing, Grid Computing, and Utility Computing.
- Grid computing provides a virtual pool of computation resources it uses several computers in parallel to solve a particular, individual problem, or to run a specific application.
- Cloud computing, on the other hand, uses multiple resources, including computing resources, to provide a required "service" to the user.
- Cloud computing provides on-demand services such as computing, storage, and Software "as a service."
- The cloud can be both software and infrastructure. It can be an application you access through the Web or a server like Gmail and it can be also an IT infrastructure that can be used as per user's request. Whether a service is software or hardware, the following is a simple test to determine whether that service is a cloud service :
- If you can walk into any place and sit down at any computer without preference for operating system or browser and access a service, that service is cloud-based.
- Generally, there are three measures used to decide whether a particular service is a cloud service or not :
  1. The service is accessible via a web browser or web services API.

2. Zero capital expenditure is necessary to get started.
3. You pay only for what you use.
- Cloud computing is a pay-per-use model for allowing convenient, on-demand network access to a shared pool of computing resources like networks, servers, storage, applications, services.

6.1.1 Services Provided by Cloud Computing

(a) Infrastructure as a Service (IaaS)
- It provides virtualized resources computation, storage, and communication on demand.
- Amazon Web Services mainly offers IaaS.
- Its EC2 service offers Virtual Machines with a software stack that can be modified to a normal physical server which could be customized.
- Users are allowed to perform various activities on the server, such as : starting and stopping it, modifying it by installing software packages, connecting virtual disks to it, and by deciding access permissions and firewalls rules.

(b) Platforms as a Service (PaaS)
- A cloud can be easily programmed when using Platform as a Service.
- A cloud platform offers an environment on which developers create and deploy applications and without having knowledge of many processors are used or how much memory that applications will be using.
- Google AppEngine is an example of Platform as a Service. It allows for developing and hosting Web applications in an environment which is scalable.
- Applications are written using programming languages such as Python or Java, and use the services' own proprietary structured object data store.
- Building blocks contain mail service, instant messaging service (XMPP), an image manipulation service.

(c) Software as a Service(SaaS)
- Applications are located on the top of the cloud stack.
- End users use web portals to access services provided by these layers.
- Therefore, consumers are more interested in using on-line software services than locally installed computer programs.
- Desktop applications such as Word and Excel are accessed as a service in the Web.

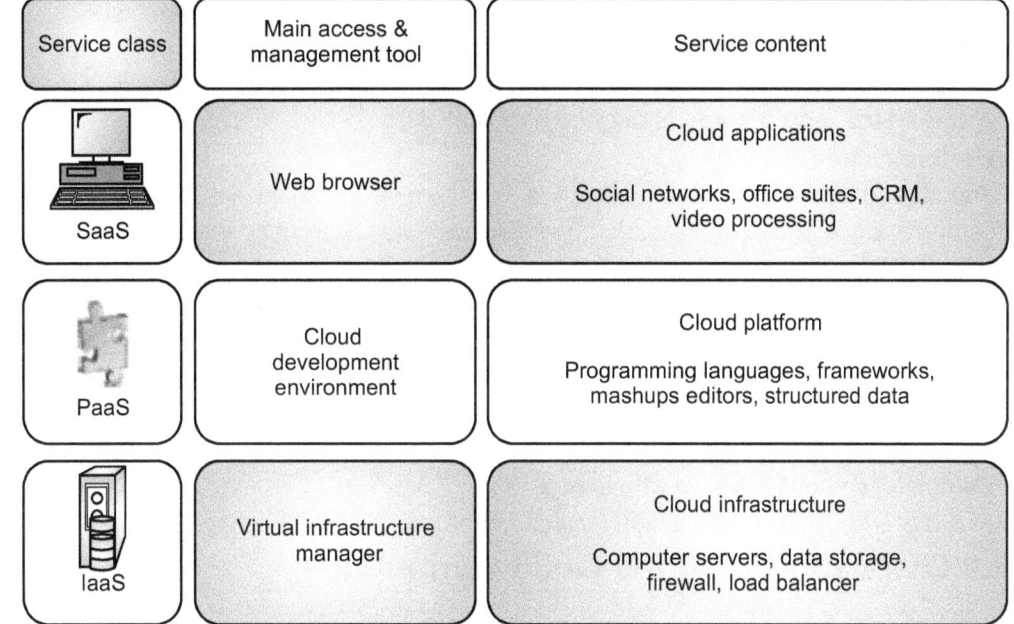

Fig. 6.1 : Services Provided by Cloud Computing

- Salesforce.com, which uses the SaaS model, provides business productivity applications (CRM) that exist totally on their servers, which let customers to change and use applications whenever needed.
- SaaS systems have some defining characteristics :

1. Availability Via Web Browser

SaaS software never requires the installation of software on your laptop or desktop. Refer Fig. 6.2.

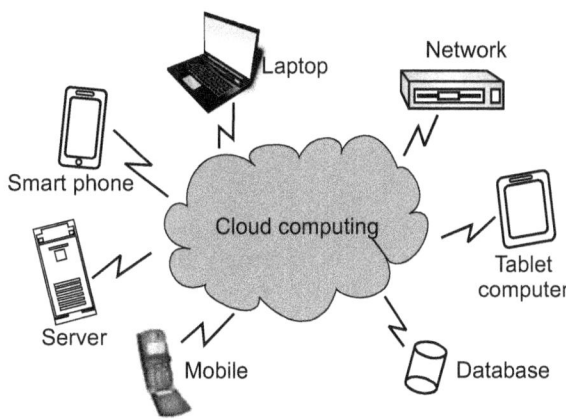

Fig. 6.2 : Cloud Computing – Availability of Accessing Devices

You access it through a web browser using open standards or a browser plug-in. That means application, resources or data files can be accessed independent of any operating system any hardware platform. Only need is that the device from which you are using accessing the service supports the web browser.

2. **On-Demand Availability**

   You should not have to go through a sales process to gain access to SaaS based software. Once you have access, you should be able to go back into the software any time, from anywhere.

3. **Pay per use Policy**

   SaaS does not need any infrastructure investment or complex setup, so you should not have to pay any huge cost for set up purpose. You should simply pay for the parts of the service you use as you use them. When you no longer need those services, you simply stop paying.

4. **Minimal Need of Technical Knowledge**

   SaaS systems don't require a high technical knowledge for their configuration.

6.1.2 Characteristics of the Cloud Computing

Following are some essential characteristics of cloud computing :

1. **On-Demand Self-Service**

   A service consumer accessing the servicing can automatically make use of the computing capabilities, such as server processing time and network storage without requiring human interaction with each service's provider.

2. **Broad Network Access**

   Cloud capabilities, both hardware and software are available over the network and accessed through various devices such as mobile phones, laptops, and tablets. Only the need is that these devices must web browser.

3. **Resource Pooling**

   The provider's computing resources (HW and SW) are pooled to serve multiple consumers using a multi-tenant model, with different physical and virtual resources dynamically assigned and reassigned according to user's demand. Multi-tenancy is the most important feature of the cloud-based application. It is characterized by the location independence feature in which the customer has no control or knowledge over the exact location of the provided resources but may be able to specify location at a higher level of abstraction (e.g., country, state, or datacenter). Examples of resources include storage, processing, memory, network bandwidth, and virtual machines.

4. **Rapid Flexibility**

   Capabilities can be rapidly and elastically provisioned; it can be quickly scaled out, and quickly scaled in. For the user, the capabilities available for provisioning appear to be unlimited and can be purchased in any quantity at any time.

5. **Monitoring Service**

   Cloud systems automatically control and optimize use by using a metering ability in which resources' usage can be monitored, controlled, and reported, providing transparency for both the provider and consumer who is utilizing the service. The advantage here is that you are paying for exactly what you are using.

6.1.3 Understanding Public and Private Clouds

- Enterprises can deploy the applications developed in their premises on Public, Private or Hybrid clouds. Cloud Integrators can play a vital part in determining the right cloud path for each organization.

Public Cloud

- Public clouds are owned and operated by third parties; they deliver superior economies of scale to customers, as the infrastructure costs are spread among a mix of users, giving each individual client an attractive low-cost, "Pay per Use" model.
- All customers share the same infrastructure pool with limited configuration, security protections, and availability variances. These are managed and supported by the cloud provider.
- One of the advantages of a Public cloud is that they may be larger than an enterprises cloud, thus providing the ability to scale seamlessly, on demand.
- Disadvantages of public cloud are less data security and lack of control.

Private Cloud

- Private clouds are built exclusively for a single enterprise. They aim to address concerns on data security and offer greater control, which is typically lacking in a public cloud.
- There are two variations to a private cloud :

On-Premise Private Cloud

- On-premise private clouds, also known as internal clouds are hosted within one's own data center. This model provides a more standardized process and protection, but is limited in aspects of size and scalability.
- IT departments would also need to sustain the capital and operational costs for the physical resources. This is best suited for applications which require complete control and configurability of the infrastructure and security.

Externally Hosted Private Cloud

- This type of private cloud is hosted externally with a cloud provider, where the provider facilitates an exclusive cloud environment with full guarantee of privacy.
- This is best suited for enterprises that don't like a public cloud due to sharing of physical resources.

Hybrid Cloud
- Hybrid Clouds combine both public and private cloud models.
- With a Hybrid Cloud, service providers can utilize third party Cloud Providers in a full or partial manner thus increasing the flexibility of computing. The Hybrid cloud environment is capable of providing on-demand, externally provisioned scale.
- The ability to expand a private cloud with the resources of a public cloud can be used to manage any unexpected surges in workload.

6.1.4 Cloud Computing Benefits

Cloud computing offers number of benefits to the enterprise and individual. Some of the typical benefits are listed below :

1. Increased Scalability
- An enterprise can rapidly and elastically provide services, in some cases automatically, to quickly "scale up" their computing capabilities, and rapidly release those services to quickly "scale in."
- To the enterprise, the capabilities available for provisioning often appear to be unlimited and can be purchased in any quantity at any time.

2. On-Demand Self-Service
- Enterprises can provide computing capabilities, such as server time and network storage, as needed automatically without requiring human intervention by the cloud service provider (CSP).

3. Energy Efficiency
- IT organizations usually have large data centers and server farms, which require energy 24/7 to power and cool the servers. Data centers typically have large carbon outcomes due to their enormous energy consumption and have to comply with strict environmental controls.
- Cloud computing can be viewed as the green computing option, as it has a much smaller carbon footprint by limiting redundant systems and using computing power more efficiently.

4. Resource Pooling
- The provider's computing resources (storage, processing power, memory etc.) are pooled to serve multiple agencies using a "multi-tenant" model.
- For example, resources that belong to different agencies may co-exist on the same physical device and the resources of one agency may be spread across multiple physical devices.
- Cloud service providers dynamically assign and reassign resources according to user's demands, which are more cost-effective and enable them to charge lower fees.

5. **Metered Service**

   CSPs automatically control, optimize, and meter the use of their computing resources such as, storage, processing power, bandwidth, and active user accounts. They monitor, control, report, and bill the resources that the agency uses.

6. **Universal Access**

   Organization staff can acquire, access, and configure their cloud services over the Internet from any place and at any time. Cloud services are flexible enough to enable staff members to use the device of their choice such as a desktop, laptop, or mobile device.

7. **Cost Savings and Cost Avoidance**

   Organizations only pay for the computing capabilities they use. In addition, cloud computing allows for less capital expenditure: instead of an agency purchasing and maintaining the infrastructure for their computing needs, a third party provides and maintains the infrastructure.

8. **Disaster Recovery**

   Data replication is instant and automatic so you don't need to worry about losing data. Furthermore, the start-up after a system failure is almost instantaneous, enabling you to rise up your processing power and get your system back up as quickly as possible.

9. **Mobile Impact**

   Cloud computing has added a whole new functionality to mobile devices. Mobile applications can now take advantage of cloud-based processing and data storage, making mobile devices significantly more functional.

10. **Faster Deployment**

    Cloud computing allows organizations to get their applications up and running more quickly due to improved manageability and lower maintenance requirements. Additionally, organization IT departments have more flexibility to rapidly adjust resources with fluctuating demands.

11. **Easier Collaboration**

    Cloud computing enables organizations to store documents in a central and virtual location where multiple users can access and edit them. This allows for real time collaboration on documents, a tool that was not possible before. Cloud computing also facilitates collaboration by enabling agency staff to share multimedia files, have online discussions, and subscribe to dynamic content.

12. **Reduced IT Infrastructure Total Cost of Ownership**

    Organizations can take advantage of commodity cloud computing services (common low-cost hardware and software solutions deployed in the cloud) to reduce the total cost of ownership of IT infrastructure and services.

6.1.5 Cloud Computing Challenges

In spite of growing influence of cloud computing technology, concerns regarding cloud computing still remain. Some common challenges are :

1. **Data Protection**
   - Data Security is a crucial element that warrants scrutiny. Enterprises are reluctant to buy an assurance of business data security from vendors. They fear losing data to competition and the data confidentiality of consumers.
   - In many instances, the actual storage location is not disclosed, adding onto the security concerns of enterprises.
   - In the existing models, firewalls across data centers (owned by enterprises) protect this sensitive information. In the cloud model, Service providers are responsible for maintaining data security and enterprises would have to rely on them.

2. **Data Recovery and Availability**
   - All business applications have Service level agreements that are rigorously followed. Operational teams play a key role in management of service level agreements and runtime governance of applications.
   - In production environments, operational teams support
   1. Appropriate clustering and Fail over.
   2. Data Replication.
   3. System monitoring (Transactions monitoring, logs monitoring and others).
   4. Maintenance (Runtime Governance).
   5. Disaster recovery.
   6. Capacity and performance management.
   - If, any of the above mentioned services is under-served by a cloud provider, the damage and impact could be severe.

3. **Management Capabilities**
   - Although there being multiple cloud providers, the management of platform and infrastructure is still in its immaturity. Features like "Auto-scaling" for example, is a crucial requirement for many enterprises. There is huge potential to improve on the scalability and load balancing features provided today.

4. **Regulatory and Compliance Restrictions**
   - In some of the European countries, Government regulations do not allow customer's personal information and other sensitive information to be physically located outside the state or country.
   - In order to meet such requirements, cloud providers need to setup a data center or a storage site exclusively within the country to comply with regulations. Having such an infrastructure may not always be feasible and is a big challenge for cloud providers.

- With cloud computing, the action moves to the interface, that is, to the interface between service suppliers and multiple groups of service consumers. Cloud services will demand expertise in distributed services, procurement, risk assessment and service negotiation areas that many enterprises are only moderately equipped to handle.

6.2 Introduction to Mobile Computing

- In simple terms Mobile computation is the process of computation on a mobile device. Mobile computing refers to computing systems that are movable and its computing facilities can be used while they are being moved.
- Mobile computing is the ability to use the technology to wirelessly connect to and use centrally located information and/or application software through the application of small, portable, and wireless computing and communication devices.
- In mobile computing, a set of distributed computing systems or service provider servers participate, connect, and synchronize through mobile communication protocols.
- Mobile computing provides decentralized (distributed) computations on number of heterogeneous devices, systems, and networks, which are mobile, synchronized, and interconnected via mobile communication standards and protocols.
- Mobile device does not restrict itself to just one application, such as, voice communication.
- Mobile computing basically offers mobility with computing power and also facilitates a large number of applications on a single device.
- Mobile computing is the discipline for creating an information management platform, which is free from spatial and temporal constraints. The freedom from these constraints allows its users to access and process desired information from anywhere in the space. The state of the user, static or mobile, does not affect the information management capability of the mobile platform.
- A user can continue to access and manipulate desired data while traveling on plane, in car, on ship, etc. Thus, the discipline creates an illusion that the desired data and sufficient processing power are available on the spot, whereas in reality they may be located far away.
- The discipline of mobile computing has its origin in Personal Communications Services (PCS). PCS refers to a wide variety of wireless access and personal mobility services provided through a small terminal (e.g., cell phone), with the goal of enabling communications at any time, at any place, and in any form. PCS are connected to Public Switched Telephone Network (PSTN) to provide access to wired

- telephones. PCS include digital cellular systems and telecommunication system standards for residential, business, and public cordless access applications.
- In mobile computing platform information between processing units flows through wireless channels. The processing units (client in client/server paradigm) are free from temporal and spatial constraints. That is, a processing unit (client) is free to move about in the space while being connected to the server. This temporal and spatial freedom provides a powerful facility allowing users to reach the data site (site where the desired data is stored) and the processing site (the geographical location where a processing must be performed) from anywhere. This capability allows organizations to set their offices at any location.
- Mobile Computing is a technology that allows transmission of data, voice and video via a computer or any other wireless enabled device without having to be connected to a fixed physical link.

6.2.1 Basic Components of Mobile Computing System

- Following are the basic components of Mobile Computing System :
    1. Mobile communication
    2. Mobile hardware
    3. Mobile software

Mobile Communication

- The mobile communication in this case, refers to the infrastructure put in place to ensure that seamless and reliable communication. These would include entities such as Protocols, Services, Bandwidth, and Portals necessary to facilitate and support of the stated services. The data format is also defined at this stage. This ensures that there is no collision with other existing systems which offer the same service.
- Since the media is unguided/ unbounded, the overlaying infrastructure is more of radio wave oriented. That is, the signals are carried over the air to intended devices that are capable of receiving and sending similar kinds of signals.

Mobile Hardware

- Mobile hardware includes mobile devices or device components that receive or access the service of mobility. They would range from Portable laptops, Smart phones, Tablet PC's, Personal Digital Assistants.
- These devices will have receptor medium that are capable of sensing and receiving signals. These devices are configured to operate in full-duplex, whereby they are capable of sending and receiving signals at the same time. They don't have to wait until one device has finished communicating for the other device to initiate communications.
- Above mentioned devices use an existing and established network to operate on. In most cases, it is a wireless network.

Mobile Software
- Mobile software is the actual program that runs on the mobile hardware. It deals with the characteristics and requirements of mobile applications. This is the engine of the mobile device. In other terms, it is the operating system of that appliance. It is the essential component that makes the mobile device operate.
- Since portability is the main factor, this type of computing ensures that users are not tied or pinned to a single physical location, but are able to operate from anywhere. It will incorporate all aspects of wireless communications.

6.2.2 Mobile Computing Current Trends
- In today's computing world, different technologies are emerging rapidly. These have grown to support existing computer networks all over the world.
- With mobile computing, we find that the need to be confined within one physical location has been eliminated. We hear of terms such as tele-communication, pervasive computing, and ubiquitous computing.
- All these technologies let the people to work from home or any location but at the same time accessing resources as if one is in the office.
- The emergence of portable computers and laptops, Personal Digital Assistants (PDA), PC Tablets and Smart phones, has in turn made mobile computing very convenient.
- The portability of the devices ensures and enables user to access all services as if they were in the internal network of their company. This new technology enables users to update documents, surf the internet, send and receive e-mail, stream live video files, take photographs and also support video and voice conferencing.
- The constant and ever increasing demand for superior and robust smart devices has been as a mechanism for market share. Each manufacturer is trying to create a well reputation in the market. These devices are invented and innovated to provide top of the class applications and services.
- With cellular phones, different manufacturers have come up with unique Smart phones that are capable of performing the same tasks as computers and at the same processing speed. The market share for different competitors is constantly being fought for. For example the manufacturers of Apple's I phone OS, Google's Android', Microsoft Windows Mobile, Research In Motion's Blackberry OS, are constantly competing to offer better products with each release.
- The need for better, portable, affordable, and robust mobile devices has also made these vendors to constantly be innovative. Market figure and statistics show an ever rapidly growing need to purchase and use such devices for either professional or home use.

- Since technology is driven by market needs, it's in this light that services suited for a long term implementation are developed or innovated. This has also pushed other industry vendors to adopt services that will provide better service delivery. For example, cellular service providers are forced to improve and be innovative to capture more subscribers. This can be in terms of superior services such as high speed internet and data access, voice and video service etc. hence the adoption of different generations of networks like of 2G, 2.5G, 3G, 4G networks services.
- The essence of mobile computing is to work from any location. The use of I pads, Tablets, Smart phones, and notes books, have in turn pushed the demand for these devices.
- Modern day workers have such devices that enable them carry out their work from the confines or comfort of their present location. These devices are configured to access and store large amounts of vital data. Executive and top management can act of decisions based on ready information without going to the office. For example, sales reports and market forecasts can be accessed through this devices or meeting carried out via video or audio conferencing through the device. With such features being high in demand, manufacturers are always and constantly coming up with applications geared to supporting different service delivery in terms of mobile computing.

6.2.3 Mobile Computing Classification

- Mobile computing is not limited to Mobile Phones only, but also there are various gadgets available in the market helping mobile computing. They are usually classified in the following categories :

1. **Personal Digital Assistant (PDA)**
- The main purpose of this device was to act as an electronic organizer or day planner that is portable, easy to use and capable of sharing information with your computer systems.
- PDA was an extension of the PC, not a replacement. These systems were capable of sharing information with a computer system through a process or service known as synchronization. Where both devices will access each other to check for changes or updates in the individual devices. The use of infrared and Bluetooth connections enabled these devices to always be synchronized.
- With PDA devices, a user could; browsers the internet, listen to audio clips, watch video clips, edit and modify office documents, and many more services. They had a stylus and a touch sensitive screen for input and output purposes.

2. **Smart Phones**
- This kind of phone combines the features of a PDA with that of a mobile phone or camera phone. It has a superior edge over other kinds of mobile phones.

- Smart phone have the capability to run multiple programs concurrently. These phones include high-resolution touch enabled screens, web browsers that can access and properly display standard web pages rather than just mobile-optimized sites, and high-speed data access via Wi-Fi and high speed cellular broadband.
- The most common mobile operating systems (OS) used by modern smart phones include Google's Android, Apple's iOS, BlackBerry OS, Microsoft's Windows Phone, and embedded Linux distributions such as Maemo and MeeGo. Such operating systems can be installed on many different phone models, and typically each device can receive multiple OS software updates over its lifetime.

3. **Tablet PC and I Pads**
- This mobile device is larger than a mobile phone or a Personal Digital Assistant and integrates into a touch screen and operated using touch sensitive motions on the screen. They are often controlled by a pen or touch of a finger. They are usually in slate form and are light in weight. Examples would include; I pads, Galaxy Tabs, Blackberry Playbooks etc.
- They offer the same functionality as portable computers. They support mobile computing to a far superior way and have enormous processing horse power. User can edit and modify document files, access high speed internet, stream video and audio data, receive and send e-mails, perform lectures and presentations among very many other functions. They have excellent screen resolution and clarity.

6.2.4 Mobile Computing Major Advantages

Mobile computing has drastically changed the human being life. Following are the clear advantages of Mobile Computing :

1. **Location Flexibility**
- This has enabled user to work from anywhere as long as there is a connection established.
- A user can work without being in a fixed position. Their mobility ensures that they are able to carry out numerous tasks at the same time perform their stated jobs.

2. **Saves Time**
- The time consumed or wasted by travelling from different locations or to the office and back, have been slashed. One can now access all the important documents and files over a secure channel or portal and work as if they were on their computer.
- It has enhanced telecommunicating in many companies. This also reduces unnecessary expenses that might be incurred.

3. **Enhanced Productivity**
- Productive nature has been boosted by the fact that a worker can simply work efficiently and effectively from whichever location they see comfortable and suitable.
- Users are able to work with comfortable environments.

4. Ease of Research
- Research has been made easier, since users will go to the field and search for facts and feed them back to the system.
- It has also made it easier for field officer and researchers to collect and feed data from wherever they without making unnecessary trip to and from the office to the field.

5. Entertainment
- Video and audio recordings can now be streamed on the go using mobile computing.
- It is easy to access a wide variety of movies, educational and informative material. With the improvement and availability of high speed data connections at considerable costs, one is able to get all the entertainment they want as they browser the internet for streamed data.
- One can be able to watch news, movies, and documentaries among other entertainment offers over the internet. This was not such before mobile computing dawned on the computing world.

6. Streamlining of Business Processes
- Business processes are now easily available through secured connections. Basing on the factor of security, adequate measures have been put in place to ensure authentication and authorization of the user accessing those services.
- Some business functions can be run over secure links and also the sharing of information between business partners. Also it's worth noting that lengthy travelling has been reduced, since there is the use of voice and video conferencing.
- Meetings, seminars and other informative services can be conducted using the video and voice conferencing. This cuts down on travel time and expenditure.
- Being an ever growing and emerging technology, mobile computing will continue to be a core service in computing and Information Communication and Technology.

6.2.5 Mobile Computing Security Issues

- Mobile computing has its fair share of security concerns as any other technology. Due to their roaming nature, it is not easy to monitor the proper usage. User might have different intentions on how to utilize this privilege. Improper and unethical practices such as hacking, industrial espionage, pirating, online fraud and malicious destruction are some but few of the problems experienced by mobile computing.
- Another big problem that infected mobile computing is credential verification. It is not possible to that the person using that person is the true barrier. Other users share username and passwords. This is also a major threat to security. This being a very sensitive issue, most companies are very reluctant to implement mobile computing to the dangers of misrepresentation.

- The problem of identity theft is very difficult to contain or destroy. Issues with unauthorized access to data and information by hackers, is also a major problem. They gain access to steal vital data from companies. This problem has been a major headache and hindrance in rolling out mobile computing services.
- No company wants to lay open their secrets to hacker and other intruders, who will in terms, sell them to their competitors. It is also important to take the necessary precautions to minimize these threats from taking place. Some of those measures include :

1. Hiring qualified personnel.
2. Installing Security Hardware and Software.
3. Educating the Users on proper Mobile computing ethics.
4. Auditing and developing sound, effective policies to govern mobile computing.
5. Enforcing proper access rights and permissions.

These are just few ways to determine possible threats to any company planning to offer mobile computing. Since information is vital, all possible measures should be evaluated and implemented for safeguard purposes.

- In the absence of such measures, it is possible for exploits and other unknown threats to infiltrate and cause irrefutable harm that would cost a huge of damage. These may be in terms of reputation or financial penalties. In such cases, it is very easy to be misused in different unethical practices.
- The other issue would be online security. If this factor is not properly worked on, it might be an avenue for constant threat. Theft and Espionage can be also another fact limiting its full utilization. Various threats to security still exist in implementing this kind of technology.

6.2.6 Mobile Computing Future Trends

- This subsection enlists the current and future mobile technologies starting from 3G technologies which is the hottest mobile technology available in the market.

1. **3G**
- 3G or third generation mobile telecommunication is a generation of standards for mobile phones and mobile telecommunication services fulfilling the International Mobile Telecommunications-2000 (IMT-2000) specifications by the International Telecommunication Union (ITU).
- Application services include wide-area wireless voice telephone, mobile Internet access, video calls and mobile TV, all in a mobile environment.

2. **GPS (Global Positioning System)**
- The Global Positioning System (GPS) is a space-based satellite navigation system that provides location and time information in all weather, anywhere on or near the Earth, where there is an unobstructed line of sight to four or more GPS satellites.

- The GPS program provides critical capabilities to military, civil and commercial users around the world. In addition, GPS is the backbone for modernizing the global air traffic system, weather, location services.

3. **Long Term Evolution (LTE)**
- LTE is a standard for wireless communication of high-speed data for mobile phones and data terminals. It is based on the GSM/EDGE and UMTS/HSPA network technologies, increasing the capacity and speed using new modulation techniques. Its related with the implementation of forth Generation (4G) technology.

4. **WiMax**
- WiMAX (Worldwide Interoperability for Microwave Access) is a wireless communications standard designed to provide 30 to 40 megabit-per-second data rates, with the latest update providing up to 1 Gbit/s for fixed stations. It is a part of a fourth generation, or 4G of wireless-communication technology.
- WiMax surpasses the 30 metres wireless range of a conventional Wi-Fi local area network (LAN), offering a metropolitan area network with a signal radius of about 50 km.
- WiMax offers data-transfer rates that can be superior to conventional cable-modem and DSL connections, however, the bandwidth must be shared among multiple users and thus yields lower speeds in practice.

5. **Near Field Communication**
- Near Field Communication (NFC) is a set of standards for Smart phones and similar devices to establish radio communication with each other by touching them together or bringing them into close proximity, usually no more than a few centimeters.
- Present and anticipated applications include contactless transactions, data exchange, and simplified setup of more complex communications such as Wi-Fi. Communication is also possible between an NFC device and an unpowered NFC chip, called a "tag".

6.2.7 Limitations of Mobile Computing

- There are some general limitations for mobile computing devices. They are described in brief as follow :

1. **Insufficient Bandwidth**

Mobile Internet access is generally slower than direct cable connections, using technologies such as GPRS and EDGE, and more recently HSDPA and HSUPA 3G networks. These networks are usually available within range of commercial cell phone towers. Higher speed wireless LANs are inexpensive but have very limited range.

2. **Security Standards**

   When working mobile, one is dependent on public networks, requiring careful use of VPN. Security is a major concern while concerning the mobile computing standards. One can easily attack the VPN through a huge number of networks interconnected through the line.

3. **Power Consumption**

   When a power outlet or portable generator is not available, mobile computers must rely entirely on battery power. Combined with the compact size of many mobile devices, this often means unusually expensive batteries must be used to obtain the necessary battery life.

4. **Transmission Interferences**

   Weather, ground, and the range from the nearest signal point can all interfere with signal reception. Reception in tunnels, some buildings, and rural areas is often poor.

5. **Potential Health Hazards**

   People who use mobile devices while driving are often distracted from driving and are thus assumed more likely to be involved in traffic accidents. While this may seem obvious, there is considerable discussion about whether banning mobile device use while driving reduces accidents or not.

   Cell phones may interfere with sensitive medical devices. Questions concerning mobile phone radiation and health have been raised.

6. **Human Interface with Device**

   Screens and keyboards tend to be small, which may make them hard to use. Alternate input methods such as speech or handwriting recognition require training.

6.3 CUDA BLOCKS AND THREADS

6.3.1 Introduction to CUDA

Compute Unified Device Architecture (CUDA) is a scalable parallel programming model and a software environment for parallel computing.

- CUDA is parallel computing platform and programming model invented by NVIDIA.
- It enables drastic increases in computing performance by utilizing the power of graphics processing unit (GPU). With CUDA it is possible to send C, C++ and FORTRAN code straight forward to GPU, no assembly language is required.

- Using high-level languages, GPU-accelerated applications run the sequential part of their workload on the CPU – which is optimized for single-threaded performance – while accelerating parallel processing on the GPU. This is called "GPU computing."
- GPU computing is possible because today's GPU does much more than render graphics. It sizzles with a teraflop of floating point performance and crunches application tasks designed for anything from finance to medicine.
- Single Instruction Multiple Data (SIMD) architecture works well when similar operation is applied to a large dataset. It does not work well for heterogeneous serial-parallel programming.
- CUDA is small extension to familiar C, C++ environment that provides a small amount of additional syntax to C or C++ which allows parallel "kernels" to be run on the device.

6.3.2 CUDA Physical Architecture

- CUDA architecture exposes GPU for general purpose computing.
- The architecture is built around Streaming Multiprocessors (SMs). Each SM has 8 processing cores. These 8 cores can run simultaneously. Refer Fig. 6.3

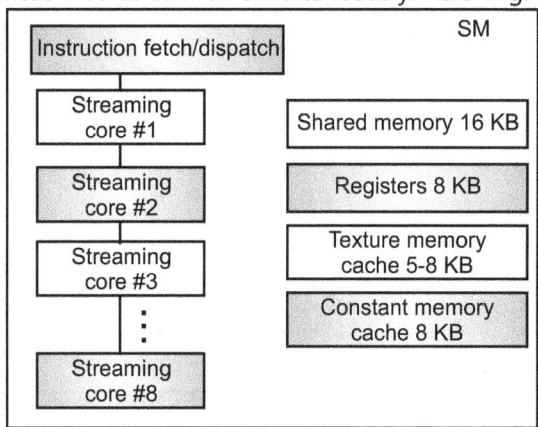

Fig. 6.3 : Device Architecture : Streaming Multiprocessor

- Each core executes identical instruction set. SM is responsible for scheduling instructions across cores with 0 overhead.
- Each thread is mapped to one SM. Threads are managed in groups of 32 – warps (basically, a SIMD group). That means up to 32 threads may be scheduled at a time. But maximum 24 wraps are active in 1 SM. Warp elements free to branch, though device will then serialize. Refer Fig. 6.4.

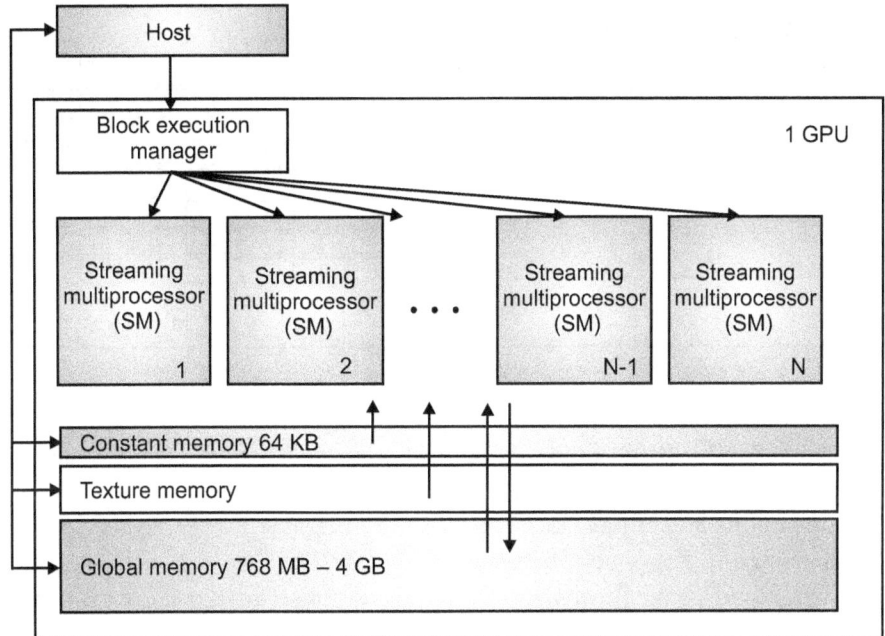

Fig. 6.4 : Role of Streaming Multiprocessors in Scheduling Instructions

- In CUDA thread level memory sharing is supported via Shared Memory.
- Register memory is local to thread, and it is divided amongst all blocks on SM.
- Computing capability of CUDA is given as follows :
  (a) 13 nodes
  (b) 4 Tesla S1070 Units / Node
  (c) 240 Streaming Processors / S1070
  (d) 12,480 total CUDA cores
- CUDA can scale to 100's of cores and 1000's of parallel threads.
- CUDA lets the programmers to focus on parallel algorithms and not on the mechanisms of parallel computing language.
- CUDA enables heterogeneous systems (CPU + GPU) for computing purpose. CPU and GPU are separate processing devices with separate DRAMs. Refer Fig. 6.5.
- GPU is a specialized processor that addresses the demands of real time high resolution 3D graphics compute intensive tasks.
- GPUs have transformed into highly parallel multi-core systems allowing very efficient manipulation of large blocks of data.
- This design is more effective than general purpose CPUs for algorithms where processing of large blocks of data is done in parallel.

6.3.3 CPUs Versus GPUs

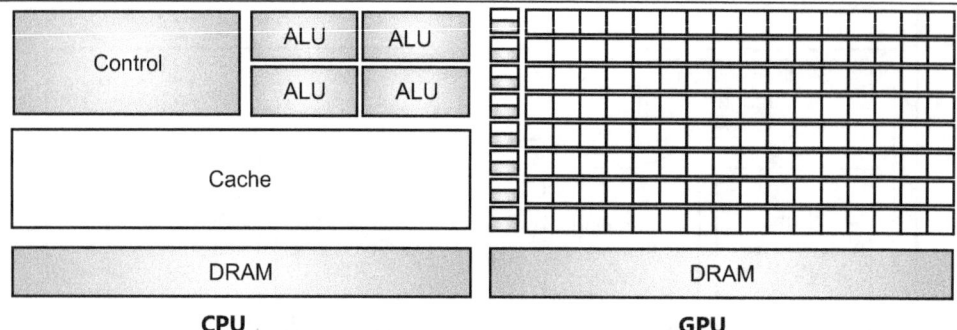

Fig. 6.5 : CPU and GPU

- Architecture of GPUs and CPUs is very different. GPUs have many parallel execution units and higher transistor counts dedicated for computation, while CPUs have few execution units and higher clock speeds.
- Small number of probably quite complex tasks can be run on CPUs number of probably quite complex whereas GPUs are designed to run large number of quite simple tasks.
- The CPU design is aimed at systems that execute a number of isolated and unconnected tasks. The GPU design is aimed at problems that can be broken down into thousands of tiny fragments and worked on individually. Thus, CPUs are very suitable for running operating systems and application software where there are a vast variety of tasks a computer may be performing at any given time.
- CPUs and GPUs consequently support threads in very different ways. The CPU has a small number of registers per core that must be used to execute any given task. To achieve this, they rapidly perform context switch between tasks. Context switching on CPUs is expensive in terms of time, in that the entire register set must be saved to RAM and the next one restored from RAM. GPUs, by comparison, also use the same concept of context switching, but instead of having a single set of registers, they have multiple banks of registers. Consequently, a context switch simply involves setting a bank selector to switch in and out the current set of registers, which is several orders of magnitude faster than having to save to RAM.
- Both CPUs and GPUs must deal with stall conditions. These are generally caused by I/O operations and memory fetches. The CPU does this by context switching. Providing there are enough tasks and the runtime of a thread is not too small, this works reasonably well. If there are not enough processes to keep the CPU busy, it will idle. If there are too many small tasks, each blocking after a short period, the CPU will spend most of its time context switching and very little time doing useful work.

- CPU scheduling policies are often based on time slicing, dividing the time equally among the threads. As the number of threads increases, the percentage of time spent context switching becomes increasingly large and the efficiency starts to rapidly drop off.
- GPUs are designed to handle stall conditions and expect this to happen with high frequency. The GPU model is a data-parallel one and thus it needs thousands of threads to work efficiently. It uses this pool of available work to ensure it always has something useful to work on. Thus, when it hits a memory fetch operation or has to wait on the result of a calculation, the streaming processors simply switch to another instruction stream and return to the stalled instruction stream sometime later.
- One of the major differences between CPUs and GPUs is the total number of processors on each device. CPUs are typically dual- or quad-core devices. The CPU executes any given task the set of registers that are present on per core. CPUs are typically dual- or quad-core devices. That is to say they have a number of execution cores available to run programs on. The current Fermi GPUs have 16 SMs, which can be thought of a lot like CPU cores. CPUs often run single-thread programs, meaning they calculate just a single data. CPUs and GPUs maintain threads in very different ways.
- CUDA uses 1000's of threads to achieve efficiency whereas multi core CPUs can use only few. CPUs often run single-thread programs, meaning they calculate just a single data point per core, per iteration. GPUs run in parallel by default. Parallel portions of an application are executed on the devices as kernels. One kernel is executed at a time and many threads execute each kernel. We should know the difference between CUDA threads and CPU threads. CUDA threads are extremely lightweight as compared to CPU threads. Very little overhead is involved in creating CUDA threads. CUDA threads also require minimal switching.
- A CUDA kernel is executed by an array of threads. All these threads run the same code. Each thread has an ID that it uses to compute memory address and make control decisions. Refer Fig. 6.6.

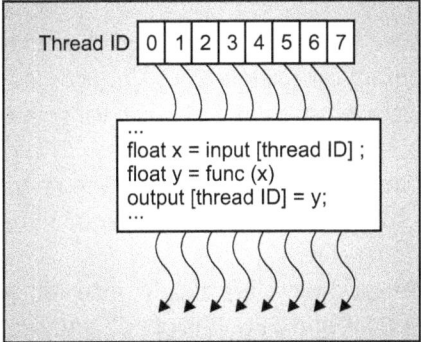

Fig. 6.6 : Array of Threads

- Thread co-operation is very important part of kernel execution. Threads need to co-operate because,
    1. Results of computation are shared to avoid redundant computation.
    2. To enable shared memory access.
    3. To enable drastic bandwidth reduction.

    This thread co-operation is powerful feature of CUDA.
- Here one important point to note that is co-operation between monolithic array of threads is not scalable but cooperation within smaller batches of threads is scalable.

6.3.4 CUDA Logical Architecture and GPU Programming

- NVIDIA uses SPMD (single program, multiple data) a variant of SIMD model for its scheduling.
- We know that parallel programming is greatly influenced by the idea of a thread. The CUDA programming model groups threads into special groups it calls warps, blocks, and grids.

Threads

- A thread is the fundamental building block of a parallel program.
- Most C programmers are familiar with the concept of thread if they have performed any multicore programming.
- Even the basic C programmers are aware of this concept as they have executed through any serial piece of code.
- With the advancements in dual core, quad core, octal core processors, more stress is on the programmer to make use of such hardware. Most programs written in the past few decades were single-thread programs because the primary hardware on which these programs would execute was a single-core CPU.
- However, considering the advantages of parallel programming it is better to decompose single large problem into number of sub-problems (divide and conquer approach) and execute each of these sub-problem threads.

Problem Decomposition

- Parallelism in the usual CPU domain is influenced by the desire to run more than one (single-threaded) program on a single CPU. This is called as task parallelism.
- Task parallelism is a parallelism model in which we split the task in N parts where N is the number of CPU cores available. Normally each CPU core calculates one "frame" of data where there are no interdependencies between frames.
- It is also possible to split each frame into N segments and allocate each one of the segments to an individual core.
- In the GPU domain, these choices are clearly observed when attempting to speed up games by using more than one GPU. It is possible to send complete, alternate frames to each GPU.

CUDA Threads, Blocks and Grids

- Threads are grouped into blocks, and blocks are grouped into a grid. Each thread has a unique local index in its block. Each block has a unique index in the grid. Blocks are independent i.e. they can be executed in any order.
- Parallel code (kernel) is launched and executed on a device by many threads. Such parallel code is written for the utilization of threads only.
- Basically, thread block is a group of threads that can perform following tasks :
  1. Synchronize the execution of threads.
  2. Communicate via shared memory.
- Note that threads in different blocks cannot cooperate.
- Threads in a single block will be executed on a single multiprocessor, sharing the software data cache, and can synchronize and share data with threads in the same block using '_syncthreads()'.
- Warp will always be a subset of threads from a single block.
- Threads in different blocks may be assigned to different multiprocessors concurrently, to the same multiprocessor concurrently (using multithreading), or may be assigned to the same or different multiprocessors at different times, depending on how the blocks are scheduled dynamically. Refer Fig. 6.7.

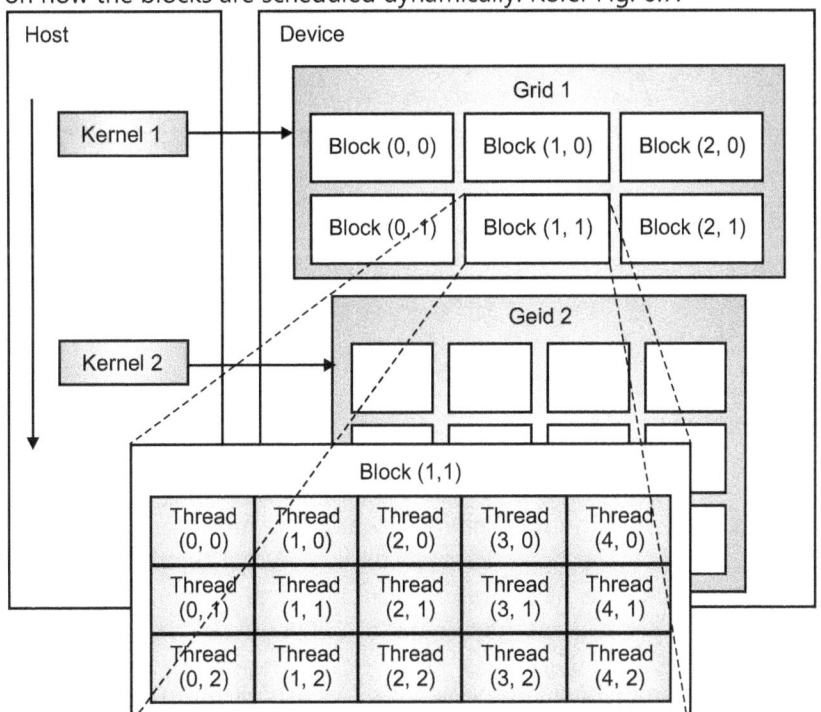

Fig. 6.7 : NVIDIA Thread Batching, Grids and Blocks

- There is a hard upper limit on the size of a thread block, 1,024 threads or 32 warps for Kepler.
- Thread blocks are always created in warp-sized units, all thread blocks in the whole grid will have the same size and shape.
- A Kepler multiprocessor can have 2,048 threads simultaneously active, or 64 warps. These can come from 2 thread blocks of 32 warps, or 3 thread blocks of 21 warps, 4 thread blocks of 16 warps, and so on up to 16 blocks of 4 warps. Another hard upper limit is 16 thread blocks can be simultaneously active on a single multiprocessor.
- NVIDIA GPUs are programmed as a sequence of kernels. Typically, each kernel completes execution before the next kernel begins, with implicit barrier synchronization between kernels. CUDA (Compute Unified Device Architecture) offers heterogeneous serial and parallel programming model that is supported on NVIDIA GPUs. NVIDIA uses SPMD (single program, multiple data) model for its scheduling which is based on the underlying hardware implementation.
- Transparent scalability is another important feature of CUDA. Hardware is free to schedule thread blocks on any processor and kernel scales across parallel multiprocessors. Refer Fig. 6.8.

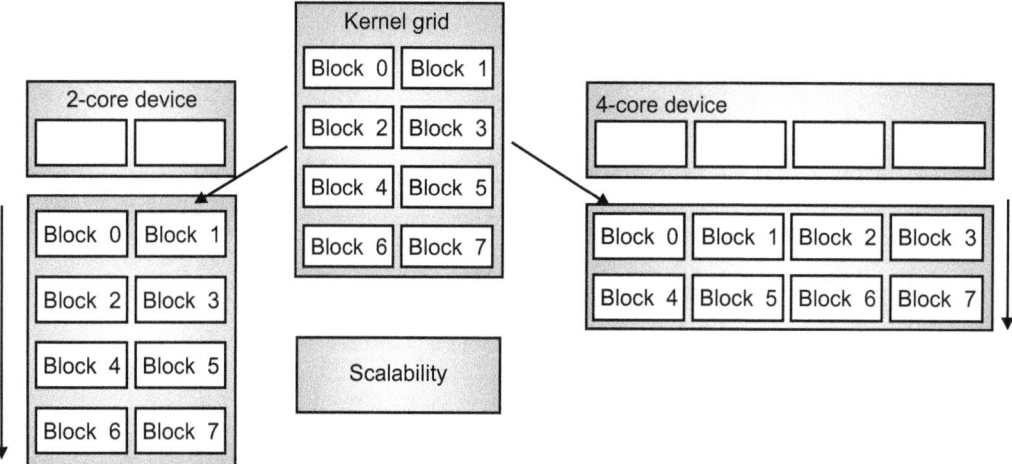

Fig. 6.8 : Transparent Scalability of CUDA

Kernels and Kernels Call Syntax

CUDA C extends C by allowing the programmer to define C functions, called kernels, that, when called, are executed N times in parallel by N different CUDA threads. These kernels are opposite to normal C functions which are executed once. A kernel is defined using the __global__ declaration specifier and the number of CUDA threads that execute that kernel for a given kernel call is specified using a new <<<...>>>execution configuration syntax. Each thread that executes the kernel is given a unique thread ID that is accessible within the kernel through the built-in threadIdx variable.

Kernels are called with the <<< >>> syntax. Certain kernel parameters can be specified with this syntax. For example : <<<Dg, Db, Ns, S>>>

Where :

Dg = Dimensions of the grid (type dim3).

Db = Dimensions of the block (type dim3).

Ns = Number of bytes shared memory dynamically allocated / block (type size_t).

0 is taken as default value for Ns.

S = associated cudaStream_t. Default value is 0 for S.

CUDA Function Type Qualifiers

Kernels are defined as __global__. This specifies that the function runs on the device and is callable from the host only __device__ and __host__ are other available qualifiers.

1. __device__ is executed on device and it is callable only from device.
2. __host__ is executed on host and it is callable from host only. Default is not specified.

The following sample code adds two vectors A and B of size N and stores the result into vector C :

```
// Kernel definition
__global__ void VecAdd(float* A, float* B, float* C)
{
    int i = threadIdx.x;
    C[i] = A[i] + B[i];
}
int main()
{
    ...
    // Kernel invocation with N threads
    VecAdd<<<1, N>>>(A, B, C);
    ...
}
```

Here, each of the N threads that execute VecAdd() performs one pair-wise addition.

Thread Hierarchy

For convenience, threadIdx is a 3-component vector, so that threads can be identified using a one-dimensional, two-dimensional, or three-dimensional thread index, forming a one-dimensional, two-dimensional, or three-dimensional thread block. This provides a natural way to invoke computation across the elements in a domain such as a vector, matrix, or volume. The index of a thread and its thread ID relate to each other in a straightforward way : For a one-dimensional block, they are the same; for a two-dimensional block of size (Dx, Dy), the thread ID of a thread of index (x, y) is (x + y Dx); for a three-dimensional block of size (Dx, Dy, Dz), the thread ID of a thread of index (x, y, z) is (x + y Dx + z Dx Dy).

As an example, the following code adds two matrices A and B of size N × N and stores the result into matrix C :

```
// Kernel definition
__global__ void MatAdd(float A[N][N], float B[N][N],
            float C[N][N])
{
    int i = threadIdx.x;
    int j = threadIdx.y;
    C[i][j] = A[i][j] + B[i][j];
}

int main()
{
    ...
    // Kernel invocation with one block of N * N * 1 threads
    int numBlocks = 1;
    dim3 threadsPerBlock(N, N);
    MatAdd<<<numBlocks, threadsPerBlock>>>(A, B, C);
    ...
}
```

There is a limit to the number of threads per block, since all threads of a block are expected to reside on the same processor core and must share the limited memory resources of that core. On current GPUs, a thread block may contain up to 1024 threads.

However, a kernel can be executed by multiple equally-shaped thread blocks, so that the total number of threads is equal to the number of threads per block times the number of blocks.

Blocks are organized into a one-dimensional, two-dimensional, or three-dimensional grid of thread blocks as illustrated by Fig 6.9. The number of thread blocks in a grid is usually dictated by the size of the data being processed or the number of processors in the system, which it can greatly exceed.

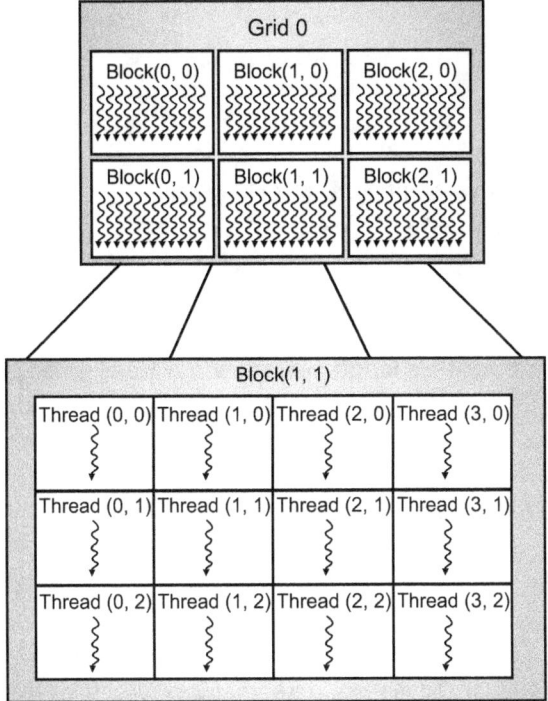

Fig. 6.9 : Grid of Thread Blocks

The number of threads per block and the number of blocks per grid specified in the <<<...>>> syntax can be of type int or dim3. Two-dimensional blocks or grids can be specified as in the example above.

Each block within the grid can be identified by a one-dimensional, two-dimensional, or three-dimensional index accessible within the kernel through the built-in blockIdx variable. The dimension of the thread block is accessible within the kernel through the built-in blockDim variable.

Extending the previous MatAdd() example to handle multiple blocks, the code becomes as follows :

```
// Kernel definition
__global__ void MatAdd(float A[N][N], float B[N][N],
float C[N][N])
{
   int i = blockIdx.x * blockDim.x + threadIdx.x;
   int j = blockIdx.y * blockDim.y + threadIdx.y;
   if (i < N && j < N)
      C[i][j] = A[i][j] + B[i][j];
}
```

```
int main()
{
    ...
    // Kernel invocation
    dim3 threadsPerBlock(16, 16);
    dim3 numBlocks(N / threadsPerBlock.x, N / threadsPerBlock.y);
    MatAdd<<<numBlocks, threadsPerBlock>>>(A, B, C);
    ...
}
```

A thread block size of 16 x 16 (256 threads), although arbitrary in this case, is a common choice. The grid is created with enough blocks to have one thread per matrix element as before. For simplicity, this example assumes that the number of threads per grid in each dimension is evenly divisible by the number of threads per block in that dimension, although that need not be the case.

Thread blocks are required to execute independently. It must be possible to execute them in any order, in parallel or in series. This independence requirement allows thread blocks to be scheduled in any order across any number of cores as illustrated by Fig. 6.9, enabling programmers to write code that scales with the number of cores.

Threads within a block can cooperate by sharing data through some shared memory and by synchronizing their execution to co-ordinate memory accesses. More precisely, one can specify synchronization points in the kernel by calling the __syncthreads() intrinsic function; __syncthreads() acts as a barrier at which all threads in the block must wait before any is allowed to proceed. Shared Memory gives an example of using shared memory.

For efficient cooperation, the shared memory is expected to be a low-latency memory near each processor core (much like an L1 cache) and __syncthreads() is expected to be lightweight.

Threading on GPUs

Look at the following section of code :

```
void some_func(void)
{
int i;
for (i=0;i<128;i++)
{
a[i] =b[i] * c[i];
}
}
```

This piece of code is very simple. It stores the result of a multiplication of "b" and "c" value for a given index in the result variable "a" for that same index. The "for" loop iterates 128 times (indexes 0 to 127).

In CUDA you could translate this to 128 threads, each of which executes the line
a[i] = b[i] * c[i];
This is possible because there is no dependency between one iteration of the loop and the next.

Thus, to transform this into a parallel program is actually quite easy. This is called loop parallelization and is very much the basis for one of the more popular parallel language extensions, OpenMP.

On a quad-core CPU we can also translate this to four blocks, where CPU core 1 handles indexes 0–31, core 2 indexes 32–63, core 3 indexes 64–95, and core 4 indexes 96–127.

Some compilers will either automatically translate such blocks or translate them where the programmer marks that this loop can be parallelized.

This gives two levels of parallelism and is not too different from the GPU model.

In CUDA, we can translate this loop by creating a kernel function, which is a function that executes on the GPU only and cannot be executed directly on the CPU. In the CUDA programming model the CPU handles the serial code execution, which is where it excels. When we come to a computationally intense section of code the CPU hands it over to the GPU to make use of the huge computational power it has.

Applications that used a large amount of floating-point math ran many times faster on machines fitted with such coprocessors. Exactly the same is true for GPUs. They are used to accelerate computationally intensive sections of a program.

The GPU kernel function, conceptually, looks identical to the loop body, but with the loop structure removed. Thus, we can write as :

```
__global__ void some_kernel_func(int * const a, const int * const b, const int * const c)
{
a[i] = b[i] * c[i];
}
```

Note that we have lost the loop and the loop control variable, 'i' We also have a __global__ prefix added to the C function that tells the compiler to generate GPU code and not CPU code when compiling this function, and to make that GPU code globally visible from within the CPU.

The CPU and GPU have separate memory spaces, meaning you cannot access CPU parameters in the GPU code and vice versa. As a consequence, the global arrays a, b, and c at the CPU level are no longer visible on the GPU level. We have to declare memory space on the GPU, copy over the arrays from the CPU, and pass the kernel function pointers to the GPU memory space to both read and write from. When we are done with this, we copy that memory back into the CPU.

The next problem you have is that 'i' is no longer defined; instead, the value of 'i' is defined for you by the thread you are currently running. Initially, we will be using 128 instances of this function, and initially this will be in the form of 128 threads. CUDA provides a special parameter, different for each thread, which defines the thread ID or number. We can use this to directly index into the array. This is very similar to MPI, where you get the process rank for each process.

The thread information is provided in a structure. As it is a structure element, we will store it in a variable, thread_idx for now to avoid having to reference the structure every time. Thus, the code becomes :

```
__global__ void some_kernel_func(int * const a, const int * const b, const int * const c)
{
const unsigned int thread_idx = threadIdx.x;
a[thread_idx] =b[thread_idx] * c[thread_idx];
}
```

Note, some people prefer idx or tid as the name for the thread index since these are somewhat shorter to type.

What is happening, now, is that for thread 0, the thread_idx calculation returns 0. For thread 1, it returns 1, and so on, up to thread 127, which uses index 127. Each thread does exactly two reads from memory, one multiply and one store operation, and then terminates. Note that the code executed by each thread is identical, but the data changes. This is at the heart of the CUDA and SPMD model.

OpenMP and MPI have similar blocks of code. They extract, for a given iteration of the loop, the thread ID or thread rank allocated to that thread. This is then used to index into the dataset.

We actually have N cores on each SM, so question arises here is how can you run 128 threads? Like the CPU, each thread group is placed into the SM and the N SPs start running the code. The first thing we do after extracting the thread index is fetch a parameter from the b and c array. Before beginning with this fetching some 400–600 GPU clocks pass by before the memory subsystem comes back with the requested data. During this time the set of N threads gets suspended.

Threads are, in practice, actually grouped into 32 thread groups, and when all 32 threads are waiting on something such as memory access, they are suspended. The group of 32 threads is a warp (32 threads) and a half warp (16 threads). Thus, the 128 threads translate into four groups of 32 threads. The first set all run together to extract the thread ID and then calculate the address in the arrays and issue a memory fetch request.

The next instruction, a multiply, requires both operands to have been provided, so the thread is suspended. When all 32 threads in that block of 32 threads are suspended, the hardware switches to another warp.

Note that when warp 0 is suspended pending its memory access completing, warp 1 becomes the executing warp. The GPU continues in this manner until all warps have moved to the suspended state.

Prior to issuing the memory fetch, fetches from consecutive threads are usually grouped together. This reduces the overall latency (time to respond to the request), as there is an overhead associated in the hardware with managing each request.

These threads are then placed in the ready state and become available for the GPU to switch in the next time it hits a blocking operation, such as another memory fetch from another set of threads.

Having executed all the warps (groups of 32 threads) the GPU becomes idle waiting for any one of the pending memory accesses to complete. At some point later, a sequence of memory blocks being returned from the memory subsystem is obtained. It is likely, but not guaranteed, that these will come back in the order in which they were requested.

Let's assume that addresses 0–31 were returned at the same time. Warp 0 moves to the ready queue, and since there is no warp currently executing, warp 0 automatically moves to the executing state. Gradually, all the pending memory requests will complete, resulting in all of the warp blocks moving back to the ready queue.

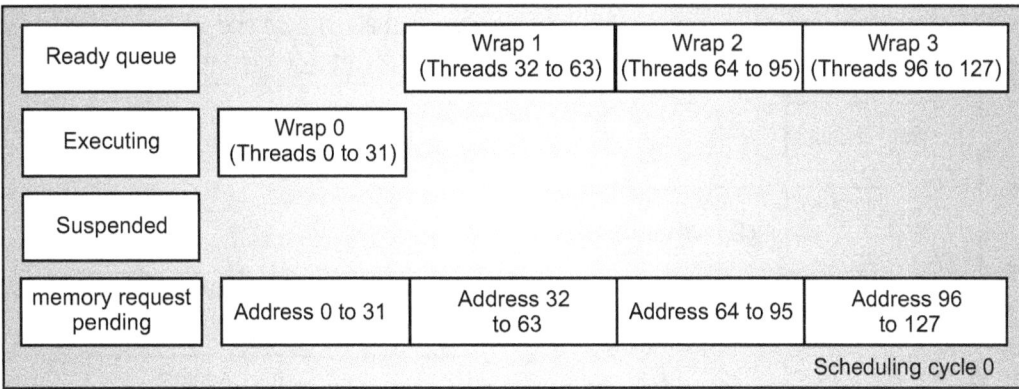

Fig. 6.10 : Scheduling Cycle 0

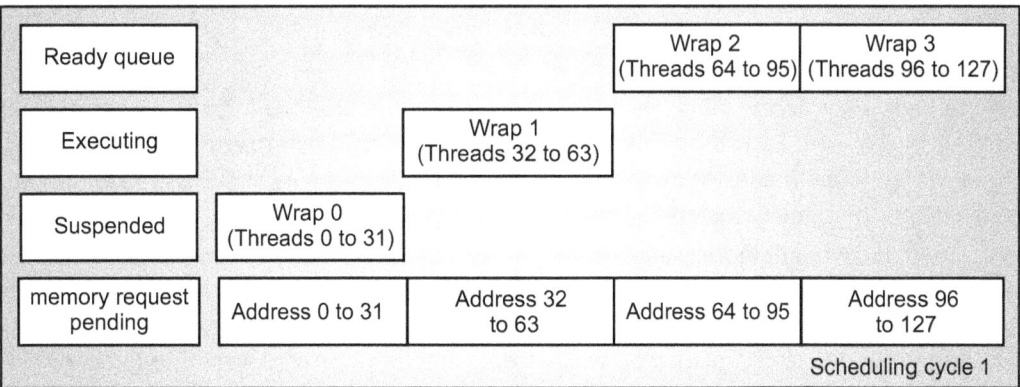

Fig. 6.11 : Scheduling Cycle 1

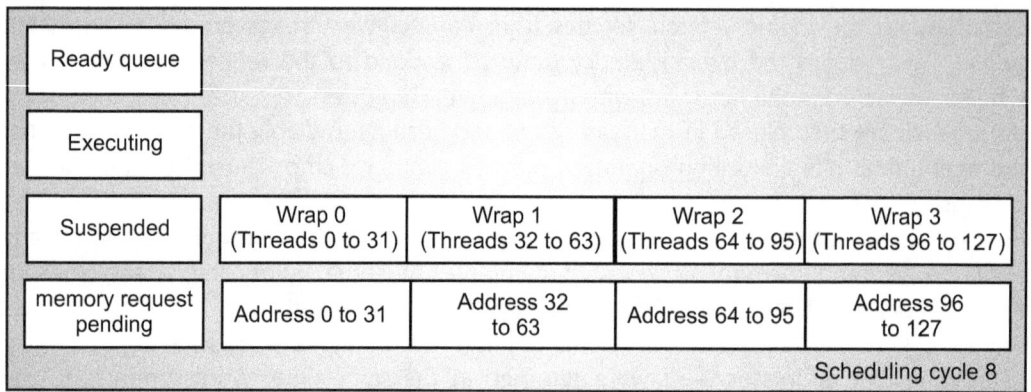

Fig. 6.12 : Scheduling Cycle 8

Once warp 0 has executed, its final instruction is a write to the destination array a. As there are no dependent instructions on this operation, warp 0 is then complete and is retired. The other warps move through this same cycle and eventually they have all issued a store request. Each warp is then retired, and the kernel completes, returning control to the CPU.

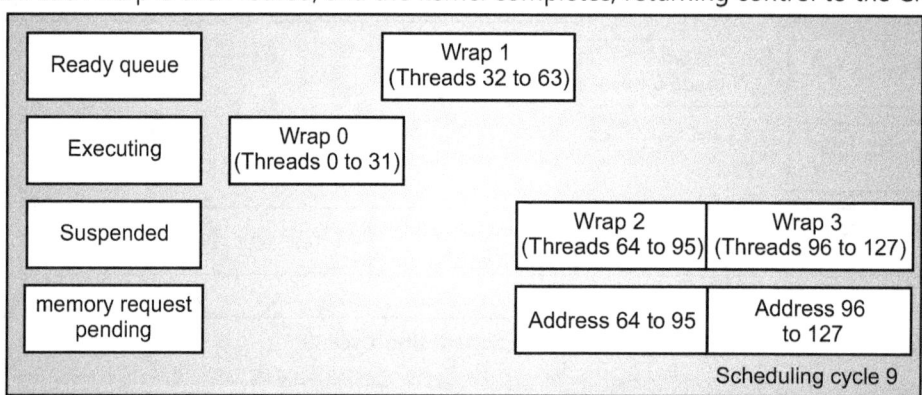

Fig. 6.13 : Scheduling Cycle 9

Memory Hierarchy

CUDA threads may access data from multiple memory spaces during their execution as illustrated by Fig 6.14. Each thread has private local memory. Each thread block has shared memory visible to all threads of the block and with the same lifetime as the block. All threads have access to the same global memory.

There are also two additional read-only memory spaces accessible by all threads: the constant and texture memory spaces. The global, constant, and texture memory spaces are optimized for different memory usages (see Device Memory Accesses). Texture memory also offers different addressing modes, as well as data filtering, for some specific data formats (see Texture and Surface Memory).

The global, constant, and texture memory spaces are persistent across kernel launches by the same application.

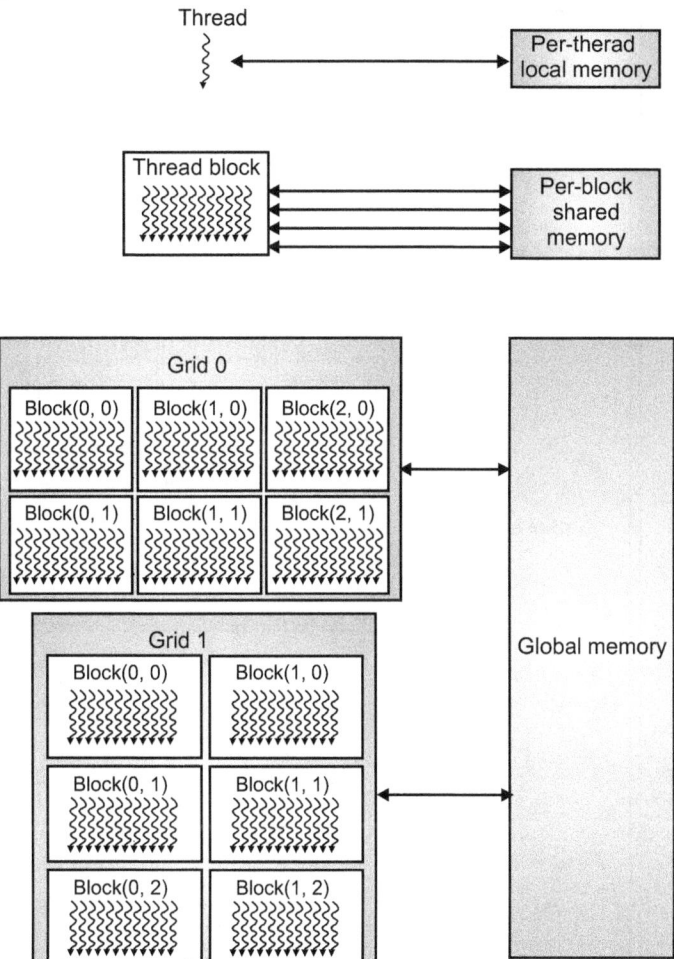

Fig. 6.14 : Memory Hierarchy

Heterogeneous Programming

As illustrated by Fig 6.15, the CUDA programming model assumes that the CUDA threads execute on a physically separate device that operates as a coprocessor to the host running the C program. This is the case, for example, when the kernels execute on a GPU and the rest of the C program executes on a CPU. The CUDA programming model also assumes that both the host and the device maintain their own separate memory spaces in DRAM, referred to as host memory and device memory, respectively. Therefore, a program manages the global, constant, and texture memory spaces visible to kernels through calls to the CUDA runtime (described in Programming Interface). This includes device memory allocation and deallocation as well as data transfer between host and device memory.

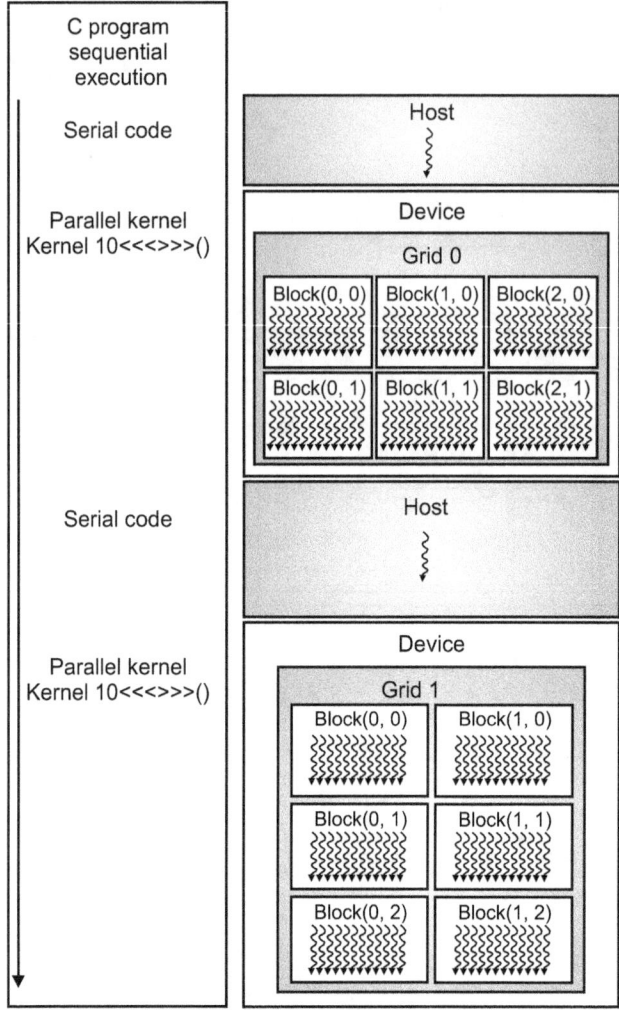

Fig. 6.15 : Heterogeneous Programming

Note : Serial code executes on the host while parallel code executes on the device.

Compute Capability

The compute capability of a device is represented by a version number which is called as its "SM version". This version number identifies the features supported by the GPU hardware. Some features those are present in latest version will not be available with older versions. This version number is used by applications at runtime to determine which hardware features and/or instructions are available on the present GPU.

The compute capability revision comprises a major and a minor revision number (x.y):

Devices with the same major revision number are of the same core architecture. The major revision number is 5 for devices based on the Maxwell architecture, 3 for devices based on the Kepler architecture, 2 for devices based on the Fermi architecture, and 1 for devices based on the Tesla architecture.

The minor revision number corresponds to an incremental improvement to the core architecture, possibly including new features.

Compute Levels

CUDA supports a number of compute levels. The original G80 series graphics cards were used with the first version of CUDA. The compute capability is fixed into the hardware. To upgrade to a newer version users had to upgrade their hardware. When upgrading a compute level it is possible move from an older platform to a newer one, which doubles the compute capacity of the card at the same price of original card. Since NVIDIA putforth new technologies and up gradations almost every year, results into almost double computing power availability.

Compute 1.0

Compute level 1.0 is found on the older graphics cards. Most of the series 8000 cards come under this category. The main features lacking in compute 1.0 card are those for atomic operations. Atomic operations are the class of operations which continues to execution without any interruptions. That means either all operations are executed or none of them. Compute 1.0 cards are now obsolete, so the restrictions and other disadvantages of these cards can be ignored.

Compute 1.1

9000 series cards, such as the 9800 GTX, come under the category of compute 1.1. These cards were extremely popular. One major change brought in with compute 1.1 devices was support for overlapped data transfer and kernel execution. This support was provided on most of the devices.

The kernel cudaGetDeviceProperties() returns the device Overlap property, which defines if this functionality is available. Double buffering is very important feature supported by compute 1.1 level.

Double memory space is required to use this technique when 512 MB card is available. However, with Tesla cards, we can have up to 6 GB of GPU memory, which makes such techniques very useful.

Cycle 0 : CPU fills the first buffer when two areas of memory are allocated in the GPU memory space.

Cycle 1 : The CPU then invokes a CUDA kernel (a GPU function) on the GPU, which returns immediately to the CPU. The CPU then fetches the CUDA kernel. Meanwhile, the GPU is processing away in the background on the CUDA kernel provided. When the CPU is ready, it starts filling the other buffer.

Cycle 2 : When the CPU is done filling the buffer, it invokes a kernel to process buffer 1. It then checks if the kernel from cycle 1, which was processing buffer 0, has completed. If not, it waits until this kernel has finished and then fetches the data from buffer 0 and then loads the next data block into the same buffer. During this time the kernel kicked off at the start of the cycle is processing data on the GPU in buffer 1.

Cycle N : Then repeat cycle 2 alternating between which buffer we read and write to on the CPU with the buffer being processed on the GPU.

GPU-to-CPU and CPU-to-GPU transfers keeps both the CPU and GPU busy.

Compute 1.2

Compute 1.2 devices were influenced by low-end GT200 series hardware.

GTX260 and GTX280 cards fall under this category. With the GT200 series hardware, NVIDIA approximately doubled the number of CUDA core processors on a single card by doubling the number of multiprocessors present on the card. Warps are blocks of code that execute within a multiprocessor, and increasing the amount of available warps per multiprocessor helps to get better performance.

Issues like global memory and bank conflicts in the shared memory found in compute 1.0 and compute 1.1 devices were greatly reduced. This make the GT200 series hardware far easier to program and it greatly improved the performance of many previous, poorly written CUDA programs.

Compute 1.3

Extension of GT200- GT200 a/b revisions of the hardware fall under compute 1.3 category. This is after the initial release of the GT200 series. Almost all higher-end cards from this period were compute 1.3 compatible.

The major change that occurs with compute 1.3 hardware is the introduction of support for limited double-precision calculations. GPUs are primarily aimed at graphics which creates a need for fast single-precision calculations, but limited need for double-precision ones.

Compute 2.0

Compute 2.0 devices changed to Fermi hardware.

Some of the main changes in compute 2.x hardware are as follows :

- Introduction of 16 K to 48 K of L1 cache memory on each SP.
- Introduction of a shared L2 cache for all SMs.
- Support in Tesla-based devices for ECC (Error Correcting Code) based memory checking and error correction.
- Support in Tesla-based devices for dual-copy engines.
- Extension in size of the shared memory from 16 K per SM up to 48 K per SM.

- For optimum coalescing of data, it must be 128-byte aligned.
- The number of shared memory banks increased from 16 to 32.

A level one (L1) cache is a cache present on a device and is the fastest cache type available. Compute 1.x hardware has no cache, except for the texture and constant memory caches. The introduction of a L1 cache makes it much easier for many programmers to write programs that work well on GPU hardware.

On Fermi hardware the L2 cache is up to 768 K in size and it is a unified cache. It means it is shared and provides a consistent view for all the SMs. This allows for much faster inter block communication through global atomic operations. Shared cache memory is faster than global memory on GPU.

Compute 2.0 also supports ECC memory which provides automatic error detection and correction.

Shared memory was transformed into a combined L1 cache.

The L1 cache size is 64 K. However, to preserve backward compatibility, a minimum of 16 K must be allocated to the shared memory, meaning the L1 cache is really only 48 K in size. Using a switch, shared memory and L1 cache usage can be swapped, giving 48 K of shared memory and 16 K of L1 cache. Going from 16 K of shared memory to 48 K of shared memory is a huge benefit for certain programs.

Shared memory banks also increased from 16 to 32 bits. This is a major benefit over the previous generations. It allows each thread of the current warp (32 threads) to write to exactly one bank of 32 bits in the shared memory without causing a shared bank conflict.

Compute 2.1

Compute 2.1 is specifically designed for targeting the games market, such as the GTX460 and GTX560. These devices use the following architecture :

- 48 CUDA cores per SM instead of the usual 32 per SM.
- Eight single-precision, special-function units for transcendental per SM instead of the usual four.
- Dual-warp dispatcher instead of the usual single-warp dispatcher.

Most games make little use of double-precision floating-point data, but significant use of single-precision floating-point and integer math. So compute 2.1 has sacrificed the double precision hardware and increased the number of CUDA cores.

Single warp dispatcher on compute 2.0 hardware takes two clock cycles to dispatch instructions of an entire warp. On compute 2.1 hardware, instead of the usual two instruction dispatchers per two clock cycles, we have four.

In the hardware, there are three banks of 16 CUDA cores, 48 CUDA cores in total, instead of the usual two banks of 16 CUDA cores.

The compute 2.1 hardware is actually a superscalar approach which is already followed in CPUs from the original Pentium CPU onwards. To make use of all the cores, the hardware needs to identify instruction-level parallelism (ILP) within a single thread.

6.4 Memory Handling with DUDA

In the traditional CPU model we have a linear memory model, also known as flat memory model. In linear memory model single CPU core can access any memory location without restriction. In practice, for CPU hardware we have a level one (L1), level two (L2), and level three (L3) cache. For understanding CPU based system and performance on CPU based system, we must first understand how the cache works. So in this sub section we will see cache from both the perspectives CPU and GPU and how memory handling is done in CUDA.

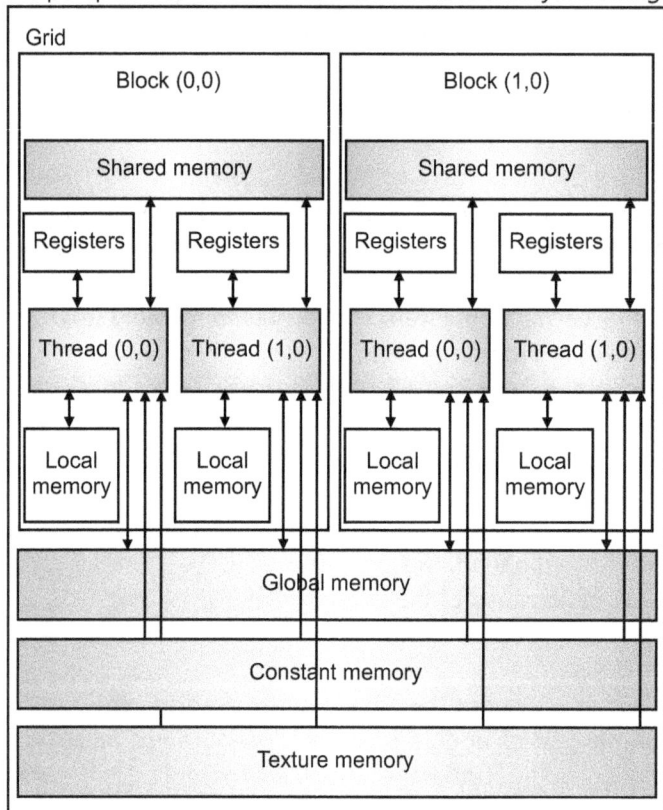

Fig. 6.16 : NVIDIA CUDA Memory Space Overview

In CUDA host (CPU) and device (GPU) have separate memory spaces.
- Host manages memory on device by using functions allocate/set/copy/free memory on device using functions similar to C functions.
- The GPU, has thousands of registers per SM (streaming multiprocessor).
- An SM can be thought of like a multithreaded CPU core.
- On a GPU we have N SM cores. GPUs, application threads are pipelined, context switched, and dispatched to multiple SMs, meaning the number of active threads across all SMs in a GPU device is usually in the tens of thousands range.

- The GPU uses threads to hide memory fetch and instruction execution latency, so too few threads on the GPU means the GPU will become idle, usually waiting on memory transactions.
- The GPU also does not use register renaming, but instead dedicates real registers to each and every thread. Thus, when a context switch is required, it has near zero overhead. All that happens on a context switch is the selector (or pointer) to the current register set is updated to point to the register set of the next warp that will execute.
- Each CUDA device has several memories that can be used by programmers to achieve high Computation to Global Memory Access (CGMA) ratio and thus high execution speed in their kernels. Variables that reside in registers and shared memories can be accessed at very high speed in a highly parallel manner.
- Registers are allocated to individual threads; each thread can only access its own registers. A kernel function typically uses registers to hold frequently accessed variables that are private to each thread. Shared memories are allocated to thread blocks; all threads in a block can access variables in the shared memory locations allocated to the block. Shared memories are efficient means for threads to cooperate by sharing the results of their work.
- At the middle of the table, we see global memory, constant memory. These are the memories that the host code can write (W) and read (R) by calling API functions. The global memory can be accessed by all the threads at anytime of program execution. The constant memory allows read-only access by the device and provides faster and more parallel data access paths for CUDA kernel execution than the global memory.

Types of CUDA Memory

Table 6.1 : Types of CUDA Memory

Memory	Location	Cached	Access	Who
Local	Off-chip	No	Read/write	One thread
Shared	On-chip	N/A - resident	Read/write	All threads in a block
Global	Off-chip	No	Read/write	All threads + host
Constant	Off-chip	Yes	Read	All threads + host
Texture	Off-chip	Yes	Read	All threads + host

CACHES

A cache is a high-speed memory bank which is physically close to the processor core. The maximum speed of a cache is inversely proportional to the size of the cache. The L1 cache is the fastest, but is limited in size to usually around 16 K, 32 K, or 64 K. It is usually allocated to a single CPU core.

The L2 cache is slower, but size is larger than L1 cache which is around 256 K to 512 K. The L3 cache may or may not be present and is often several megabytes in size. The L2 and/or L3 cache may be shared between processor cores or maintained as separate caches and can be directly linked to processor cores. On traditional CPUs L3 cache is shared between processor cores. This allows fast inter core communication via this shared memory within the device.

The G80 and GT200 series GPUs have no equivalent CPU-like cache. But they have a hardware-managed cache that is treated as a read-only CPU cache in terms of constant and texture memory. However GPU relies primarily on a programmer-managed cache, or shared memory.

Architecture of non-program managed data cache consists of an L1 cache (per SM) that is both programmer managed and hardware managed. It also has a shared L2 cache across all SMs.

This architecture allows inter processor communication, without having the availability global memory. This is particularly useful for atomic operations where, because the L2 cache is unified, all SMs get a consistent value at a given memory location. The processor does not have to write to the slow global memory, to read it back again, just to ensure consistency between processor cores.

Types of Data Storage

On a GPU, numbers of places are available for storing the data, each place is characterized by its potential bandwidth and latency. Most preferred places are registers inside the device. Then we have the following memories :

- Shared memory
- Programmer-managed L1 cache
- Constant memory
- Texture memory
- Device memory
- Host memory.

Global memory plays an important role in performance. Global memory should looked first in order to get optimal performance.

Most CUDA programs are developed progressively, using global memory exclusively. Once this initial development is completed, then the use of other memory types such as zero copy and shared, constant, and ultimately registers is considered. For an optimal program, programmers often consider the above mentioned issues. Programmers should continuously think about not only how to access global memory efficiently, but also how those accesses, especially for data that is reused in some way, can be eliminated.

REGISTER USAGE

The GPU has thousands of registers per SM (streaming multiprocessor). An SM can be thought of like a multithreaded CPU core. On a typical CPU we have two, four, six, or eight cores. On a GPU we have N SM cores. For example, a Fermi GF100 series have16 SMs on the top-end device. The GT200 series has up to 32 SMs per device. The G80 series has up to 16 SMs per device.

Due to the different number of SPs per core, a major difference in the number of threads per core can be observed. A typical CPU will support one or two hardware threads per core. A GPU has between 8 and 192 SPs per core, meaning each SM can at any time be executing this number of concurrent hardware threads.

In practice on GPUs, application threads are pipelined, context switched, and dispatched to multiple SMs, meaning the number of active threads across all SMs in a GPU device is usually in the tens of thousands range.

One major difference between CPU and GPU architectures is how CPUs and GPUs map registers. The CPU runs lots of threads by using register renaming and the stack. To run a new task the CPU needs to do a context switch, which involves storing the state of all registers onto the stack (the system memory) and then restoring the state from the last run of the new thread. This can take several hundred CPU cycles. If you load too many threads onto a CPU it will spend all of the time simply swapping out and in registers as it context switches. The effective throughput of useful work rapidly drops off as soon as you load too many threads onto a CPU. On the other hand GPU uses threads to hide memory fetch and instruction execution latency, so too few threads on the GPU means the GPU will become idle, usually waiting on memory transactions. The GPU also does not use register renaming, but instead dedicates real registers to each and every thread. Thus, when a context switch is required, it has near zero overhead. All that happens on a context switch is the selector (or pointer) to the current register set is updated to point to the register set of the next warp that will execute.

A warp is simply a grouping of threads that are scheduled together. In the current hardware, this is a group of 32 threads. Thus, we swap in or swap out, and schedule, groups of 32 threads within a single SM.

Each SM can schedule a number of blocks. Blocks at the SM level are simply logical groups of independent warps. The number of registers per kernel thread is calculated at compile time. All blocks are of the same size and have a known number of threads, and the register usage per block is known and fixed. Consequently, the GPU can allocate a fixed set of registers for each block scheduled onto the hardware.

At a thread level, this is transparent to the programmer. However, a kernel that requests too many registers per thread can limit the number of blocks the GPU can schedule on an SM, and thus the total number of threads that will be run. Thus, underutilization of the hardware could be there because less number of threads and the performance starts to rapidly drop off. Too many threads can mean you run short of resources and whole blocks of threads are dropped from being scheduled to the SM.

Depending on the particular hardware we are using there is 8 K, 16 K, 32 K or 64 K of register space per SM for all threads within an SM. Remember that one register is required per thread. Thus, a simple local float variable in C results in N registers usage, where N is the number of threads that are scheduled. For example : with the Fermi-level hardware, you get 32 K of register space per SM. With 256 threads per block ((32,768/4 bytes per register)/256 threads) 32 registers per thread available.

The CUDA programming model assumes a system composed of a host and a device, each with their own separate memory. Kernels operate out of device memory, so the runtime provides functions to allocate, deallocate, and copy device memory, as well as transfer data between host memory and device memory.

Device memory can be allocated either as *linear memory* or as *CUDA arrays.*

CUDA arrays are unclear memory layouts optimized for texture fetching.

Linear memory exists on the device in a 32-bit address space for devices of compute capability 1.x and 40-bit address space of devices of higher compute capability, so separately allocated entities can reference one another via pointers or selectors.

Linear memory is typically allocated using **cudaMalloc()** and freed using **cudaFree()** and data transfer between host memory and device memory are typically done using **cudaMemcpy()**.

In the vector addition code sample of Kernels, the vectors need to be copied from host memory to device memory :

```
// Device code
__global__ void VecAdd(float* A, float* B, float* C, int N)
{
int i = blockDim.x * blockIdx.x + threadIdx.x;
if (i < N)
C[i] = A[i] + B[i];
}
// Host code
int main()
{
int N = ...;
size_t size = N * sizeof(float);
// Allocate input vectors h_A and h_B in host memory
float* h_A = (float*)malloc(size);
float* h_B = (float*)malloc(size);
// Initialize input vectors
...
// Allocate vectors in device memory
float* d_A;
cudaMalloc(&d_A, size);
```

```
float* d_B;
cudaMalloc(&d_B, size);
float* d_C;
cudaMalloc(&d_C, size);
// Copy vectors from host memory to device memory
cudaMemcpy(d_A, h_A, size, cudaMemcpyHostToDevice);
cudaMemcpy(d_B, h_B, size, cudaMemcpyHostToDevice);
// Invoke kernel
int threadsPerBlock = 256;
int blocksPerGrid =
(N + threadsPerBlock - 1) / threadsPerBlock;
VecAdd<<<blocksPerGrid, threadsPerBlock>>>(d_A, d_B, d_C, N);
// Copy result from device memory to host memory
// h_C contains the result in host memory
cudaMemcpy(h_C, d_C, size, cudaMemcpyDeviceToHost);
// Free device memory
cudaFree(d_A);
cudaFree(d_B);
cudaFree(d_C);
// Free host memory
...
}
```

Shared Memory

Variable Type Qualifiers shared memory is allocated using the __shared__ qualifier.

Shared memory is expected to be much faster than global memory. So whenever possible use of global memory should be replaced by shared memory accesses.

The following code sample is a straightforward implementation of matrix multiplication that does not take advantage of shared memory. Each thread reads one row of A and one column of B and computes the corresponding element of C.

A is therefore read B.width times from global memory and B is read A.height times.

```
// Matrices are stored in row-major order:
// M(row, col) = *(M.elements + row * M.width + col)
typedef struct {
int width;
int height;
float* elements;
```

} Matrix;
// Thread block size
#define BLOCK_SIZE 16
// Forward declaration of the matrix multiplication kernel
__global__ void MatMulKernel(const Matrix, const Matrix, Matrix);
// Matrix multiplication - Host code
// Matrix dimensions are assumed to be multiples of BLOCK_SIZE
void MatMul(const Matrix A, const Matrix B, Matrix C)
{
// Load A and B to device memory
Matrix d_A;
d_A.width = A.width; d_A.height = A.height;

size_t size = A.width * A.height * sizeof(float);
cudaMalloc(&d_A.elements, size);
cudaMemcpy(d_A.elements, A.elements, size,
cudaMemcpyHostToDevice);
Matrix d_B;
d_B.width = B.width; d_B.height = B.height;
size = B.width * B.height * sizeof(float);
cudaMalloc(&d_B.elements, size);
cudaMemcpy(d_B.elements, B.elements, size,
cudaMemcpyHostToDevice);
// Allocate C in device memory
Matrix d_C;
d_C.width = C.width; d_C.height = C.height;
size = C.width * C.height * sizeof(float);
cudaMalloc(&d_C.elements, size);
// Invoke kernel
dim3 dimBlock(BLOCK_SIZE, BLOCK_SIZE);
dim3 dimGrid(B.width / dimBlock.x, A.height / dimBlock.y);
MatMulKernel<<<dimGrid, dimBlock>>>(d_A, d_B, d_C);
// Read C from device memory
cudaMemcpy(C.elements, Cd.elements, size,

```
cudaMemcpyDeviceToHost);
// Free device memory
cudaFree(d_A.elements);
cudaFree(d_B.elements);
cudaFree(d_C.elements);
}
// Matrix multiplication kernel called by MatMul()
__global__ void MatMulKernel(Matrix A, Matrix B, Matrix C)
{
// Each thread computes one element of C
// by accumulating results into Cvalue
float Cvalue = 0;

int row = blockIdx.y * blockDim.y + threadIdx.y;
int col = blockIdx.x * blockDim.x + threadIdx.x;
for (int e = 0; e < A.width; ++e)
Cvalue += A.elements[row * A.width + e]
* B.elements[e * B.width + col];
C.elements[row * C.width + col] = Cvalue;
}
```

The following code sample is an implementation of matrix multiplication that does take advantage of shared memory. In this implementation, each thread block is responsible for computing one square sub-matrix *Csub* of C and each thread within the block is responsible for computing one element of *Csub*.

Csub is equal to the product of two rectangular matrices: the sub-matrix of *A* of dimension (*A.width*, *block_size*) that has the same row indices as *Csub*, and the sub-matrix of *B* of dimension (*block_size*, *A.width*)that has the same column indices as *Csub*. In order to fit into the device's resources, these two rectangular matrices are divided into as many square matrices of dimension *block_size* as necessary and *Csub* is computed as the sum of the products of these square matrices. Each of these products is performed by first loading the two corresponding square matrices from global memory to shared memory with one thread loading one element of each matrix, and then by having each thread compute one element of the product. Each thread accumulates the result of each of these products into a register and once done writes the result to global memory.

By blocking the computation this way, we take advantage of fast shared memory and save a lot of global memory bandwidth since *A* is only read (*B.width / block_size*) times from global memory and *B* is read (*A.height / block_size*) times.

The *Matrix* type from the previous code sample is augmented with a *stride* field, so that sub-matrices can be efficiently represented with the same type. __device__ functions are used to get and set elements and build any sub-matrix from a matrix.

```
// Matrices are stored in row-major order:
// M(row, col) = *(M.elements + row * M.stride + col)
typedef struct {
int width;
int height;
int stride;
float* elements;
} Matrix;
// Get a matrix element
__device__ float GetElement(const Matrix A, int row, int col)
{
return A.elements[row * A.stride + col];
}
// Set a matrix element
__device__ void SetElement(Matrix A, int row, int col, float value)
{
A.elements[row * A.stride + col] = value;
}
// Get the BLOCK_SIZExBLOCK_SIZE sub-matrix Asub of A that is
// located col sub-matrices to the right and row sub-matrices down from the upper-left corner of A
__device__ Matrix GetSubMatrix(Matrix A, int row, int col)
{
Matrix Asub;
Asub.width = BLOCK_SIZE;
Asub.height = BLOCK_SIZE;
Asub.stride = A.stride;
Asub.elements = &A.elements[A.stride * BLOCK_SIZE * row + BLOCK_SIZE * col];
return Asub;
}
// Thread block size
#define BLOCK_SIZE 16
```

```
// Forward declaration of the matrix multiplication kernel
__global__ void MatMulKernel(const Matrix, const Matrix, Matrix);
// Matrix multiplication - Host code
// Matrix dimensions are assumed to be multiples of BLOCK_SIZE
void MatMul(const Matrix A, const Matrix B, Matrix C)
{
// Load A and B to device memory
Matrix d_A;
d_A.width = d_A.stride = A.width; d_A.height = A.height;
size_t size = A.width * A.height * sizeof(float);
cudaMalloc(&d_A.elements, size);
cudaMemcpy(d_A.elements, A.elements, size,
cudaMemcpyHostToDevice);
Matrix d_B;
d_B.width = d_B.stride = B.width; d_B.height = B.height;
size = B.width * B.height * sizeof(float);
daMalloc(&d_B.elements, size);
cudaMemcpy(d_B.elements, B.elements, size,
cudaMemcpyHostToDevice);
// Allocate C in device memory
Matrix d_C;
d_C.width = d_C.stride = C.width; d_C.height = C.height;
size = C.width * C.height * sizeof(float);
cudaMalloc(&d_C.elements, size);
// Invoke kernel
dim3 dimBlock(BLOCK_SIZE, BLOCK_SIZE);
dim3 dimGrid(B.width / dimBlock.x, A.height / dimBlock.y);
MatMulKernel<<<dimGrid, dimBlock>>>(d_A, d_B, d_C);
// Read C from device memory
cudaMemcpy(C.elements, d_C.elements, size,
cudaMemcpyDeviceToHost);
// Free device memory
cudaFree(d_A.elements);
cudaFree(d_B.elements);
```

```
cudaFree(d_C.elements);
}
// Matrix multiplication kernel called by MatMul()
__global__ void MatMulKernel(Matrix A, Matrix B, Matrix C)
{
// Block row and column
int blockRow = blockIdx.y;
int blockCol = blockIdx.x;
// Each thread block computes one sub-matrix Csub of C
Matrix Csub = GetSubMatrix(C, blockRow, blockCol);
// Each thread computes one element of Csub
// by accumulating results into Cvalue
float Cvalue = 0;
// Thread row and column within Csub
int row = threadIdx.y;
int col = threadIdx.x;
// Loop over all the sub-matrices of A and B that are required to compute Csub
// Multiply each pair of sub-matrices together and accumulate the results
for (int m = 0; m < (A.width / BLOCK_SIZE); ++m) {
// Get sub-matrix Asub of A
Matrix Asub = GetSubMatrix(A, blockRow, m);
// Get sub-matrix Bsub of B
Matrix Bsub = GetSubMatrix(B, m, blockCol);
// Shared memory used to store Asub and Bsub respectively
__shared__ float As[BLOCK_SIZE][BLOCK_SIZE];
__shared__ float Bs[BLOCK_SIZE][BLOCK_SIZE];
// Load Asub and Bsub from device memory to shared memory
// Each thread loads one element of each sub-matrix
As[row][col] = GetElement(Asub, row, col);
Bs[row][col] = GetElement(Bsub, row, col);
// Synchronize to make sure the sub-matrices are loaded before starting the computation
__syncthreads();
// Multiply Asub and Bsub together
for (int e = 0; e < BLOCK_SIZE; ++e)
```

```
Cvalue += As[row][e] * Bs[e][col];
// Synchronize to make sure that the preceding computation is done before loading two new
// sub-matrices of A and B in the next iteration
__syncthreads();
}
// Write Csub to device memory
// Each thread writes one element
SetElement(Csub, row, col, Cvalue);
}
```

Page-Locked Host Memory

The runtime provides functions to allow the use of *page-locked* host memory (as opposed to host memory allocated by **malloc()**). These functions are **cudaHostAlloc()** and **cudaFreeHost()** allocate and free page-locked host memory; **cudaHostRegister()** page-locks a range of memory allocated by **malloc()**.

Using page-locked host memory has several benefits :

- Copies between page-locked host memory and device memory can be performed concurrently with kernel execution for some devices as mentioned in Asynchronous Concurrent Execution.
- On some devices, page-locked host memory can be mapped into the address space of the device, eliminating the need to copy it to or from device memory as detailed in Mapped Memory.
- On systems with a front-side bus, bandwidth between host memory and device memory is higher if host memory is allocated as page-locked and even higher if in addition it is allocated as write-combining as described in Write-Combining Memory.

Page-locked host memory is insufficient resource however, so allocations in page-locked memory will start failing long before allocations in pageable memory. In addition, by reducing the amount of physical memory available to the operating system for paging, consuming too much page-locked memory reduces overall system performance.

Portable Memory

A block of page-locked memory can be used in conjunction with any device in the system but by default. The benefits of using page-locked memory described above are only available in conjunction with the device that was current when the block was allocated (and with all devices sharing the same unified address space, if any, as described in Unified Virtual Address Space). To make these advantages available to all devices, the block needs to be allocated by passing the flag **cudaHostAllocPortable** to **cudaHostAlloc()** or pagelocked by passing the flag **cudaHostRegisterPortable** to **cudaHostRegister()**.

Write-Combining Memory

By default page-locked host memory is allocated as cacheable. It can optionally be allocated as *write-combining* instead by passing flag **cudaHostAllocWriteCombined** to **cudaHostAlloc()**. Write-combining memory frees up the host's L1 and L2 cache resources, making more cache available to the rest of the application. In addition, write-combining memory is not snooped during transfers across the PCI Express bus, which can improve transfer performance by up to 40%.

Reading from write-combining memory from the host is prohibitively slow, so write-combining memory should in general be used for memory that the host only writes to.

Mapped Memory

A block of page-locked host memory can also be mapped into the address space of the device by passing flag **cudaHostAllocMapped** to **cudaHostAlloc()** or by passing flag **cudaHostRegisterMapped** to **cudaHostRegister()**. Such a block has therefore in general two addresses: one in host memory that is returned by **cudaHostAlloc()** or **malloc()**, and one in device memory that can be retrieved using **cudaHostGetDevicePointer()** and then used to access the block from within a kernel. The only exception is for pointers allocated with **cudaHostAlloc()** and when a unified address space is used for the host and the device as mentioned in Unified Virtual Address Space.

Accessing host memory directly from within a kernel has several advantages :

- There is no need to allocate a block in device memory and copy data between this block and the block in host memory; data transfers are implicitly performed as needed by the kernel.
- There is no need to use streams to overlap data transfers with kernel execution; the kernel-originated data transfers automatically overlap with kernel execution.
- Since mapped page-locked memory is shared between host and device however, the application must synchronize memory accesses using streams or events to avoid any potential read-after-write, write-after-read, or write-after-write hazards.

To be able to retrieve the device pointer to any mapped page-locked memory, pagelocked memory mapping must be enabled by calling **cudaSetDeviceFlags()** with the **cudaDeviceMapHost** flag before any other CUDA call is performed. Otherwise, **cudaHostGetDevicePointer()** will return an error. **cudaHostGetDevicePointer()** also returns an error if the device does not support mapped page-locked host memory. Applications may query this capability by checking the **canMapHostMemory** device property which is equal to 1 for devices that support mapped page-locked host memory.

Texture and Surface Memory

CUDA supports a subset of the texturing hardware that the GPU uses for graphics to access texture and surface memory. Reading data from texture or surface memory instead of global memory can have several performance benefits.

There are two different APIs to access texture and surface memory :
- The texture reference API that is supported on all devices.
- The texture object API that is only supported on devices of compute capability 3.x.

Texture reference API has several limitations over texture reference API.

Texture Memory

Texture memory is read from kernels using the device functions. The process of reading a texture calling one of these functions is called a texture *fetch*. Each texture fetch specifies a parameter called a texture object for the texture object API or a texture reference for the texture reference API.

The texture object or the texture reference specifies :
- The texture, which is the piece of texture memory that is fetched. Texture objects are created at runtime and the texture is specified when creating the texture object. Texture references are created at compile time and the texture is specified at runtime by bounding the texture reference to the texture through runtime functions.
- Several distinct texture references might be bound to the same texture or to textures that overlap in memory. A texture can be any region of linear memory or a CUDA array.
- Its dimensionality that specifies whether the texture is addressed as a one dimensional array using one texture co-ordinate, a two-dimensional array using two texture co-ordinates, or a three-dimensional array using three texture co-ordinates. Elements of the array are called texels, short for texture elements. The texture width, height, and depth refer to the size of the array in each dimension. Table lists the maximum texture width, height, and depth depending on the compute capability of the device.
- The type of a texel isdefined in char, short, int, long, longlong, float, double that are derived from the basic integer and single-precision floating-point types.
- The *read mode* is either **cudaReadModeNormalizedFloat** or **cudaReadMode ElementType**. If it is **cudaReadModeNormalizedFloat** and the type of the texel is a 16-bit or 8-bit integer type, the value returned by the texture fetch is actually returned as floating-point type and the full range of the integer type is mapped to [0.0, 1.0] for unsigned integer type and [–1.0, 1.0] for signed integer type; for example, an unsigned 8-bit texture element with the value 0xff reads as 1. If it is **cudaReadModeElementType**, no conversion is performed.

    Whether texture co-ordinates are normalized or not, by default, textures are referenced using floating-point co-ordinates in the range [0, N-1] where N is the size of the texture in the dimension corresponding to the co-ordinate. For example, a texture that is 64 × 32 in size will be referenced with co-ordinates in the range [0, 63] and [0, 31] for the x and y dimensions, respectively. Normalized texture co-ordinates cause the co-ordinates to be specified in the range [0.0, 1.0-1/N] instead of [0, N-1], so the same 64 × 32 texture would be addressed by normalized co-ordinates in the range [0, 1-1/N] in both the x and y dimensions. Normalized texture co-ordinates are a natural fit to some applications requirements, if it is preferable for the texture co-ordinates to be independent of the texture size.

The Addressing Mode
- It is valid to call the device functions with co-ordinates that are out of range. The addressing mode defines what happens when device functions are called with co-ordinates that are out of range. The default addressing mode is to fix the co-ordinates to the valid range : [0, N) for non-normalized co-ordinates and [0.0, 1.0) for normalized co-ordinates. If the border mode is specified instead, texture fetches with out of-range texture co-ordinates return zero. For normalized co-ordinates, the warp mode and the mirror mode are also available. When using the wrap mode, each co-ordinate x is converted to frac(x)=x floor(x) where floor(x) is the largest integer not greater than x. When using the mirror mode, each co-ordinate x is converted to frac(x) if floor(x) is even and 1-frac(x) if floor(x) is odd. The addressing mode is specified as an array of size three whose first, second, and third elements specify the addressing mode for the first, second, and third texture co-ordinates, respectively; the addressing mode are **cuda Address Mode Border**, **cuda Address Mode Clamp**, **cuda Address Mode Wrap**, and **cuda Address Mode Mirror**; **cuda Address Mode Wrap** and **cuda Address Mode Mirror** are only supported for normalized texture co-ordinates.

The Filtering Mode
- This mode specifies how the value returned when fetching the texture which is computed based on the input texture co-ordinates. Linear texture filtering may be done only for textures that are configured to return floating-point data. It performs low-precision interpolation between neighboring texels. When enabled, the texels surrounding a texture fetch location are read and the return value of the texture fetch is interpolated based on where the texture co-ordinates that fell between the texels.
- Simple linear interpolation is performed for one-dimensional textures, bilinear interpolation for two-dimensional textures, and trilinear interpolation for three dimensional textures. The filtering mode is equal to **cuda Filter Mode Point** or **cuda Filter Mode Linear**. If it is **cuda Filter Mode Point**, the returned value is the texel whose texture co-ordinates are the closest to the input texture co-ordinates. If it is **cuda Filter Mode Linear**, the returned value is the linear interpolation of the two (for a one dimensional texture), four (for a two dimensional texture), or eight (for a three dimensional texture) texels whose texture co-ordinates are the closest to the input texture co-ordinates. **cuda Filter Mode Linear** is only valid for returned values of floating-point type.

A texture object is created using **cuda Create Texture Object()** from a resource description of type struct **cuda Resource Desc**, which specifies the texture, and from a texture description defined as such :

```
struct cudaTextureDesc
{
enum cudaTextureAddressMode addressMode[3];
enum cudaTextureFilterMode filterMode;
enum cudaTextureReadMode readMode;
int sRGB;
int normalizedCoords;
unsigned int maxAnisotropy;
enum cudaTextureFilterMode mipmapFilterMode;
float mipmapLevelBias;
float minMipmapLevelClamp;
float maxMipmapLevelClamp;
};
```

The following code sample applies some simple transformation kernel to a texture.

```
// Simple transformation kernel
__global__ void transformKernel(float* output, cudaTextureObject_t texObj)
int width, int height;
float theta;
{
// Calculate normalized texture co-ordinates
unsigned int x = blockIdx.x * blockDim.x + threadIdx.x;
unsigned int y = blockIdx.y * blockDim.y + threadIdx.y;
float u = x / (float)width;
float v = y / (float)height;
// Transform co-ordinates
u -= 0.5f;
v -= 0.5f;
float tu = u * cosf(theta) - v * sinf(theta) + 0.5f;
float tv = v * cosf(theta) + u * sinf(theta) + 0.5f;
// Read from texture and write to global memory
output[y * width + x] = tex2D<float>(texObj, tu, tv);
// Host code
```

```
int main()
{
// Allocate CUDA array in device memory
cudaChannelFormatDesc channelDesc = cudaCreateChannelDesc(32, 0, 0, 0,
cudaChannelFormatKindFloat);
cudaArray* cuArray;
cudaMallocArray(&cuArray, &channelDesc, width, height);
// Copy to device memory some data located at address h_data in host memory
cudaMemcpyToArray(cuArray, 0, 0, h_data, size,
cudaMemcpyHostToDevice);
// Specify texture
struct cudaResourceDesc resDesc;
memset(&resDesc, 0, sizeof(resDesc));
resDesc.resType = cudaResourceTypeArray;
resDesc.res.array.array = cuArray;
// Specify texture object parameters
struct cudaTextureDesc texDesc;
memset(&texDesc, 0, sizeof(texDesc));
texDesc.addressMode[0] = cudaAddressModeWrap;
texDesc.addressMode[1] = cudaAddressModeWrap;
texDesc.filterMode = cudaFilterModeLinear;
texDesc.readMode = cudaReadModeElementType;
texDesc.normalizedCoords = 1;
// Create texture object
cudaTextureObject_t texObj = 0;
cudaCreateTextureObject(&texObj, &resDesc, &texDesc, NULL);
// Allocate result of transformation in device memory
float* output;
cudaMalloc(&output, width * height * sizeof(float));
// Invoke kernel
dim3 dimBlock(16, 16);
dim3 dimGrid((width + dimBlock.x - 1) / dimBlock.x, (height + dimBlock.y - 1) / dimBlock.y);
transformKernel<<<dimGrid, dimBlock>>>(output, texObj, width, height, angle);
// Destroy texture object
```

```
cudaDestroyTextureObject(texObj);
// Free device memory
cudaFreeArray(cuArray);
cudaFree(output);
return 0;
}
```

Texture Reference API

Some of the attributes of a texture reference are undeniable and must be known at compile time. They are specified when declaring the texture reference. A texture reference is declared as a variable of type **texture** :

texture<DataType, Type, ReadMode> texRef;

where :

- **Data Type** specifies the type of the texel;
- **Type** specifies the type of the texture reference and is equal to **cudaTexture Type1D**, **cudaTextureType2D**, or **cudaTextureType3D**, for a one-dimensional, two-dimensional, or three-dimensional texture, respectively, or **cudaTexture Type1DLayered** or **cudaTextureType2DLayered** for a onedimensional or two-dimensional layered texture respectively; Type is an optional field whose default value is **cudaTextureType1D**;
- **ReadMode** specifies the read mode; it is an optional field whose default value is **cudaReadModeElementType**.
- A texture reference can only be declared as a static global variable and cannot be passed as an argument to a function.

The other attributes of a texture reference are mutable and can be changed at runtime through the host runtime. The **texture** type is defined in the high-level API as a structure publicly derived from the **textureReference** type defined in the low-level API as such :

```
struct textureReference {
int normalized;
enum cudaTextureFilterMode filterMode;
enum cudaTextureAddressMode addressMode[3];
struct cudaChannelFormatDesc channelDesc;
int sRGB;
unsigned int maxAnisotropy;
enum cudaTextureFilterMode mipmapFilterMode;
float mipmapLevelBias;
float minMipmapLevelClamp;
```

```
float maxMipmapLevelClamp;
}
```
Here channelDesc describes the format of the texel; it must match the DataType argument of the texture reference declaration.

channelDesc is of the following type:
```
struct cudaChannelFormatDesc {
int x, y, z, w;
enum cudaChannelFormatKind f;
};
```

where x, y, z, and w are equal to the number of bits of each component of the returned value and f is :

- **cudaChannelFormatKindSigned** if these components are of signed integer type.
- **cudaChannelFormatKindUnsigned** if they are of unsigned integer type.
- **cudaChannelFormatKindFloat** if they are of floating point type.
- **normalized**, **addressMode**, and **filterMode** may be directly modified in host code.

Before a kernel can use a texture reference to read from texture memory, the texture reference must be bound to a texture using **cudaBindTexture()** or **cudaBindTexture2D()** for linear memory, or **cudaBindTextureToArray()** for CUDA arrays. **cudaUnbindTexture()** is used to unbind a texture reference. Once a texture reference has been unbound, it can be safely rebound to another array, even if kernels that use the previously bound texture have not completed.

6.5 MULTI-CPU AND MULTI-GPU SOLUTION

6.5.1 Introduction

In modern computing systems it is common to have multiple devices, both CPUs and GPUs. CPUs are all about sockets and cores. A socket is a physical entity on the motherboard into which a CPU is placed. A CPU may contain one or more cores. Each core is effectively a separate entity.

A number of CPU and GPU sockets are located on a single node or computer system.

Knowing the physical arrangement of cores, sockets, and nodes allows for effective scheduling or distribution of tasks.

6.5.2 Locality

The principle of locality is often seen in GPUs and CPUs. Memory closer to the device (shared memory on the GPU, cache on the CPU) is quicker to access. Communication between cores is much quicker than communication to another core in a different socket.

Communication to a core on another node is very much slower than within the node. Software that is aware of this concept can make a huge difference to the overall performance of the system. Such socket-aware software can split data along the lines of the hardware layout, ensuring one core is working on a consistent dataset and this software also ensures cores that need to co-operate are within the same socket or node.

6.5.3 Multi-CPU Systems

- Single-socket, multicore desktop is the most common multi-CPU system. Almost any PC available today such as desktop machines, media PCs, laptops will have a multicore CPU. Workstations and low-end servers are another type of multi-CPU systems. These are often dual-socket machines, typically powered by multicore Xeon CPUs. Data center–based servers are multi-CPU systems which have typically 4, 8, or 16 sockets, each with a multicore CPU. Such hardware is often used to create a virtualized set of machines, allowing companies to centrally support large numbers of virtual PCs from one large server.
- One of the major problems with any multi-CPU system is memory coherency. Both CPUs and GPUs allocate memory to individual devices. In the case of GPUs, this is the global memory that is available on each GPU card. In the CPU case, this is the system memory on the motherboard.
- When you have independent programs using just a single core, scaling can be easily done in this case as each program can be localized to a given core. The program then accesses its own data and makes good use of the CPU core's cache. But problem arises when we have two cores cooperating with one another. This can be better understood with the help of the following example.
- To speed up access to memory locations, CPUs make extensive use of caches. When the value of a parameter is to be updated say x++, then which value of x is actually written to memory? Suppose two cores need to update x, one core wants to perform increment the value of x and other core want to decrement the value of x. Both cores must have a consistent view of the memory location holding the parameter x.
- This is the issue of cache coherency and is limited by the maximum number of cores that can practically cooperate on a single node. When core 1 writes to x, it informs all other cores that the value of x has now changed and then does a slow write out to the main memory instead of a quick write back to cache access.
- In a simple coherency model, the other cores then mark the entry for x in their caches as invalid.
  The next access to x then causes x to be reloaded from the slow main memory. As subsequent cores write to x, the process is repeated and the next core to access parameter x must again fetch it from memory and write it back again. In effect, the parameter x becomes non-cached. This is called as a huge performance hit on CPU system.

- In more complex coherency models, instead of invalidating x the invalidation request is replaced with an update request. Thus, every write has to be distributed to N caches. As the number of N grows, the time to synchronize the caches becomes impractical. This often limits the practical number of nodes that can be placed into a symmetrical multiprocessor (SMP) system.
- Now remember that caches are supposed to run at high speed. Within a single socket, this is not hard. As the number of sockets increased the more difficult it becomes to keep everything synchronized.
- Memory access time is another major problem. To make programming easier on such systems the memory is logically arranged as a huge linear address space. When a core from socket 1 tries to access a memory address from socket 2, it has to be done by socket 2, as only socket 2 can physically address that memory. This is called non uniform memory access (NUMA). Although conceptually it makes a programmer's life easier, this is not optimal in terms of memory locality and such programs might perform very slowly.

6.5.4 Multi-GPU Systems

- Almost all the computing systems available today have multiple GPUs inside them. As a programmer you should always try to produce the best experience possible on whatever hardware is available.
- If the user has a dual-GPU system and use only one GPU, then it is not good programming practice. You should understand how cores works and you must utilize them for your benefits.
- If you are writing an application or working with known hardware, you should try for multi-GPU solutions. Almost all PCs support at least two PCI-E slots, allowing at least two GPU cards to be put into almost any PC. CUDA does not use or require SLI (Scalable Link Interface), so absence of an SLI-certified motherboard is no obstacle to using multiple GPUs in CUDA applications. Adding one additional GPU card, will result into doubling the level of performance, and the current execution time reduces to half.

6.5.5 Algorithms on Multiple GPUs

- The CUDA environment does not support a helpful multi-GPU model. The model is based more on a single-core, single-GPU relationship. This model works for tasks that are independent of one another, but this model is not useful in situation where GPUs need to cooperate in some way.
- On a multi-GPU system large task is spawned into N tasks, where N is equal to the number of GPUs in the system. Each task gets a separate data packet or job from a central server. As GPUs finish tasks, it simply requests additional tasks from the central server (task dispatcher).

- Consider an example of video encoding where we need cooperation. Encoding video is typically done by applying a JPEG-type algorithm to each individual frame and then looking for the motion vectors between frames. Thus, we have an operation within a frame that can be distributed to N GPUs, but then an operation that requires the GPUs to share data and has a dependency on the first task (JPEG compression) completing.
- The easiest way to do this is to use two passes, one kernel that simply does the JPEG compression on N independent frames, and a second kernel that does the motion vector analysis–based compression. We can do this because motion vector–based compression uses a finite window of frames, so frame 1 does not affect frame 1000. Thus, we can split the work into N independent jobs. The downside of this approach, as with any multi pass algorithm, is we read the data more than once. As the dataset is typically quite large and will involve slow mass storage devices, this is generally a bad approach.
- A single-pass method is more efficient, but more difficult to program. You can transform the problem, if you consider the set of frames on which you do motion vector compression to be the dataset.

    Each set of frames is independent and can be dispatched to a separate GPU card. The GPU kernel first does JPEG compression on all frames within the set it was provided. It then calculates, over those same frames, the motion aspects. By using this approach, you have managed to keep the data on the GPU card.

This eliminates the major bottleneck with this type of problem that of moving data around the system.

In this case it was possible to restructure the algorithm so it could be broken down into independent chunks of data. This may not always be possible and many types of problems require at least a small amount of data from the other GPUs. When you require another GPU's data, you have to explicitly share that data and explicitly sequence the access to that data between the GPUs. This approach is appropriate if it is at all possible to break down the problem into independent chunks.

This could be done using GPU peer-to-peer communication model, or you can use CPU-level primitives to cooperate at the CPU level.

6.5.6 Choice of GPU

When there is more than one GPU on a system then the following question arise :
1. Are they the same or different?
2. How does the programmer know?
3. Does it matter?

All this questions have a great influence on the type of GPUs. All depends largely on the type of application. Several binary images are embedded in the CUDA binary, one of each generation of GPUs. At a minimum a binary for the lowest compute–capability GPU should be present. However, additional binaries, optimized for higher-level compute devices, may also be present. The CUDA runtime will automatically select the highest level of binary based on the compute device when executing a kernel.

Certain functions are only available on certain compute-level devices; running such code (incompatible) on a lower-level compute device results in the kernel failing to run. Therefore, for certain programs at least, we have to care which GPU is used. Other programs run much better or worse on newer hardware, due to the effects of caching and block size selection by the application. For example other applications may have been written to use large numbers of registers on the G80/G200 series devices, something that was reduced on the Fermi architecture and then restored with Kepler.

Some user or administration-level knowledge is required about which is the best platform on which to run a given kernel, or the programmer has to adapt the program so it runs well on all platforms. This can be done by either avoiding compute device–specific routines, which can often make things much harder to program, or by providing some alternative kernels that avoid the compute-level issue. However this issue is often driven by commercial concerns.

6.5.7 Single-Node Systems

Before 4.0 SDK versions of CUDA single-node systems were the only multi-GPU model available as shown in Fig. 6.17. A single CPU-based task would be associated with a single-GPU. A task on this GPU would be either a process or a thread. In the background CUDA runtime would bind the CPU process/thread ID to the GPU context. Thus, all subsequent CUDA calls (e.g., cudaMalloc) would allocate memory on the device that was bound to this GPU

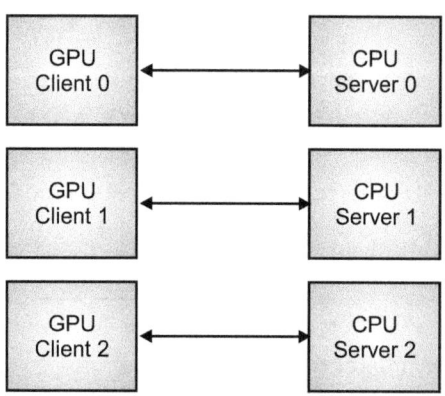

Fig. 6.17 : Single Node System

This approach had a number of drawbacks but some advantages. From a programming perspective, the process/thread model on the host side is fragmented by the OS type. A process is a program that runs as an independent schedulable unit on a CPU and has its own data space. To conserve memory, multiple instances of the same process usually share the code space and the OS maintains a set of registers (or context) for each process. A thread on the other hand is a much more lightweight element of the CPU scheduling. It shares both the code and data space used by its parent process. However, as with a process, each thread requires the OS to maintain a state (instruction pointer, stack pointer, registers, etc.).

Threads may communicate and cooperate with other threads within the same process. Processes may communicate and cooperate with other processes through interprocess communication. Such communication between processes may be within a CPU core, within a CPU socket, within a CPU node, within a rack, within a computer system, or even between computer systems.

CPU threads are similar to the GPU threads except that they do not execute in groups or warps as the GPU ones do. GPU threads communicate via shared memory and explicitly synchronize to ensure every thread has read/written to that memory. The shared memory is local to an SM, which means threads can only communicate with other threads within the same SM. Because a block is the scheduling unit to an SM, thread communication is actually limited to a per-block basis.

Processes on the CPU can be thought of in the same way as blocks on the GPU. A process is scheduled to run on one of N CPU cores. A block is scheduled to run one of N SMs on the GPU. In this sense the SMs act like CPU cores.

CPU processes can communicate to one another via host memory on the same socket. However, due to processes using a separate memory space, this can only happen with the assistance of a third-party interprocess communications library, as neither process can physically see the address space of the other. The same is not true, however, for GPU blocks, as they access a common address space on the GPU global memory.

Systems with multiple CPUs using shared host memory can also communicate with one another via this shared host memory, but again with the help of a third-party interprocess communication library. Multiple GPUs can communicate to one another on the same host, using host memory or directly via the PCI-E bus peer-to-peer communication model. However peer-to-peer communication is only supported for 64-bit OSs using Fermi or later cards. For Windows this is only supported with the TCC (Tesla compute cluster) driver, which effectively means it's only supported for Tesla cards.

6.5.8 Streams

Streams are virtual work queues on the GPU. They are used for asynchronous operation, that is, when GPU is used to operate separately from the CPU. Certain operations implicitly cause a synchronization point, for example, the default memory copies to and from the host or device. This is actually what the programmer wants. After copying the results back from the GPU they will instantly do something with those results on the CPU. When application is debugged then partial results may be appeared but the application may fail to run at full speed.

By creating a stream you can push work and events into the stream which will then execute the work in the order in which it is pushed into the stream. Streams and events are associated with the GPU context in which they were created. Have a look at following program how to create a couple of streams and events on multiple GPUs.

```
void fill_array(u32 * data, const u32 num_elements)
{
for (u32 i=0; i< num_elements; i++)
{
data[i] =i;
}
}
void check_array(char * device_prefix,
u32 * data,
const u32 num_elements)
{
bool error_found = false;
for (u32 i=0; i< num_elements; i++)
{
if (data[i] != (i*2))
{
printf("%sError: %u %u", device_prefix,i,data[i]);
error_found = true;
}
}
if (error_found== false)
printf("%sArray check passed", device_prefix);
}
```

In the first function we simply fill the array with a value from 0 to num_elements. The second function simply checks GPU results. It is possible to replace both the functions as

```
__global__ void gpu_test_kernel(u32 * data)
{
const int tid = (blockIdx.x * blockDim.x)
+ threadIdx.x;
```

```
data[tid] *= 2;
}
```
Kernel function is defined as follows.
```
// Define maximum number of supported devices
#define MAX_NUM_DEVICES (4)
// Define the number of elements to use in the array
#define NUM_ELEM (1024*1024*8)
// Define one stream per GPU
cudaStream_t stream[MAX_NUM_DEVICES];
// Define a string to prefix output messages with so we know which GPU generated it
char device_prefix[MAX_NUM_DEVICES][300];
// Define one working array per device, on the device
u32 * gpu_data[MAX_NUM_DEVICES];
// Define CPU source and destination arrays, one per GPU
u32 * cpu_src_data[MAX_NUM_DEVICES];
u32 * cpu_dest_data[MAX_NUM_DEVICES];
```
Following function declares a number of values, each of which is indexed by device_num. This allows us to use the same code for every device and just increment the index.
```
// Host program to be called from main
__host__ void gpu_kernel(void)
{
// No dynamic allocation of shared memory required
const int shared_memory_usage = 0;
// Define the size in bytes of a single GPU's worth of data
const size_t single_gpu_chunk_size = (sizeof(u32) * NUM_ELEM);
// Define the number of threads and blocks to launch
const int num_threads = 256;
const int num_blocks = ((NUM_ELEM þ (num_threads-1))
/ num_threads);
// Identify how many devices
int num_devices;
CUDA_CALL(cudaGetDeviceCount(&num_devices));
if (num_devices > MAX_NUM_DEVICES)
num_devices = MAX_NUM_DEVICES;
```
The first task is to identify how many GPUs we have available with the cudaGetDeviceCount call.
```
// Run one memcpy and kernel on each device
for (int device_num=0;device_num < num_devices;device_num++)
{
```

```
// Select the correct device
CUDA_CALL(cudaSetDevice(device_num));
```
The first section of each loop then sets the current device context to the device_num parameter to ensure all subsequent calls then work with that device.
```
// Generate a prefix for all screen messages
struct cudaDeviceProp device_prop;
CUDA_CALL(cudaGetDeviceProperties(&device_prop, device_num));
sprintf(&device_prefix[device_num][0], "\nID:%d %s:", device_num, device_prop.name);
// Create a new stream on that device
CUDA_CALL(cudaStreamCreate(&stream[device_num]));
// Allocate memory on the GPU
CUDA_CALL(cudaMalloc((void**)&gpu_data[device_num],single_gpu_chunk_size));
// Allocate page locked memory on the CPU
CUDA_CALL(cudaMallocHost((void **)&cpu_src_data[device_num], single_gpu_chunk_size));
CUDA_CALL(cudaMallocHost((void **)&cpu_dest_data[device_num], single_gpu_chunk_size));
// Fill it with a known pattern
fill_array(cpu_src_data[device_num], NUM_ELEM);
// Copy a chunk of data from the CPU to the GPU asynchronous
CUDA_CALL(cudaMemcpyAsync(gpu_data[device_num], cpu_src_data[device_num], single_gpu_chunk_size, cudaMemcpyHostToDevice, stream[device_num]));
// Invoke the GPU kernel using the newly created stream - asynchronous invokation
gpu_test_kernel<<<num_blocks, num_threads, shared_memory_usage, stream[device_num]>>>(gpu_data[device_num]);
cuda_error_check(device_prefix[device_num], "Failed to invoke gpu_test_kernel");
// Now push memory copies to the host into the streams
// Copy a chunk of data from the GPU to the CPU asynchronous
CUDA_CALL(cudaMemcpyAsync(cpu_dest_data[device_num],gpu_data[device_num], single_gpu_chunk_size, cudaMemcpyDeviceToHost, stream[device_num]));
}
```

In the above program we create a stream, or work queue, for each GPU present in the system. Into this stream we place a copy from the host (CPU) memory to the GPU global memory followed by a kernel call and then a copy back to the CPU. They will execute in this order, so the kernel will not start executing until the preceding memory copy has completed.

6.5.9 Multiple-Node Systems

- A single computer forms a single node on a network. Cluster of machines can be obtained by connecting many single machines together. Typically, such a cluster will be composed of a set of rack-mounted nodes. The rack may then itself be interconnected with one or more additional racks.
- Example of fastest GPU systems in the world as of 2014, are GeForce GTX 980, 970 Maxwell GPU, Tianhe-1A. Tianhe-1A consists of over 14,000 CPUs with over 7000 Tesla Fermi GPUs. These 7000 Tesla Fermi GPUs are split into 112 cabinets (racks), each of which contains 64 compute nodes. It runs a custom interconnect that supports up to 160 GB/s of communications bandwidth.
- The number of CPU cores and GPUs depends on the application and what percentage of the code is serial. If the ration of number of CPU cores and GPUs is very little, then the simple one CPU core to multiple GPUs works well enough. However, if the CPU load is significant, then the throughput will be limited. To overcome this we need to allocate less GPUs per CPU core, moving to a 1 : 2 or 1 : 1 ratio as the application demands. The simplest and most scalable method is via assigning one process to each set of CPU/GPUs on the node. This model is highly scalable. However as we go on scaling the model it has significant impact on network communications. For such models we need a communications mechanism that allows us to schedule work to a given CPU/GPUs set, regardless of where they are on the network. ZeroMQ, socket are very lightweight and fairly user-friendly communications library. Once initialized, ZeroMQ runs in the background and allows the application to use synchronous or asynchronous communication without having to worry about buffer management.
- ZeroMQ supports a number of transports between threads (INPROC), between processes (IPC), broadcast to many nodes (MULTICAST), and a network-based system (TCP). Multicast transport is widely used transport technique as it provides the most flexibility in terms of connecting multiple nodes on the network.
- The first task we need to perform with ZeroMQ is to set up a connection point. Refer Fig. 6.18. At this point we have one master (server) that distributes the work packets to clients. Client is a CPU/GPU set (not a physical node). Each client connects to a specific point on the network. This point of connection is provided by the server. At this point client works for work to be given to it. This point is called as access point and it is created when server binds with a port. All clients then connect to this access point. ZeroMQ sets up an internal queue for each client that connects to this access point.

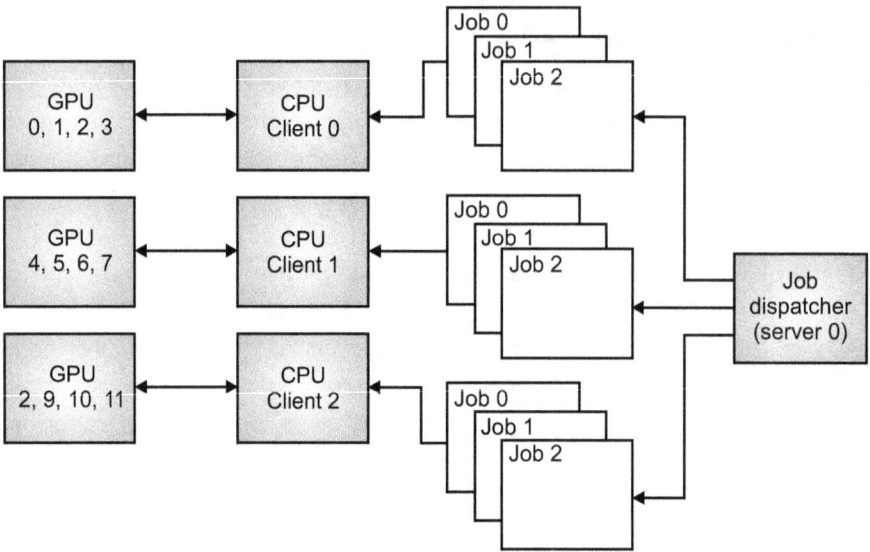

Fig. 6.18 : Multiple Node System

- The next step is to decide on a messaging pattern, the simplest being the request/reply pattern. This is similar to MPI in that we have a send and recv function, and that for every send, there must be a response. This is done as follows :

Client:
zmq::context_t context(1);
zmq::socket_t socket(context, ZMQ_REQ);
socket.connect("tcp://localhost:5555");

Server:
zmq::context_t context(1);
zmq::socket_t socket(context, ZMQ_REP);
socket.bind("tcp://*:5555");

The CPU client then maintains a work queue, usually at least two items to allow for GPU double buffering.

The protocol used in the application is that the CPU client connects to the server and asks the server for a batch of work. The server then responds with a range that it would like the client to work on. The client then does any work necessary on the CPU to generate data for that work packet.

```
// Host program to be called from main
__host__ void gpu_kernel_client(const u32 pid)
{
printf("\nRunning as Client");
```

```cpp
// Init Network
zmq::context_t context(1);
zmq::socket_t socket(context, ZMQ_REQ);
socket.connect("tcp://localhost:5555");
// GPU params
size_t chunk_size;
u32 active_streams;
u32 num_devices;
// Setup all available devices
setup_devices(&num_devices,
&active_streams,
&chunk_size);
u32 results_to_process;
get_work_range_from_server(pid,
&results_to_process,
&socket);
// Generate CPU data for input data
generate_cpu_data_range(0, results_to_process);
// Keep track of pending results
u32 pending_results = results_to_process;
// While there is still work to be completed
while (pending_results != 0)
{
// Try to distribute work to each GPU
u32 work_distributed = distribute_work(num_devices, chunk_size, pending_results);
// Collect work from GPU
u32 work_collected = collect_work(num_devices, chunk_size);
// Decrement remaining count
pending_results -= work_collected;
// Post completed work units to server
if (work_collected > 0)
{
send_completed_units_to_server(pid,
chunk_size,
&socket);
}
// If no work was distributed, or collected and we've not finished yet then sleep
if ( (work_distributed == 0) &&
(work_collected == 0) &&
```

```
(pending_results != 0) )
{
printf(".");
fflush(stdout);
snooze(100);
}
}
// Print summary of how many each device processed
for (u32 device_num=0u;
device_num < num_devices;
device_num++)
{
printf("%s processed: %u",
device_prefix[device_num],
num_processed[device_num]);
}
printf("\nTotal: src:%u dest:%u",
unprocessed_idx, completed_idx);
cleanup_devices(num_devices);
}
```

The client code, after receiving the initial work from the server and generating the GPU work queue, runs over a loop until the work is complete. This loop distributes work to the available GPUs, processes work that is already complete, and posts any completed work to the server. Finally, if it was not able to do any of the above, it sleeps for 100 ms and then tries again. At this point of time additional buffer space is required to post out the completed units to the server and some time to push the data into the transmission queue. Thus, we no longer immediately reschedule work onto the GPU, but schedule additional work later. This allows for a simpler approach where we distribute work, collect any finished work, process it locally if necessary, and post it to the server.

```
__host__ u32 distribute_work(const int num_devices, const size_t chunk_size, u32 pending_results)
{
u32 work_units_scheduled = 0;
// Cycle through each device
for (u32 device_num = 0;
device_num < num_devices;
device_num++)
{
u32 stream_num = 0;
```

```
bool allocated_work = false;
while ( (allocated_work == false) &&
(stream_num < streams_per_device[device_num]) )
{
// If there is more work to schedule
if (pending_results > 0)
{
// If the device is available
if (processed_result[device_num][stream_num] == true)
{
// Allocate a job to the GPU
push_work_into_queue(device_num, chunk_size, stream_num);
// Set flag to say GPU has work pending
processed_result[device_num][stream_num] = false;
// Keep track of how many new units were issued
work_units_scheduled++;
// Move onto next device
allocated_work = true;
pending_results--;
}
}
stream_num++;
}
}
return work_units_scheduled;
}
```

Advantages of Multi GPU system

As multi GPU system transformed the design process by utilizing the graphics capability and high performance computing power of Graphics Processing Units, this technology intelligently scales the performance of applications and dramatically speeds up the production workflow.

Following are some advantages of multi GPU system from the performance perspective :

- **Time Saving :** A multi GPU system helps address the pressure of delivering a high quality product into market more quickly by utilizing the high computing capability, renderings and visual aids of GPUs.
- **Multiple Iterations :** Better results are obtained by revising the product multiple times in a resource and time constrained environment. Multiple iterations provide additional refinement to the product revisions.

- **Flexibility :** A multi GPU system also offers tremendous flexibility in its implementation. Irrespective of using traditional desktop workstation or high end virtualized server, multiple GPUs help optimize the workflow across a range of professional applications with dramatic increase in performance.

QUESTIONS

1. Explain the concept of Cloud Computing with the help of the following points :
   a. Definition
   b. Services provided by cloud computing
   c. Characteristics
   d. Types of clouds
   e. Advantages
2. What are the challenges before Cloud Computing ?
3. Write short note on Mobile Computing. Explain the basic components of Mobile Computing System.
4. Write short note on Mobile Computing classification.
5. What are the advantages of Mobile Computing?
6. What are the security issues before Mobile Computing ?
7. Explain the various future trends of Mobile Computing.
8. What are the limitations of Mobile Computing ?
9. What is CUDA? Explain the physical and logical architecture of CUDA.
10. Explain the difference between CPU and GPU.
11. Write short notes on CUDA threads, blocks and grids. Draw the suitable the diagram to explain the above concepts.
12. Explain the concept of threading on GPU.
13. Explain the CUDA kernel with the help of :
    a. Kernel call syntax
    b. Function type qualifiers
    c. Thread hierarchy
14. Draw and explain the CUDA memory hierarchy concept.
15. Write short note on heterogeneous programming.
16. Write short note on compute capability of CUDA and explain different compute levels.
17. Explain different types of memories in CUDA. How memory handling is done in CUDA?

Model Question Papers For In-Semester University Exam.
(30 Marks)

Model Question Paper – I   (30 Marks)

1. Explain different computation models with suitable example. (3 M)
2. Write short note on different approaches for writing concurrent programs. (6 M)
3. Explain following distributed programming languages : (3 M)
   (a) LISP
   (b) YACC
4. Write short note on Inter Process Communication. (3 M)
5. Explain the relationship between co-operating threads. Draw suitable diagram. (3 M)
6. What is concurrent LISP. Explain different LISP programming languages that support concurrency. (3 M)
7. Explain various alternatives to CUDA. (3 M)
8. Explain the hardward overview and physical architecture of CUDA with neat diagram. (3 M)
9. Explain various metrics used for evaluating the performance of parallel algorithms. (3 M)

Model Question Paper – II   (30 Marks)

1. Explain different declarative programming techniques with suitable examples. (3 M)
2. What are the techniques to implement concurrency control. (3 M)
3. Write short note on specialized computation models. (3 M)
4. Explain various synchronization mechanisms. (3 M)
5. Write short note on shared memory. (3 M)
6. Write short note on : (3 M)
   (a) Cl – CUDA
   (b) Cl – GPU
   Explain with suitable example.
7. How parallelism can be achieved with the help of GPU. (3 M)
8. Differentiate between serial computing and parallel computing. (3 M)
9. Write short note on classification of parallel architectures. Draw suitable diagram. (6 M)

Notes

www.ingramcontent.com/pod-product-compliance
Lightning Source LLC
Chambersburg PA
CBHW081145230426

43664CB00018B/2805